Chronos, Kairos, Christos

Jack Finegan

Chronos, Kairos, Christos

Nativity and Chronological Studies Presented to Jack Finegan

Edited by
Jerry Vardaman
and
Edwin M. Yamauchi

Eisenbrauns
Winona Lake
1989

Library of Congress Cataloging-in-Publication Data

Chronos, kairos, Christos: nativity and chronological studies
presented to Jack Finegan/edited by Jerry Vardaman and
Edwin M. Yamauchi.
    p.   cm.
  Bibliography: p.
  ISBN 0-931464-50-1
  1. Jesus Christ—Date of birth. 2. Jesus Christ—Date of
death. 3. Bible. N.T.—Criticism, interpretation, etc.
4. Finegan, Jack, 1908-. I. Finegan, Jack, 1908-. II. Vardaman,
Jerry. III. Yamauchi, Edwin M.
BT318.C47 1989
232.9'08—dc20   89-34759
                                         CIP

Contents

Contents

A Tribute to Jack Finegan on his Eightieth Birthday

Jerry Vardaman

The articles contained in this volume represent a variety of viewpoints on different aspects of New Testament study, especially concerning the birth of Jesus. This is what one would expect in a field still alive with research and still searching for as much light as can be shed on *still* unanswered questions. Not one contributor, however, has any difference of opinion concerning his appreciation for and high esteem of Professor Jack Finegan. Professor Finegan's list of writings (listed below) will demonstrate how active he has been, not only in Nativity research, but also in all phases of biblical study: world religions, pastoral work, textual studies, religious novels, commentaries, archaeological investigations, and a number of other related fields of specialization.

Professor Finegan turned eighty years of age on 11 July 1988. It is my happy privilege, along with each of the other contributors to this book, to express warm greetings and congratulations to him on this joyful occasion. Through these studies, we wish to express gratitude to him for pointing us to academic excellence in our own search for truth.

This volume has been in production longer than any of us have desired. A Nativity Conference was conducted at Mississippi State University on 16 December 1983, and it was at that time that most of these studies were publicly delivered. Jack Finegan presided over this conference with his rich wisdom, and because he turned seventy-five years of age in that year, it was decided at that time that the articles, when prepared for press, would be published as a *Festschrift* to honor him. The one value in the delay in publication is to remind us on his eightieth birthday, also, of our debt to him!

I owe a debt to each contributor who has made this book possible, especially Edwin Yamauchi, my coeditor. The money to fund the Nativity Conference, and partly to fund this book, was provided by Ashland Oil, and made available to us through the added generosity and helpfulness of the Ken Davis family of Ashland, Kentucky, each member of which family we thank. Help was also given by numerous colleagues at Mississippi State University.

Finally, all contributors and, no doubt, future readers desire to thank James Eisenbraun and David Aiken of Eisenbrauns. They have provided wise technical expertise and generous financial support to make this *Festschrift* available. Their patience with our slowness has allowed considerable revisions in most of these studies and conscientious attempts to make each article quite current with the latest discoveries, as careful readers will note. Scholarly abbreviations follow the guidelines established in the *Journal of Biblical Literature*.

Jack Finegan: A Tribute

Bastiaan Van Elderen

Recently while I was paging through Webster's *New Collegiate Dictionary* (1981) in a cursory way, my eye fell on the word "habilitate" and to my pleasant surprise I saw that Jack Finegan was quoted in the entry. Rightly or wrongly, I am assuming that this is the man who was my *Doktorvater* and the man who is honored in this festschrift. In fact, I am convinced it is, because the quote reflects his years of study in Germany where he wrote under Hans Lietzmann a doctoral dissertation entitled *Die Überlieferung der Leidens- und Auferstehungsgeschichte Jesu* (1934).

I met Jack Finegan, the scholar and professor, in 1958 while I was doing graduate study in Berkeley at the University of California and Pacific School of Religion. However, it was soon that I also met Jack Finegan, the pastor, the man, and a lasting friend.

He was a multifaceted man. His youth in the southwest of the United States exposed him to that life and culture, traces of which continued in later life as he continued to do "cowboy" rope tricks equal to that of rodeo experts. He had a broad interest in transport and recreation. He expertly maneuvered his yacht in the San Francisco Bay. He incongruously arrived on campus in his Jaguar. And he piloted planes all over the western United States.

In the realm of scholarship and research he was a man of rigor, precision, thoroughness, and innovation. What he practiced he also demanded in his students. Scholarship and research for him were and remain serious business. These qualities are evident in his publications. A brief look at his *Handbook of Biblical Chronology* (1964) astounds one at the detailed research and comprehensive presentation of the data. Many of the essays in this collection have used this work not only as a source, but also as a publication that has had a formative influence on chronological discussions since.

Perhaps the name of Prof. Jack Finegan is best known for his contributions in the field of biblical archeology. He not only made me aware of the importance of this field but also inspired me to pursue this specialization in my research and teaching. For decades his *Light from the Ancient Past* (1946; 2d ed. in 1959) has been both a source book and textbook in numerous universities, colleges, and seminaries. As an "armchair archeologist," Jack Finegan was able to digest and summarize archeological reports (which often are as dry as the dust out of which the artifacts come!), integrate the data, and present an informative and meaningful interpretation that both the layman could comprehend and the scholar could respect and use. He had such a high and wholesome respect for the biblical text and its interpretation that for him all data must be considered and followed—even if some traditional or cherished ideas are challenged.

It is not my purpose nor within the scope of this tribute possibly to review all the publications of Jack Finegan. The bibliography on pp. xi–xix will give the reader an idea of the depth, spread, and amount of writing this scholar has done and continues to do. However, I would like to single out a few items.

Chapters and sections in his basic work, *Light from the Ancient Past*, were later expanded into specialized studies: *The Archeology of the New Testament: The Life of Jesus and the Beginning of the Early Church* (1969), *Archaeological History of the Ancient Middle East* (1979), *The Archeology of the New Testament: The Mediterranean World of the Early Christian Apostles* (1981). And these works in the archeology of the Middle East have become standard source books and textbooks for all phases of biblical and early Christian studies. Another chapter in *Light from the Ancient Past* became the basis for an informative guide in the textual criticism of the New Testament: *Encountering New Testament Manuscripts* (1974). This excellent and lucid introduction to a complex field of study remains one of the best on the market.

In 1969 Jack Finegan published a book that I consider outstanding in its field but has not received proper recognition and use. It is entitled *Hidden Records of the Life of Jesus*. In this book are collected all the data (in original text with translation and numerous photographs of the manuscripts) relating to Jesus in early Christian literature. All these sources are accompanied by informative and judicious introductions and evaluations. One is deeply impressed by all the sources consulted by Finegan in the preparation of this volume. Perhaps, in view of the recent interest in the apocryphal Gospels and related literature, scholars will turn more and more to this valuable source book. In my judgment anyone working in this area cannot ignore this book. May it in due time receive its proper recognition!

Through the use of Prof. Finegan's publications on the archeology of the biblical world, it is truly possible either in actuality or in imagina-

tion and study to go "to the East . . . to the place where these things
were preached and done," as Melito of Sardis did in A.D. 160 (cited by
Finegan in his preface to *Archeology of the New Testament* [1969]).

On the other hand, my portrait of Jack Finegan as author would
not be complete without a reference to his work as a novelist. In one of
his fiction books entitled *Mark of the Taw* (1972) he weaves together an
interesting and delightful story about the biblical John Mark by making
use of his knowledge of the Middle East and its literature. At first
glimpse this may seem a bit incongruous, but in reality is further
demonstration of Jack Finegan's versatility, imagination, and creativity.

For many years Jack Finegan was Professor of New Testament
History and Archeology at the Pacific School of Religion in Berkeley,
California. His lectures were masterpieces of organization and structure,
loaded with pertinent information, spiced with personal experiences,
and filled with perceptive insights and judgments. The world of the
New Testament came alive in his presentation, and his enthusiastic
interest in the history and archeology of the ancient Middle East was
contagious. However, his horizons were also worldwide. Many times he
has traveled around the world in his investigation and study of other
religions—results of which are evident in his bibliography (e.g., *The
Archeology of World Religions* [1952]). In recent days his study of religion
has included travel in Tibet.

The scholar Jack Finegan was also the preacher Jack Finegan. For
years he preached weekly at the University Christian Church in
Berkeley. These masterful sermons, many of which have been published, not only presented the data of recent biblical scholarship, but
also applied these data to the present-day needs of the parishoners. And
that was essentially the mark of the man Jack Finegan—he was a deeply
committed Christian for whom the Christian Gospel had a significant
relevance in this confused and troubled world. Because he so faithfully
served his Lord and Master, he was able to serve us in such a rich and
varied way. Thanks be to God!

Of Time and History

Jack Finegan

In Gal 4:4 the Apostle Paul says that it was in the fulness of the time (*chronos*) that God sent forth his Son; therefore *chronos logos*—or the time science that is chronology—has always been of interest in Christian studies. Along with *chronos* as time in the sense of duration, *kairos* is time in the sense of particular time, especially right or proper time, as in Rom 5:6 where Paul says that while we were yet helpless, at the right time (*kairos*) Christ died for the ungodly. Therefore in Christian studies there is an endeavor not only to have an appreciation of the long sweep of history but also to identify the particular points by which that history is notably punctuated.

On chronological questions there has not always been unanimity of opinion. In Christianity's commemoration of the *kairos* of Christ's death and resurrection the "fourteeners" (*quartodecimans*), for example, held that the annual observance should be on the exact calendar date, that is, the fourteenth day of the Jewish month Nisan regardless of the day of the week on which it fell, but others felt that the observance should be adjusted as necessary to fall always on a particular day, namely, on Sunday.

Although there has not been unanimity of judgment there has been an effort to marshal the best resources to deal with the problems. Thus, from Apollonius in the third century B.C. to Ptolemy in the second century A.D., the city of Alexandria was recognized as preeminent in astronomy, and therefore the church of Alexandria and the bishop of Alexandria were given special responsibility for determining the proper date of the annual Easter observance. Accordingly, the festal letters of Bishop Athanasius of Alexandria regularly begin with some remark about the approach of the important festival and conclude with the communication of the date for the year in question. Also, upon an occasion when Athanasius was in exile and his Arian opponents announced a date that proved to be erroneous, it was accounted a matter of disgrace for them.

Even so today we do not yet have unanimous agreement on many questions of chronology, and it is still appropriate that scholars, dealing as far as possible with all relevant evidence, endeavor to understand *chronos* and *kairos* in regard to Christian history.

The papers in the present volume—the dedication of which to myself I acknowledge with much appreciation—deal along the lines of my own special interests with historical matters in general and often with chronological questions in particular, and the authors, if not in agreement—yet—on all conclusions, are in agreement, I believe, that there are in these fields significant materials with which to work, and that such work is important.

A number of the papers were presented originally at a Nativity Conference held prior to Christmas 1983 at the Cobb Institute of Archaeology at Mississippi State University, at which I had the honor to preside. As the name indicates, the particular point in the long sweep of time with which the conference chiefly dealt is the birth of Jesus, which is the point from which Dionysius Exiguus preferred to reckon time—rather than from the reign of Diocletian, which to the Christians marked the beginning of the "era of the martyrs." The reckoning by Dionysius *ab incarnatione Domini*—established perhaps not entirely correctly—was generally followed from then on in the Christian world and even beyond.

As the Gospel of Matthew shows by reference to Herod, the King of the Jews, and as the Gospel of Luke shows by reference not only to rulers of the Jews but also to the Caesars of Rome and other rulers, the birth and life of Jesus were framed by the events of wider history; therefore the dates of the birth and life are to be dealt with in relation to the dates of surrounding events—and the latter also are not always without question—hence the difficulty and the challenge of this and related investigations.

Bibliography of the Writings of Jack Finegan

This list does not include all the foreign translations of Finegan's books, nor does it include the many articles in the following encyclopedias: *Twentieth Century Encyclopedia of Religious Knowledge: An Extension of the New Schaff-Herzog Encyclopedia of Religious Knowledge* (ed. Lefferts A. Loetscher; 2 vols.; Grand Rapids: Baker, 1955), *The Interpreter's Dictionary of the Bible* (ed. G. A. Buttrick; 4 vols.; Nashville: Abingdon, 1962), *Collier's Encyclopedia* (ed. W. D. Halsey; 1963 ed.), *Encyclopaedia Britannica* (1965 ed.), *Encyclopaedia Americana*. In addition, Finegan did a great deal of the illustrative work on the *Good News New Testament*, obtaining the photographs and writing the captions for the illustrations appearing with most of the books.

Books and Monographs

1934

1. *Die Überlieferung der Leidens- und Auferstehungsgeschichte Jesu.* Beiheft zur Zeitschrift für die neutestamentliche Wissenschaft 15. Giessen: Alfred Töpelmann.

1946

2. *Light from the Ancient Past: The Archeological Background of the Hebrew-Christian Religion.* Princeton: Princeton University Press.
   [See also nos. 12, 19, 22, 35, 41]

3. *Book of Student Prayers.* New York: Association Press.

4. *A Highway Shall Be There.* St. Louis: Bethany.

1949

5. *Youth Asks about Religion.* New York: Association Press.
   [See also nos. 20, 39]

6. *Like the Great Mountains.* St. Louis: Bethany.

1952

7. *The Archeology of World Religions: The Background of Primitivism, Zoroastrianism, Hinduism, Jainism, Buddhism, Confucianism, Taoism, Shinto, Islam, and Sikhism.* Princeton: Princeton University Press.
   [See also nos. 14, 27, 33]

8. *Rediscovering Jesus.* New York: Association Press.

1953

9. *Clear of the Brooding Cloud.* Nashville: Abingdon-Cokesbury.

1954

10. *The Orbits of Life.* St. Louis: Bethany.

1955

11. *India Today!* St. Louis: Bethany.
    [See also no. 13]

12. *Kodaibunka no Hikari.* Tokyo: Iwanami Shoten.
    [Japanese translation of no. 2, by Prince Takahito Mikasa]

13. *Indien!* Munich: Drömer.
    [German translation of no. 11]

14. *Splendori delle antichi religioni.* 2 vols. Milan: Aldo Martello.
    [Italian translation of no. 7, by Glauco Cambon]

1956

15. *Wanderer upon Earth.* New York: Harper.
    [See also no. 16]

16. *Viajando por el Mundo.* Mexico City: Editora Latinao Americana.
    [Spanish translation of no. 15, by José Villalba Pinyana]

17. *Beginnings in Theology.* New York: Association Press.
    [See also nos. 18, 23, 25]

18. *Christian Theology.* With a Foreword by William Neil. London: English Universities Press/Teach Yourself Books.
    [British edition of no. 17]

1957

19. *Luci del lontano passato: documenti archeologici della religione Ebraica-Christiana*. Milan: Aldo Martello.
[Italian translation of no. 2, by Glauco Cambon]

1958

20. *Forty Questions and Answers on Religion*. New York: Association Press.
[Based on no. 5]

1959

21. *Space, Atoms, and God: Christian Faith and the Nuclear-space Age*. St. Louis: Bethany.

22. *Light from the Ancient Past: The Archeological Background of Judaism and Christianity*. Princeton: Princeton University Press.
[Revised edition of no. 2; see also nos. 35, 41]

1960

23. *First Steps in Theology*. New York: Association Press, Reflection Books.
[Reprint of no. 17]

1962

24. *In the Beginning: A Journey through Genesis*. New York: Harper.

25. *Step by Step in Theology*. New York: Association Press.
[Adapted by Hal Vermes and Jean Vermes from no. 17]

1963

26. *Let My People Go: A Journey through Exodus*. New York: Harper and Row.

27. *Esplendores de las antiguas religiones, argueología de las religiones*. 2 vols. Barcelona: Luis de Caralt.
[Spanish translation of no. 7, by Domingo Manfredi Cano]

28. *At Wit's End*. Richmond: John Knox.
[See also no. 29]

29. *Am Ende unserer Weisheit: Ein Buch der Lebenshilfe*. Basel: Friedrich Reinhardt.
[German translation of no. 28, by Irmgard Vogelsanger-de Roche]

1964

30. *The Three R's of Christianity*. Richmond: John Knox.

31. *Jesus, History, and You*. Richmond: John Knox.

32. *Handbook of Biblical Chronology: Principles of Time Reckoning in the Ancient World and Problems of Chronology in the Bible*. Princeton: Princeton University Press.
    [See also no. 34]

1965

33. *The Archeology of World Religions*. 3 vols. Princeton: Princeton University Press.
    [Paperback reprint of no. 7]

1967

34. *Seisho-nendaigaku*. Tokyo: Iwanami Shoten.
    [Japanese translation of no. 30, by Prince Takahito Mikasa]

1969

35. *Light from the Ancient Past: The Archeological Background of Judaism and Christianity*. 2 vols. Princeton: Princeton University Press.
    [Paperback reprint of no. 22; see also no. 41]

36. *Hidden Records of the Life of Jesus: An Introduction to the New Testament Apocrypha, and to Some of the Areas through Which They were Transmitted, Namely, Jewish, Egyptian, and Gnostic Christianity, Together with the Earlier Gospel-type Records in the Apocrypha, in Greek and Latin Texts, [with] Translations and Explanations*. Philadelphia/Boston: Pilgrim Press.

37. *The Archeology of the New Testament: The Life of Jesus and the Beginning of the Early Church*. Princeton: Princeton University Press.
    [See also nos. 44, 46]

1972

38. *Mark of the Taw*. Richmond: John Knox.

39. *Cien preguntas obre religion*. Buenos Aires: La Aurora. [Spanish translation of no. 5, by Marcelo Peréz Rivas]

1973

40. *The Christian Church (Disciples of Christ).* Royal Oak, MI: Cathedral Publishers.
[See also no. 73]

1974

41. *Light from the Ancient Past: The Archeological Background of Judaism and Christianity.* 2 vols. Princeton: Princeton University Press.
[Reprint of no. 35]

42. *Encountering New Testament Manuscripts: A Working Introduction to Textual Criticism.* Grand Rapids: Eerdmans.
[See also no. 43]

1975

43. *Encountering New Testament Manuscripts: A Working Introduction to Textual Criticism.* London: SPCK.
[British edition of no. 42]

1978

44. *The Archeology of the New Testament: The Life of Jesus and the Beginning of the Early Church.* Princeton: Princeton University Press.
[Paperback reprint of no. 37]

1979

45. *Archaeological History of the Ancient Middle East.* Boulder, CO: Westview/Folkestone, England: Dawson.
[See also nos. 48, 50]

1981

46. *The Archeology of the New Testament: The Mediterranean World of the Early Christian Apostles.* Boulder, CO: Westview/London: Croom Helm.
[Companion volume to no. 37]

47. *Discovering Israel: An Archeological Guide to the Holy Land.* Grand Rapids: Eerdmans.

1983

48. *Kokogaku kara mita Kodai-orientoshi.* Tokyo: Iwanami Shoten. [Japanese translation of no. 45, by Prince Takahito Mikasa]

1986

49. *Tibet: A Dreamt of Image.* Sambhota series. New Delhi: Tibet House and Wiley Eastern.

50. *Archaeological History of the Ancient Middle East.* New York: Dorset. [Reprint of no. 45]

Forthcoming

51. *An Archaeological History of Religions of Indian Asia.* 2 vols. New York: Paragon House.

52. *Myth and Mystery: An Introduction to the "Pagan" Religions of the Ancient World.* Grand Rapids: Baker.

Articles and Contributions

1947

53. Research Abstracts: Archeology 1947. *Journal of Bible and Religion* 15: 229–31.

1948

54. Research Abstracts: Archeology 1948. *Journal of Bible and Religion* 16: 216–19.

1949

55. Research Abstracts: Archeology 1949. *Journal of Bible and Religion* 17: 245–49.

1950

56. Research Abstracts: Archeology 1950. *Journal of Bible and Religion* 19: 76–80.

57. The Chronology of Ezekiel. *Journal of Biblical Literature* 69: 61–66.

1951

58. Prescribing for a Sick World. *Christian Century* 68: 1098–99.

1952

59. Research Abstracts: Archeology 1951–52. *Journal of Bible and Religion* 21: 21–29.

1953

60. Research Abstracts: Archeology 1952–53. *Journal of Bible and Religion* 22: 257–63.

1955

61. Research Abstracts: Archeology 1954–55. *Journal of Bible and Religion* 24: 191–99.

1956

62. The Original Form of the Pauline Collection. *Harvard Theological Review* 49: 85–103.

63. Judaeo-Christian Heritage. Pp. 43–64 in *Mid-East: World-Center, Yesterday, Today, and Tomorrow,* ed. Ruth Nanda Anshen. Science of Culture series, vol. 7. New York: Harper.
    [See also no. 71]

64. Helping Students Face the Issues of Life; Sermon: Thank God and Take Courage. Pp. 151–60 in *Life-Situation Preaching,* ed. Charles F. Kemp. St. Louis: Bethany.

1957

65. Nebuchadnezzar and Jerusalem. *Journal of Bible and Religion* 25: 203–5.

66. Too Good to Be True? *The Pulpit* 28: 87–89.

67. The Great Invitation. *Pulpit Digest* 37: 15–19.

1958

68. Research Abstracts: Archeology 1956–58. *Journal of Bible and Religion* 27: 320–32.

1961

69. Research Abstracts: Archeology 1958–61. *Journal of Bible and Religion* 29: 317–28.

1969

70. A Lonesomeness for Eternity. Pp. 82–90 in *The Vital Pulpit of the Christian Church*, ed. Hunter Beckelhymer. St. Louis: Bethany.

1975

71. Judaeo-Christian Heritage. Pp. 43–64 in *Mid-East: World-Center, Yesterday, Today, and Tomorrow*, ed. Ruth Nanda Anshen. New York: Cooper Square.
[Reprint of no. 63]

1976

72. The Death and Burial of St. Peter. *Biblical Archaeology Review* 2/4 (December): 3–8.

73. The Christian Church (Disciples of Christ). Pp. 148–75 in *Our Faiths*, ed. Martin E. Marty. New York: Pillar Books.
[Reprint of no. 40]

1977

74. Did Peter Die in Babylon? *Biblical Archaeology Review* 3/2 (June): 48.
[Letter to editor]

1979

75. Crosses in the Dead Sea Scrolls: A Waystation on the Road to the Christian Cross. *Biblical Archaeology Review* 5/6 (November/December): 41–49.

76. Chronology of the New Testament. Pp. 686–93 in *The International Standard Bible Encyclopedia*, ed. Geoffrey W. Bromiley et al. Revised edition. Vol. 1. Grand Rapids: Eerdmans.
[Revision of article by William P. Armstrong in 1919/1929 edition]

1981

77. The Churches of Macedonia. *Biblical Illustrator* 7/3 (Spring): 70–75.

78. Capernaum. Pp. 56–62 in *Where Jesus Walked*, ed. William H. Stephens. Nashville: Broadman.

1982

79. Review of *The Holy Land: An Archaeological Guide from Earliest Times to 1700*, by Jerome Murphy-O'Connor. *Biblical Archaeology Review* 8/1 (January/February): 8, 10.

1985

80. The Fall of Jerusalem in A.D. 70. *Biblical Illustrator* 11/3 (Spring): 2–3, 9–12.

1987

81. Philippi. *Biblical Illustrator* 14/1 (Fall): 68–71.

Forthcoming

82. Religions of the Past. In *Introduction to the World's Religions*, ed. Joseph Bettis. New York: Macmillan/Scribner's.

Matthew and the Magi

The Significance of
the Structure of Matthew 1

Bastiaan Van Elderen

An interesting and attractive development in recent biblical scholarship is the recognition of and concern for the literary structure of biblical literature. The biblical authors are being hailed as literary artists and skilled craftsmen. The evangelists, especially, are no longer being dubbed as "scissors-and-paste" writers, but are being identified as authors and theologians with a careful plan, definite purpose, and well-designed structure for their writings. In fact, some modern scholars have focused so heavily on these features that one of the current approaches to the biblical literature is "structuralism." The concern of this paper is not to evaluate or critique this current method, except to observe that I have serious reservations and problems with the philosophical and theological presuppositions involved in much structuralist thinking.

However, I do have a great and growing appreciation for the structural features of biblical literature and I think we can learn a great deal from the literary techniques and structural devices employed by the biblical authors. The emphasis and focus of these literary products are often embedded in their structure. In the case of the Gospels, a greater awareness of the nature of first-century literature aids in detecting literary features. And this in many instances involves a double perspective since the documents are written in Greek, the language of the Hellenistic world, by men deeply rooted in the Semitic mindset, such as even Luke through the influence of the Septuagint. Hence, this kind of study can at times be both exciting and complex.

I will examine the structure of the Gospel of Matthew, and, more specifically chap. 1. Many issues relating to this Gospel cannot be

Bastiaan Van Elderen is Professor of New Testament in the Faculty of Theology at the Free University of Amsterdam.

considered in this paper, but for orientation I will make a few observations as the setting for a more intensive study of chap. 1. Although controversy continues regarding the structural outline of Matthew's Gospel, the two major approaches focus on the use of repeated formulae. One outline centers on the five major discourses, each preceded by a narrative section and concluded by a fixed and familiar formula—καὶ ἐγένετο ὅτε ἐτέλεσεν ὁ Ἰησοῦς (7:28, 11:1, 13:53, 19:1, 26:1). One problem with this outline is the place of the opening chapters and closing chapters of the Gospel—which no one would want to denigrate to the status of introduction and epilogue.

The other approach, set forth initially by J. D. Kingsbury,[1] builds around the formula in 4:17 and 16:21—ἀπὸ τότε ἤρξατο ὁ Ἰησοῦς—and identifies three divisions:

1. The person of Jesus Messiah (1:1–4:16)
2. The public proclamation of Jesus Messiah (4:17–16:20)
3. The suffering, death, and resurrection of Jesus Messiah (16:21–28:20)

R. H. Gundry has expressed some reservations about Kingsbury's outline and notes that the Gospel of Matthew does not neatly divide into the three divisions since the material of the one spills over into the other. Furthermore, he suggests that the formulae in 4:17 and 16:21 actually signal divisions in the ministry of Jesus rather than in Matthew's gospel as a whole.[2]

These repeated formulae, on the other hand, cannot be ignored since they obviously have some kind of literary function. Hence, the tripartite division of Kingsbury and the traditional fivefold division by discourses must be seen as clearly embedded in the structure and content of Matthew. In table 1 I have tried to integrate the two by imposing the former over the latter.

In his discussion about the structure of Matthew, Gundry observes that "we should avoid imposing an outline on Matthew" and he concludes his discussion by suggesting that "the Gospel of Matthew is structurally mixed."[3] This first caveat is very proper since any outline must emerge from the document itself. However, a further problem is

1. J. D. Kingsbury, *Matthew: Structure, Christology, Kingdom* (Philadelphia: Fortress, 1975) 9.

2. R. H. Gundry, *Matthew: A Commentary on His Literary and Theological Art* (Grand Rapids: Eerdmans, 1982) 10.

3. Ibid., 10, 11.

TABLE 1.

1. Person of Jesus the Messiah 1:1–4:16	2. Public proclamation of Jesus Messiah 4:17–16:20					3. Suffering, death, and resurrection of Jesus Messiah 16:21–28:20
	First Discourse 4:12–7:29	Second Discourse 8:1–11:1	Third Discourse 11:2–13:53	Fourth Discourse 13:54–19:1	Fifth Discourse 19:2–26:1	

that often we expect to find structure in an ancient document according to the logical ordering with which our Western minds operate. I would like to suggest that the Gospel of Matthew is a finely structured document that employs some important literary devices and techniques, thus it is not proper to dismiss Matthew as structurally mixed.

In many respects an analysis of Matthew 1 can be very helpful for the understanding of the entire Gospel since one finds the major themes of Matthew in this opening section. Furthermore, Matthew has used the nativity account to introduce these major themes, which then are gradually elucidated in the body and finally presented with full content in the conclusion, or perhaps more exactly, in the climax. I have labeled this literary device: adumbrative hints of the *conclusio*.

Matthew had to use this technique because these themes were not readily acceptable to his readers and they had to be gradually conditioned to the new idea set forth in the theme. In this respect, the nativity account functions in a significant way in Matthew's Gospel and effectively sets the stage for the unfolding of the major themes in the Gospel.

First of all, I shall list the major themes that Matthew introduces in the opening section, and then I shall examine the structure of this section, which is Matthew's nativity account, to see how these themes are embedded in it.

The first motif I have called *theoparousia* (θεοπαρουσία), the presence of God. I consider this as the essence of the Kingdom of Heaven as set forth by Matthew. The first allusion to it is in the Emmanuel prophecy

cited in Matt 1:23—interpreted as "God with us." The radically new
thing occasioned by the nativity is that God is now again present with
this people. And he will remain present with them, as suggested by the
last verse of Matthew's Gospel: "I am with you always, to the close of
the age" (28:20). This theoparousia is set forth by the literary device
inclusio formed by Matt 1:23, 28:20.

Closely related to this concept of theoparousia is the second motif—
the identification of Jesus as the Son of God. Kingsbury considers this
the central christological category of Matthew's Gospel that "extends
to every phase of the 'life' of Jesus: conception, birth, and infancy;
baptism and temptation; public ministry; death; and resurrection and
exaltation."[4] This motif is subtly presented in Matthew's nativity
account, especially in the structure of the genealogy, to be considered
below.

Closely related to the above motif is the identification of Jesus as
the Son of David and hence king of Israel. Davidic Sonship and royal
lineage are set forth in the genealogy and continue as a special Matthean
christological designation.

The motif of universalism comes to full expression in the Great
Commission (Matt 28:19), but hints of it are already present in the
nativity account, and throughout the Gospel there are these adumbrative hints leading to the ultimate expression in the closing section.

Another significant motif in Matthew is the continuity from the
Old Testament people of God to the Christian church. The covenant
with Abraham, alluded to in the nativity account, reaches ultimate
fulfilment in the Great Commission at the end of the Gospel. This
continuity is also illustrated by the fulfillment of Messianic promises in
Jesus of Nazareth—already cited in the nativity accounts.

All of these motifs and themes were radically new ideas for
Matthew's Jewish readers. In fact, they ran counter to many of the
basic ideas in the first century Judaism: particularism, monotheism,
Messianism, ethnic covenantism. Hence, these had to be gradually
introduced, developed, and climaxed. An examination of the structure
and content of the nativity account in Matthew will show how these
motifs are subtly introduced.

Matthew's nativity account begins with these words: βίβλος γενέσεως Ἰησοῦ Χριστοῦ υἱοῦ Δαυὶδ υἱοῦ Ἀβραάμ. The term βίβλος γενέσεως
harks back to the same words used in the Septuagint of Gen 2:4 and

4. Kingsbury, *Matthew: Structure, Christology, Kingdom*, 82. He develops this thesis in
chapter 2 (40–83). Cf. also his *Matthew* (Proclamation Commentaries; Philadelphia: Fortress, 1977) 34–57.

5:1. Some have restricted the word γένεσις to the meaning of 'genera-tion' here and thus understood, it refers to the contents of Matt 1:2–17. However, the use of βίβλος with γένεσις might suggest a broader meaning of 'history of the origin' (as in Gen 2:4), possibly including the entire nativity account in Matthew 1.[5] Others consider the expression as the heading of superscription of the entire Gospel: 'book of history'.[6] Given the use of the nativity account with its adumbrative hints of various themes and motifs and how their full expression gradually unfolds in the Gospel, the term βίβλος γενέσεως may well describe the entire Gospel and thus parallels the divisions in Genesis expressed by *tôlĕdôt*. Thus, Matthew's Gospel is the continuation and culmination of Old Testament history.

Jesus Christ is qualified in Matt 1:1 as υἱὸς Δαυίδ and υἱὸς Ἀβραάμ. Abraham figures at the beginning of the genealogy but is not further referred to in the nativity account. However, his significance in the covenant motif in the Old Testament would be well-known to the Jewish reader (cf. Genesis 12, 15, 17). Hence, to identify Jesus as the son of Abraham is very meaningful. The introduction of Abraham here, evoking various covenant connotations, forms an *inclusio* with the Great Commission in Matt 28:19 where the covenant promise to Abra-ham in Genesis regarding the families of the earth ("by you all the families of the earth shall bless themselves"—Gen 12:3) reaches its climax and fulfilment in "Go therefore and make disciples of all nations."

The role of David figures very significantly in the genealogy. The genealogy is structured by dividing Old Testament history into three periods.[7] To do this Matthew had to take some liberties with the Old Testament record. Chronologically the three periods are unequal—although each consists of fourteen generations. The first is approxi-mately 1000 years, the second approximately 350 years, and the third approximately 580 years. Some generations are omitted—for example, Joash, Amaziah, Azariah in 1:9 (cf. 1 Chr 3:11–12) and six generations that are found in Ezra 7:3. Actually, Matthew gives only thirteen generations in the third division. His concern here is not a precise

5. W. Bauer, *A Greek-English Lexicon of the New Testament* (trans. W. F. Arndt and F. W. Gingrich; 2d ed. revised by F. W. Gingrich and F. W. Danker; Chicago: University of Chicago, 1979) 154.

6. For example, T. Zahn, *Introduction to the New Testament* (Edinburgh: T. & T. Clark, 1909), 2:531.

7. The Matthean and Lucan genealogies bristle with difficulties in their similarities and differences and in their relation to the Old Testament data. Regarding biblical genealogies, cf. M. D. Johnson, *The Purpose of Biblical Genealogies* (London: Cambridge University, 1969).

record but he wants to set up a scheme of three fourteens in order to focus on the number fourteen, which is the numerical value of the name David in Hebrew (*dwd*: $4 + 6 + 4 = 14$). *Gematria*, this use of numbers and play on numerical values (especially of names), was common practice among the Jewish rabbis.

The centrality of David in the genealogy is further demonstrated by his name culminating the first period (from Abraham to David)—a period of the formation and acme of the kingdom of Israel. From this high point in the reign of David the kingdom declined in the second period, culminating in the Babylonian Captivity. The third period is a period of recovery, which culminated in the New Age (kingdom) of Jesus. Also of significance is that only David in the entire genealogy is given the title king (1:6). Jesus' continuity with David the king is neatly affirmed in the question of the Magi—"Where is he who has been born king of the Jews?" (2:2)—addressed to the usurper and pretender King Herod! (2:1, 3).

In 2 Sam 7:12-16 the promise of the kingdom and of its greatness was given to David. This promise now culminates in this new "Son of David"—Jesus Christ. As David culminates the first period at the highest point of Old Testament history, so now Jesus culminates the entire Old Testament history and ushers in the New Age. Matthew uses this designation, Son of David, for Jesus most frequently of the evangelists. In fact, it surfaces at key points in the Gospel—9:27, 12:23, 15:22, 20:30-31—and climaxes in the acclamation of the crowds and children in the triumphal entry on Palm Sunday (21:9, 15). Another subtle Matthean use of "Son of David" in the nativity account is the occurrence with Joseph in 1:20, discussed below.

The genealogy is structured by a somewhat monotonous repetition of the same formula—A ἐγέννησεν B, B ἐγέννησεν C, etc. The same verb is used throughout: γεννάω ('to beget') in the active voice. However, the use of this repeated formula is with a purpose. In five places women are mentioned in the genealogy. The first four are found in the first period: Tamar (1:3), Rahab (1:5), Ruth (1:5), and Bathsheba ("the wife of Uriah"; 1:6). These four women were non-Jews or involved with non-Jews and were party to rather unusual activities. Their inclusion is the first adumbrative hint of universalism in Matthew's Gospel. Each of these names are added to the formula with a prepositional phrase, for example, "Boaz begat Obed *by Ruth* (ἐκ τῆς ʿΡούθ; 1:5). The prominence of the male progenitor is maintained in every generation. However in 1:16, where the birth of Jesus is reported, the male progenitor is not mentioned. Rather, the stereotyped formula suddenly is changed. The verb is put in the passive voice and Mary's role is described in the same idiom as in the case of the previous four women—by means of the prepositional clause with ἐκ. The actual father of Jesus is not mentioned, as in all the other generations. Thus, this sudden change in the repeated formula alerts the reader to an unusual and singular birth in the case of Jesus—the virgin birth. This striking conclusion of the genealogy arouses the curiosity of the reader and sets the stage for the next paragraph, which is introduced thus: "Now the birth of Jesus Christ took place in this way" (1:18).

The modern reader perhaps does not find this genealogy in Matthew very edifying and meaningful. However, it is a carefully crafted account, structured to give prominence to the fulfilment and culmination of the Abrahamic covenant promises and the Davidic kingdom. An element of universalism is introduced and the significant role of women is adumbrated in four women and highlighted in Mary, the mother of Jesus. The unusual nature of the birth of Jesus is introduced to set the stage for the following account of that birth. For the reader familiar with the Old Testament history and promises and observant of the distinctive structure of this passage in Greek, this genealogy reveals important and significant features about the life and ministry of Jesus, which are further elucidated in the Gospel and prefigured in the Old Testament.

The next section in Matthew's nativity account describes the birth of Jesus, as its introductory statement suggests. However, the actual birth is only indirectly alluded to in the closing verse of the section, Matthew is not interested in the details of the birth, as is often the case with the birth accounts of important persons. In fact, Luke's Gospel provides more of such details. Similarly, extensive details are found in to apocryphal accounts, such as the *Protevangelium of James*, frequently with apologetic interests. However, Matthew's interest is to introduce certain basic themes in this account that have numerous Old Testament allusions. The focus of this passage in vv 18-25 is on the message of the angel (ἄγγελος κυρίου) and the evangelist's commentary on it (1:23). The passage has a chiastic structure in which both beginning and end refer to the birth of Jesus, which is then interpreted by the angel and the evangelist in the central section.

    1. The unusual pregnancy of Mary and birth of Jesus (v 18)
        2. The perplexity of Joseph (v 19)
            3. The message of the angel (vv 20-21)
            3'. The commentary of the evangelist (vv 22-23)
        2'. The resolution of Joseph (v 24)
    1'. The unusual pregnancy of Mary and birth of Jesus (v 25)

The peculiar circumstances of the pregnancy of Mary are high-lighted in the opening and closing sections, emphasizing that Joseph and Mary did not cohabit until after the birth of Jesus. The message of the angel instructs Joseph and clarifies his perplexity. Nowhere is there any intimation or suspicion in the mind of Joseph or others of unseemly conduct on the part of Mary, as one finds in the *Protevangelium of James.* The divine role in Mary's pregnancy seems to be known to Joseph initially, possibly from Mary. This situation puts Joseph in a perplexing quandary. Evidence from the first century, such as the Qumran litera-ture,[8] suggests that Joseph in this circumstance was obligated to divorce Mary. However, out of love for Mary and perhaps reverence for the Holy Spirit, he decided to do this secretly (λάθρα, 1:19). Hence, the first circumstantial participle in v 19, ὤν, must be interpreted as concessive: 'although he was a just man'; and the second, θέλων, as causal: 'because he was not willing to make a public example of her'. Given these tensions and emotions, one can understand Joseph's perplexity. Nor-mally and traditionally, his course of action was clearly prescribed, but an unusual factor, no less than divine intervention, has complicated the issue.

Matthew's Jewish reader would immediately recognize the numer-ous Old Testament anaphora in this passage. The phrase 'in a dream' (κατ᾽ ὄναρ) in 1:20 has Old Testament precedents and occurs only in Matthew in the New Testament (six times). Five of these occur in the first two chapters of Matthew as a means of conveying special messages to individuals in the birth narrative. Similarly, the term 'angel of the Lord (ἄγγελος θεοῦ) has Old Testament roots and is also a Mattheanism (four times): 1:20 plus two further appearances to Joseph in 2:13, 19. Strikingly the other occurrence is in Matt 28:2, in the resurrection account that culminates the Gospel. The message of the angel is couched in Old Testament concepts and terms and culminates in the naming of the child with a definition of the name—a meaningful Old Testament practice.

Further clarification for the reader regarding this unusual preg-nancy is given by the evangelist in v 22. This is the first use of his recurring formula, ἵνα πληρωθῇ, which occurs eleven times in his Gospel—four of which are in chaps. 1 and 2. It functions as another direct link with the Old Testament, further demonstrating the conti-nuity of the life and ministry of Jesus with the Old Testament.

The Old Testament citation in v 23 has been the center of exten-sive controversy relating to the use and meaning of παρθένος in Mat-

8. 1QapGen and 11QTemple. Cf. also J. Jeremias, *Jerusalem in the Time of Jesus* (Philadelphia: Fortress, 1969) 367.

thew and of ʿalmâ (Septuagint: παρθένος) in Isa 7:14. The truth of the virgin birth, or, perhaps more precisely, virgin conception, does not and should not hinge on this single passage. In fact, there are better proof texts for it elsewhere in the nativity accounts—in both Matthew and Luke. Regrettably, the animated discussion on Matt 1:23 and Isa 7:14 has neglected what I consider the more important truth—the Emmanuel prophecy, which is even interpreted for the reader: "God with us." This is the heart of Matthew's commentary here. He introduces the key concept of theoparousia, which I described earlier, and gives its interpretation from the Septuagint in Isa 8:8, 10. As noted earlier, this forms an important *inclusio* with the last verse of Matthew—"I am with you always."

The nativity account also subtly introduces Matthew's Son of God Christology. Mary's unusual pregnancy is occasioned by the Holy Spirit—ἐκ πνεύματος ἁγίου (1:18, 20)—and through this birth God again is present with his people (theoparousia; 1:21).

A further feature of this passage in Matt 1:18–25 is to give some status to Joseph who does not function in the genealogy nor in the procreation of Jesus. This is a very delicate topic for the evangelist to handle. Joseph is needed in the nativity account to establish Matthew's Davidic Christology—an important motif in his Gospel. To do this he introduces Joseph in the genealogy but gives him no generative role—in fact, he irregularly structures the end of the genealogy to set the stage for what follows. On the other hand, Joseph becomes the chief character in this next section and the account concludes with his taking the role of father by naming the child—καὶ ἐκάλεσεν τὸ ὄνομα αὐτοῦ Ἰησοῦν (v 25)—as instructed by the angel (v 21). This elevation of Joseph from the rather benign role in the genealogy is masterful in the account. He is described immediately as a (v 19) sensitive and righteous man (cf. Zechariah and Elizabeth in Luke 1:6) whose religious convictions are rooted in the Old Testament. Strikingly, he is identified as υἱὸς Δαυίδ (1:20), recalling the earlier use of this designation for Jesus (1:1). His obedient readiness to follow the instructions of the angel is simply stated and he forthrightly carries them out. And so the account concludes with an affirmation that Joseph was not the progenitor of Jesus, but nevertheless in actuality functioned as his legal parent. The ambiguity of the concluding item in the genealogy is clarified—Joseph becomes the legal parent (through naming the child). However, the unusual feature of the account, the virgin pregnancy through divine intermediation, has been affirmed.

This same prominence of Joseph continues in the next chapter (2) where the visit of the Magi and the flight to Egypt are reported. As in the last section of chap. 1, no details about the birth of Jesus are given.

In fact, the birth is rather insignificantly and incidentally mentioned in an introductory participial clause (genitive absolute): τοῦ δὲ 'Ιησοῦ γεννηθέντος . . . (Matt 2:1). The visit of the Magi is an adumbrative hint of the universalism with which Matthew's Gospel ends. However, in the ensuing events Joseph again is the principal character in the holy family—functioning throughout as the legal father. In these events Joseph twice receives special instructions through the ἄγγελος κυρίου (2:13, 19), as earlier in 1:20. Of striking signficance is the idiom used by Matthew to emphasize this special way in which Joseph is instructed:

1:20—ἰδοὺ ἄγγελος κυρίου κατ᾽ ὄναρ ἐφάνη αὐτῷ λέγων . . . .
2:13—ἰδοὺ ἄγγελος κυρίου φαίνεται κατ᾽ ὄναρ [MS B has κατ᾽ ὄναρ ἐφάνη] τῷ 'Ιωσὴφ λέγων . . . .
2:19—ἰδοὺ ἄγγελος κυρίου φαίνεται κατ᾽ ὄναρ τῷ 'Ιωσὴφ . . . λέγων . . . .

In each case the immediate obedient response of Joseph is highlighted by the aorist participle ἐγερθείς (1:24; 2:14, 21) and the verb παραλαμβάνω with Mary and/or Jesus as direct objects.[9]

This leading role of Joseph in Matthew's nativity account stands in contrast to the prominent role of Mary in the Lucan nativity account. Clearly Matthew was intent upon showing Joseph's function as the legal parent, although not the progenitor, in order to establish Jesus' Davidic descent.[10]

The first chapter of Matthew's Gospel is very carefully structured to introduce the major themes of the document. In this first chapter one finds theoparousia, universalism, Davidic Christology, Son of God Christology, continuity of the Old Testament and this new revelation in Jesus: Israel/church/covenant/kingdom. Adumbrative hints of these themes surface throughout the Gospel (for example, the theme of universalism), and in the climax of the Gospel these are forthrightly affirmed. Matthew's nativity account was not simply written to inform and provide data—in fact, his omission of many details actually results

9. H. J. B. Combrink, "The Structure of the Gospel of Matthew as Narrative," *Tyn Bul* 34 (1983) 77, interprets Joseph's obedient response as presenting Joseph as "a prototype of a 'follower' of Jesus, obeying exactly what is commnded."

10. After the episode in Luke 2:41-52 (Jesus' visit to the temple at the age of twelve), Joseph disappears from the Gospel accounts. However, in the pericope about the rejection at Nazareth, reported by Matthew and Mark in the latter part of the Galilean ministry, Matthew has the crowd identify Jesus as ὁ τοῦ τέκτονος υἱός (13:55), whereas Mark has ὁ τέκτων (6:3). Luke reports this at the beginning of the Galilean ministry and has the crowds referring to the υἱὸς . . . 'Ιωσὴφ (4:22). Cf. John 6:42.

in an incomplete account. Rather, the account is loaded with theological motifs—even the monotonous genealogy is heavily charged theologically. My aim in this presentation has been to show the foundational role of Matthew's nativity account in his Gospel.

APPENDIX

After the completion of this paper, H. J. B. Combrink's article entitled "The Structure of the Gospel of Matthew as Narrative" appeared in *Tyn Bul* 34 (1983) 61–90. He suggested the following symmetrical composition of Matthew:

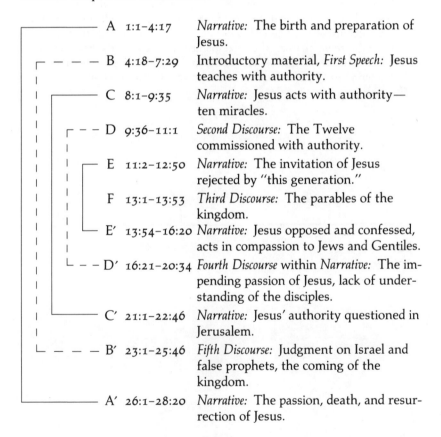

A 1:1–4:17   *Narrative:* The birth and preparation of Jesus.

B 4:18–7:29   Introductory material, *First Speech:* Jesus teaches with authority.

C 8:1–9:35   *Narrative:* Jesus acts with authority— ten miracles.

D 9:36–11:1   *Second Discourse:* The Twelve commissioned with authority.

E 11:2–12:50   *Narrative:* The invitation of Jesus rejected by "this generation."

F 13:1–13:53   *Third Discourse:* The parables of the kingdom.

E' 13:54–16:20 *Narrative:* Jesus opposed and confessed, acts in compassion to Jews and Gentiles.

D' 16:21–20:34 *Fourth Discourse* within *Narrative:* The impending passion of Jesus, lack of understanding of the disciples.

C' 21:1–22:46 *Narrative:* Jesus' authority questioned in Jerusalem.

B' 23:1–25:46 *Fifth Discourse:* Judgment on Israel and false prophets, the coming of the kingdom.

A' 26:1–28:20 *Narrative:* The passion, death, and resurrection of Jesus.

This scheme consists of alternation of *narrative* and *discourse* and recognizes the five-discourse structure of Matthew. The repeated formula in 4:17 and 16:21 functions significantly at the close of A and at

the beginning of D'—both representing significant turning points in
the Gospel of Matthew. The center of this chiastic structure is F—the
third discourse: the parables of the kingdom (chap. 13). This marks an
important transition in Jesus' address—from the ὄχλοι to his instruction
of the μαθηταί (13:36).

Combrink (p. 71) comments on this outline as follows:

> According to this pattern the pivotal point F, the parables dealing with
> kingdom of heaven, is emphasized. The larger section E–F–E' can, however,
> be taken to be a larger turning area. In this section of the Gospel the
> repeated rejection of Jesus (E) is followed by the parables (F) dealing with
> the mystery of accepting and rejecting the gospel of the kingdom—a
> speech divided into two due to a change of setting and audience. In E' Jesus
> is then confessed as Messiah and Son of God. The symmetrical pattern
> furthermore emphasizes the correspondences between the beginning and
> the end of the Gospel (A–A'), between the various speeches (B–B'; D–
> chapter 18 in D'), and even between the various narrative sections (C–C';
> E–E').

The Episode of the Magi

Edwin M. Yamauchi

Who were the biblical Magi of Matt 2:1-12, who were later transformed into the legendary "three kings of Orient"?

1. The Legend of the Christmas Magi

a. The Magi in the Apocryphal Gospels

The episode of the Magi was expanded in the genre of Infancy Gospels from the second century on.[1] One of the earliest of these, *The Protevangelium of James* (ca. A.D. 150), records the following accounts:

> And the wise men said: "We saw a very great star shining among those stars and dimming them so that the stars appeared not: and thereby knew we that a king was born unto Israel, and we came to worship him." ... And lo, the star which they saw in the east went before them until they entered into the cave: and it stood over the head of the cave.[2]

The Arabic Infancy Gospel, which may have been composed originally in Syriac, reports that the Magi came to Jerusalem following a prediction of Zoroaster.

The sixth-century Syriac *Cave of Treasures* gives the names of the Magi as Hormizdah King of Persia, Yazdegerd King of Saba, and Perozadh King of Sheba (cf. Ps 72:10).[3] The first references to the

Edwin Yamauchi is Professor of History at Miami University (Oxford, Ohio).

1. See my article, "Apocryphal Gospels," *The International Standard Bible Encyclopedia* (ed. G. W. Bromiley; rev. ed.; Grand Rapids: Eerdmans, 1979), 1:181-88.

2. M. R. James, *The Apocryphal New Testament* (Oxford: Clarendon, 1924) 47. Cf. E. Hennecke and W. Schneemelcher, *New Testament Apocrypha* (Philadelphia: Westminster, 1963), 1:386.

3. B. M. Metzger, "Names for the Nameless in the New Testament," *Kyriakon* (ed. P. Granfield and J. Jungmann; Münster: Aschendorff, 1970), 1:82.

traditional names of the Magi—Melchior, Balthasar, and Gaspar—occur in the *Excerpta Latina Barbari*, a Latin translation of a sixth-century Greek chronicle.[4] *The Armenian Infancy Gospel*, which was based on an early Syriac composition, specifies that Melqon (Melchior) came from Persia, Balthasar from Arabia, and Gaspar from India.[5] The *Excerpta et Collectanea* gives further details:

> Melchior, an old man with white hair and a long beard . . . who offered gold to the Lord as to a king. The second, Gaspar by name, young and beardless and ruddy complexioned . . . honored him as God by his gift of incense, and oblation worthy of divinity. The third, black-skinned and heavily bearded, named Balthasar . . . by his gift of myrrh testified to the Son of Man who was to die.[6]

b. *The Magi in Art*

The adoration of the Magi was one of the most popular motifs in early Christian art, appearing already in the catacomb of Santa Priscilla two centuries before the representation of shepherds adoring the Christ child.[7] The number of Magi varied from two to four but was eventually stabilized at three.[8] The three Magi, dressed in Persian garb, were usually depicted bearing gifts to the infant Jesus, resting on the lap of his mother, as in the epitaph of Severa.[9]

---

4. The name *Melchior* means "My King is Light"; *Balthasar* was probably derived from "Belteshazzar," the Babylonian name given to Daniel; and *Gaspar* may come from the Indian name Gundaphorus. See Metzger, "Names for the Nameless," 85; M. V. Scheil, "Melchior, Gaspar, Balthasar," *Florilegium ou receuil de travaux d'érudition* (ed. Melchior de Vogüé; Paris: Imprimerie Nationale, 1909) 551–54.

5. James, *Apocryphal New Testament*, 83.

6. Cited by R. E. Brown, *The Birth of the Messiah* (Garden City: Doubleday, 1977) 199. R. E. McNally, "The Three Holy Kings in Early Irish Latin Writing," *Kyriakon* (ed. P. Granfield and J. Jungmann; Münster: Aschendorff, 1970), 2:669, comments on this work: "This curious compilation, if not actually of Irish provenance, certainly reflects and parallels early Irish thinking. Largely a collection of disparate pieces of different character and origin, it was probably put together about the middle of the eighth century, possibly somewhat later."

7. Brown, *Birth of the Messiah*, 197. On the Magi in art generally, see H. Kehrer, *Die heiligen drei Könige in Literatur und Kunst* (Leipzig: Seemann, 1908–09), 2 vols.; J. C. Marsh-Edwards, "The Magi in Tradition and Art," *Irish Ecclesiastical Review* 85 (1956) 1–9.

8. C. R. Morey, *Early Christian Art* (Princeton: Princeton University, 1953) 68; André Grabar, *Christian Iconography* (Princeton: Princeton University, 1968) fig. 26; Pierre du Bourguet, *Early Christian Art* (New York: William Morrow, 1971) 46.

9. In the famous illustrated epitaph of Severa (dated to 330) a star looms above the Magi and the Madonna. The figure behind her pointing to the star has been interpreted as Balaam or as a personification of the Holy Spirit. See *The Vatican Collections: The Papacy*

The three Magi appear in the famous sixth-century mosaic from the church of St. Apollinaris Nuovo in Ravenna. Above their figures are inscribed the names: SCS. [= *Sanctus* 'Saint'] Balthassar, SCS. Melchior, and SCS. Gaspar. The purple mantle of the empress Theodora on the Church of S. Vitale in Ravenna is embroidered with figures of the Magi.[10]

The Magi were customarily portrayed in Persian dress with belted tunics, full sleeves, trousers, and peaked hats. Franz Cumont suggests that Christian artists adopted the Roman representation of Persians presenting tributes to the emperors.[11] When the Persian army under Chosroes invaded Palestine in 614, his soldiers destroyed the churches of Jerusalem but spared the Church of the Holy Nativity in Bethlehem when they saw that a mosaic of the church depicted Magi in Persian dress.[12]

At a monastic church in Deir es-Suryani in Egypt the Magi were depicted as kings:

> The Wise Men, depicted as kings, are in the bottom right-hand corner. The first is white-haired and bearded, the second middle-aged with a shorter black beard, and the third is youthful and clean-shaven. Each wears a crown and carries his gift in his left hand. The first has a purse, the second a casket, and the third a cup.[13]

---

and Art (ed. John P. O'Neill et al.; New York: Metropolitan Museum of Art, 1983) 221, no. 136.

10. Morey, *Early Christian Art*, 167; Grabar, *Christian Iconography*, fig. 252.

11. F. Cumont, "L'adoration des mages et l'art triomphal de Rome," *Atti di Pontificia Accademia di Archeologia*, ser. 11A, 111 (1932) 82–105.

12. This story was reported at the Synod of Jerusalem in 836. See Jack Finegan, *The Archeology of the New Testament* (Princeton: Princeton University, 1969) 26. Many church fathers, for example, Clement of Alexandria and Chrysostom, held that the Magi must have come from Persia. Justin Martyr asserted that the Magi came from Arabia, a view that was also followed by Tertullian and Epiphanius. Justin may have been led to this deduction by Ps 72:10 and by the knowledge that myrrh and frankincense were aromatic spices obtained from Sheba (modern Yemen in southwest Arabia). See G. Ryckmans, "De l'or (?), de l'encens et de la myrrhe," *RB* 58 (1951) 372–76; Gus W. van Beek, "Frankincense and Myrrh," *BA* 23 (1960) 70–95; *Solomon and the Queen of Sheba* (ed. J. B. Pritchard; London: Phaidon, 1974); N. Groom, *Frankincense and Myrrh* (London: Longman, 1981). The difficulty with the origin of the Magi from either Arabia or Persia is the lack of an early astrological tradition in those areas compared to Mesopotamia. E. Bishop, "Some Reflections on Justin Martyr and the Nativity Narratives," *EvQ* 39 (1967) 33, observes: "Origen, who knew the Palestine of his day, and Jerome, who lived in Bethlehem, considered favourably the claims of Babylonian astrologers, as did St. Augustine of Hippo; and it must be admitted that the concensus of three such scholars is formidable."

13. C. C. Walters, *Monastic Archaeology in Egypt* (Warminster: Aris and Phillips, 1974) 318–19.

Artists began commonly to depict the "wise men" from the east as kings from the 12th century. Between the years 1360 and 1420 one of the Three Kings was first depicted as a black.[14]

2. Was Matthew's Account Also Legendary?

As one sees how readily the biblical account of the Magi was metamorphosed over the centuries into such a multicolored tapestry of richly embroidered legends, it is not surprising that there are some who would extend the process backward into the New Testament itself. Unable to accept Matthew's account as historical because of certain supernatural or incredible elements,[15] they prefer to offer alternative theories to explain how the episode of the Magi was created either as a reflection of another historical event or as a midrashic elaboration of another biblical passage.

a. A Reflection of Tiridates' Trip?

In A.D. 66 Tiridates I, the Arsacid ruler of Armenia, visited Rome in order to receive his crown from Nero.[16] The king was accompanied by magi, and since he himself was a *magus* he sought to avoid traveling by sea (at least on his trip to Rome). According to Pliny's *Natural History* 30:6:17 Tiridates initiated Nero into "Magian" or "magical" banquets (*magicis etiam cenis eum initiaverat*).[17]

In 1902 A. Dieterich suggested that Matthew's episode of the Magi was a garbled reflection of Tiridates' trip. Like the Magi, Tiridates and his entourage came from the east. Like the Magi they came to do homage to a ruler. Like them they brought gifts.[18]

This explanation was welcomed by, among others, the Iranologist E. Herzfeld. In a recent monograph F. Zinniker has revived Dietrich's theory at some length and added the suggestion that Matthew's account may have possibly been a polemic against the "adoration" of the em-

---

14. J. Vercoutter, J. LeClant, F. M. Snowden, and J. Desanges, *The Image of the Black in Western Art* (New York: William Morrow, 1976), 1:24.

15. For example, Brown, *Birth of the Messiah*, 36; M. Hengel and H. Merkel, "Die Magier aus dem Osten und die Flucht nach Ägypten (Mt 2) im Rahmen der antiken Religionsgeschichte und der Theologie des Matthäus," *Orientierung en Jesus* (ed. P. Hoffmann; Freiburg: Herder, 1973) 139–41.

16. There are references to this trip in Suetonius, *Nero* 13 and 30; Tacitus, *Annals* 16:23; and Dio Cassius 8:146.

17. The Loeb translation takes the term *magicis* in the former sense and renders 'their banquets'.

18. "Die Weisen aus dem Morgenlande," *ZNW* 3 (1902) 1–14.

peror Nero. The recent commentary on Matthew by F. W. Beare also presents this explanation for the genesis of the Magi episode.[19]

In response to this train of interpretation I note that many of Dietrich's interpretations were highly speculative, bordering on the fantastic. He wished to interpret the encounter between Nero and the magi of Tiridates as an initiation into Mithraic mysteries, even though no mention was made of Mithras,[20] and he sought to interpret a Greek text from the magical papyri as a "Mithrasliturgie."[21]

In the context of Tiridates' visit, it is quite clear that his *magi* were priests and not astrologers—unlike Matthew's Magi. There is no reference at all to any astral phenomena. Pliny's passage indicates that Nero's interest in the Armenian magi was aroused by the emperor's fascination with magic.[22] As J. D. M. Derrett concludes, "The Magi cannot be dismissed as a fabrication, still less a fabrication based upon some embassy of a Parthian king to Nero, years after the event about to be described."[23]

b. *A Midrash of the Adoration of the Shepherds?*

Robert Gundry in his recent commentary on Matthew has proposed that Matthew transformed in a midrashic manner the Lukan episode of the adoration of the shepherds into the adoration of the Magi:

> Matthew now turns the visit of the local Jewish shepherds (Luke 2:8-20) into the adoration by Gentile magi from foreign parts. . . . The magi were astrologers. Matthew selects them as his substitute for the shepherds in order to lead up to the star, which replaces the angel and heavenly host in the tradition (Luke 2:8-15a).[24]

19. E. Herzfeld, "Sakastan" *Archäologische Mitteilungen aus Iran* 4 (1932) 111. F. Zinniker, *Probleme der sogenannten Kindheitsgeschichte bei Matthäus* (Freiburg: Paulusverlag, 1972) 128-29. F. W. Beare, *The Gospel According to Matthew* (San Francisco: Harper and Row, 1982) 74-75.

20. J. P. Kane, "The Mithraic Cult Meal in Its Greek and Roman Environment," *Mithraic Studies* (ed. J. R. Hinnells; Manchester: Manchester University, 1975), 1:317.

21. M. W. Meyer, The *"Mithras Liturgy"* (Missoula, MT: Scholars Press, 1976).

22. Pliny adds: "Yet the man [Nero] giving him a kingdom was unable to acquire from him the magic art" (*Natural History* 30:6:17). See M. Grant, *Nero: Emperor in Revolt* (New York: American Heritage, 1970) 148.

23. J. D. M. Derrett, "Further Light on the Narratives of the Nativity," *NovT* 17 (1975) 96. Cumont, "L'adoration des mages," 81, commented: "Il est oiseux de chercher comme motif de son insertion un événement politique d'une portée toute différente." See also E. Nellessen, *Das Kind und seine Mutter* (Stuttgart: Katholisches Bibelwerk, 1969) 76.

24. R. H. Gundry, *Matthew: A Commentary on His Literary and Theological Art* (Grand Rapids: Eerdmans, 1982) 26-27. Elsewhere (pp. 34-35) Gundry makes the even more

Gundry's proposals have provoked a firestorm of criticism.[25] Restricting myself to his views on the Magi episode, I find this explanation most unlikely in view of the questionable if not disreputable reputation of the magi in the first century.[26] In view of the Old Testament's condemnation of astral worship, why would Matthew choose an image that could be subject to misinterpretation (as shown by patristic comments)?[27]

The notion that God had apparently used astrology to guide the Magi to journey west troubled the church fathers. Tertullian (*On Idolatry* 9) declared:

> What then? Shall therefore the religion of those Magi act as patron now also to astrologers? . . . But, however, that science has been allowed until the Gospel, in order that after Christ's birth no one should thenceforward interpret any one's nativity by the heavens.

Ignatius, *Ephesians* 19:3, declared that when the star shone, "Thence was destroyed all magic, and every bond vanished."[28] Other church fathers maintained that the Magi were not mere astrologers like the Chaldeans but were learned followers of Zoroaster. Origen (*Contra*

---

provocative suggestion that Matthew "changes the sacrificial slaying of 'a pair of turtle-doves or two young pigeons' . . . into Herod's slaughtering the babies in Bethlehem." For studies supporting the historicity of Herod's massacres of the babes, see H. W. Montefiore, "Josephus and the New Testament," *NovT* 4 (1960) 140–48; R. T. France, "The 'Massacre of the Innocents'—Fact or Fiction?" *Studia Biblica* 2 (1978) 83–94; idem, "Herod and the Children of Bethlehem," *NovT* 21 (1979) 98–120.

25. See D. A. Carson, "Gundry on Matthew: A Critical Review," *Trinity Journal* 3 (1982) 71–91; P. B. Payne, "Midrash and History in the Gospels with Special Reference to R. H. Gundry's *Matthew*," *Gospel Perspectives 3: Studies in Midrash and Historiography* (ed. R. T. France and D. Wenham; Sheffield: JSOT Press, 1983) 177–215; D. J. Moo, "Matthew and Midrash," *Journal of the Evangelical Theological Society* 26 (1983) 31–40 and 57–70; N. L. Geisler, "Methodological Unorthodoxy," ibid., 87–94; for Gundry's responses to his critics, see ibid., 41–56, 71–86, 95–100, and 109–10.

26. I would counter the argument that shepherds also did not have a high reputation among the rabbis by noting that Jesus transformed their status by likening himself to a shepherd. J. Jeremias, *Jerusalem in the Time of Jesus* (Philadelphia: Fortress, 1969) 306: "the favourable picture of the shepherd which we are given in Jesus' teaching is quite isolated."

27. B. O. Long, "Astrology," *IDBSup* 77 comments: "To judge from the Old Testament, astrology was never assimilated into Israelite culture. It was recognized as Babylonian and was ridiculed." See Deut 4:19, Isa 47:13, Jer 10:2. R. T. France, "Scripture, Tradition, and History in the Infancy Narratives of Matthew," *Gospel Perspectives 2: Studies of History and Tradition in the Four Gospels* (ed. R. T. France and D. Wenham; Sheffield: JSOT Press, 1981) 257: "Moreover, it may be suggested that astrologers are not the most likely group to be introduced into Christian fiction by a church which soon found itself obliged to combat astrological beliefs."

28. W. R. Schoedel, *Ignatius of Antioch* (Philadelphia: Fortress, 1985) 93 comments: "It is presumably the heavenly bodies that are here said to lose their grip on humankind."

Celsum 1:58–60) took Celsus to task for failing to distinguish between the Chaldeans and the Magi. He believed that the Magi knew the prophecy of Balaam, and that they were inspired on their quest when they found their magic declining in power.

c. *A Midrash of Balaam's Prophecy of the Star?*

Numbers 22–24, a much-discussed passage, records the story of the king of Moab, Balak, enlisting the pagan prophet Balaam from Pethor (12 miles south of Carchemish) to curse the children of Israel, only to have Balaam bless them with his remarkable prophecy, which predicted that a "star" should come forth out of Jacob.[29] Though some critical scholars have been tempted to question the authenticity of this account, the historicity of such a pagan prophet named Balaam has been established by the decipherment of the Aramaic inscription (ca. 700 B.C.) from Tell Deir ʿAlla in Jordan.[30]

The Dead Sea Scrolls cite the particular passage on the star (Num 24:17) in several texts.[31] For example, the *Testimonia*, a florilegium of Messianic citations (ca. 100 B.C.), interprets the star as a reference to a Davidic Messiah. The *Damascus Document* (CD 7:18–20) declares: "The star is the Interpreter of the Law [*dôreš hattôrâ*]." The *Testament of Levi*

---

29. See S. Mowinckel, "Der Ursprung der Bilᶜamsage," *ZAW* 48 (1930) 233–71; E. Burrows, *The Oracles of Jacob and Balaam* (London: Burnes, Oates & Washbourne, 1938); O. Eissfeldt, "Die Komposition der Bileam-Erzählung," *ZAW* 57 (1939) 212–41; W. F. Albright, "The Oracles of Balaam," *JBL* 63 (1944) 208–33; A. S. Yahuda, "The Name of Balaam's Homeland," *JBL* 64 (1945) 547–51; J. Liver, "The Figure of Balaam in Biblical Tradition," *Eretz Israel* 3 (1954) 97–100; G. Vermes, "Deux traditions sur Balaam," *Cahier Sioniens* 9 (1955) 289–302; L. M. Von Pakozdy, "Theologische Redaktionsarbeit in der Bileam Perikope," *Von Ugarit nach Qumrân* (Berlin: de Gruyter, 1958) 161–76; O. Eissfeldt, "Sinaï-Erzählung und Bileam Spruche," *HUCA* 32 (1961) 179–90; J. Coppens, "Les oracles de Biléam," *Mélanges Eugène Tisserant* (Rome: Biblical Institute, 1964), 1:67–69; R. Largement, "Bileᶜam et la mantique sumero-akkadienne," *Mémorial du cinquantenaire de l'École des Langues Orientales de l'Institut Catholique de Paris* (Paris: Bloud et Gay, 1964) 37–50; H. Donner, "Balaam Pseudopropheta," *Beiträge zur alttestamentliche Theologie* (Göttingen: Vandenhoeck & Rupprecht, 1977); A. Rofé, "The Book of Balaam" (Numbers 22:2–24:25) (Jerusalem: Simor, 1979) [Hebrew].

30. J. Hoftijzer, "The Prophet Balaam in a 6th-century Aramaic Inscription," *BA* 39 (1976) 11:17; J. Hoftijzer and G. van der Kooij, *Aramaic Texts from Deir ʿAllā* (Leiden: Brill, 1976); A. Caquot and A. Lemaire, "Les textes araméens de Deir ʿAlla," *Syria* 54 (1977) 189–208; H.-P. Müller, "Einige alttestamentliche Probleme zur aramäischen Inschrift von Dēr ʿAllā," *ZDPV* 94 (1978) 56–67; P. K. McCarter, "The Balaam Texts from Deir ʿAllā; The First Combination," *BASOR* 239 (1980) 49–60; M. Delcor, "Le texte de Deir ʿAlla et les oracles bibliques de Balaᶜam," *Congress Volume: Vienna 1980* (VTSup 32; Leiden: Brill, 1981); J. A. Hackertt *The Balaam Text from Deir ʿAllā* (Chico: Scholars Press, 1984).

31. M. McNamara, "Were the Magi Essenes?" *Irish Ecclesiastical Review* 110 (1968) 312–18.

18.3 seems to refer the star to the great eschatological priest, and the War Scroll (11:5–7) to a military leader.[32]

During the Second Jewish Revolt against Hadrian (132–135) the famous Rabbi Akiva hailed Bar Koseba as "Bar Kochba," that is, "Son of the Star," thus confirming the Messianic interpretation of the Num 24:17 passage in the sense of a military leader.[33]

The suggestion that the Magi episode is a midrash based on Balaam's prophecy of the star has become quite popular. Jean Daniélou asserts: "It is very probable that the *midrash* on the star, with its leading the Magi from Jerusalem to Bethlehem and stopping over the spot where Jesus was, was inspired by Balaam."[34] This is also the conclusion reached by Raymond Brown in his magisterial study of the Nativity

> While this narrative reflects the general belief that the birth of great men was augured by astronomical phenomena, its immediate inspiration came from the story of Balaam in Num 22–24, a man with magical powers who came from the East and predicted that a star would rise from Jacob.[35]

This mode of explanation is not at all novel. But it is ironic that Catholic scholars are now accepting interpretations that were earlier proposed by antisupernatural critics of Christianity.[36] The derivation of the episode of the Magi from the Balaam prophecy was long ago

32. On the *Testimonia, Damascus Document,* and *War Scroll* see G. Vermes, *The Dead Sea Scrolls in English* (Baltimore: Penguin, 1962) 245, 104, 138. See McNamara, "Were the Magi Essenes?" 315, on the *Testament of Levi.*

33. S. Zeitlin, "Bar Kokba and Bar Kozeba," *JQR* 43 (1952) 77–80; Y. Yadin, "More on the Letters of Bar Kochba," *BA* 24 (1961) 86–95; J. A. Fitzmyer, "The Bar Kochba Period," *The Bible in Current Catholic Thought* (ed. J. L. McKenzie; New York: Herder and Herder, 1962) 133–68; Y. Yadin, *Bar Kokhba* (New York: Random House, 1971); idem, "Bar Kochba," *IDBSup* 89–92; S. Applebaum, *Prolegomena to the Study of the Second Jewish Revolt* (Oxford: British Archaeological Reports, 1976); idem, "The Second Jewish Revolt (A.D. 131–35)," *PEQ* 116 (1984) 35–41. On Akiva's declaration see A. Guttmann, "Akiba 'Rescuer of the Torah'," *HUCA* 17 (1942–43) 395–421; R. P. Benoit, "Rabbi Aquiba ben Joseph sage et héros du Judaïsme," *RB* 54 (1947) 54–89; G. S. Aleksandrov, "The Role of ᶜAqiba in the Bar-Kokhva Rebellion," *REJ* 132 (1973) 65–72.

34. J. Daniélou, *Infancy Narratives* (New York: Herder and Herder, 1968) 84. Derrett, "Narratives of the Nativity," 108 responds: "Jean Daniélou's conclusion that the Magi were an invention of Matthew and that they are merely a figuration of the admission of the gentiles into the church, may well have gone too far."

35. Brown, *Birth of the Messiah,* 117; idem, "The Meaning of the Magi; The Significance of the Star," *Worship* 49 (1975) 577–78.

36. See my "Sociology, Scripture, and the Supernatural," *Journal of the Evangelical Theological Society* 27 (1984) 169–92.

suggested as a "mythical explanation" by the early nineteenth-century critic, David Friedrich Strauss (1808-74), in his iconoclastic *Life of Jesus*, first published in 1835:

> The prophecy of Balaam (Num 24:17), *A star shall come out of Jacob*, was the cause—not indeed, as the Fathers supposed, that magi actually recognized a newly-kindled star . . . but that legend represented a star to have appeared at the birth of Jesus, and to have been recognized by astrologers as the star of the Messiah.[37]

One glaring obstacle to this view—in the light of the fact that Matthew delights in quoting Old Testament passages—is the absence of any explicit or even implicit reference to the Numbers passage or to Balaam.[38] Strauss's lame answer as to Matthew's omission was: "Because it was not he who wove this history out of the materials furnished in the Old Testament; he received it, already fashioned, from others, who did not communicate to him its real origin."[39]

In summary, to suppose that the episode of the Magi reflects the trip of Tiridates to Rome, or a metamorphosis of the adoration of the shepherds, or an elaboration of Balaam's prophecy, in my view, requires greater credulity in critical ingenuity than the faith required to accept the episode as historical. Assuming that the latter is the case, what can one discover about the background of the Magi?

3. The History of the Magi

a. The Magi and the Persians

According to Herodotus (1:101) the magi (Greek μάγος, plural μάγοι) were originally one of the tribes of the Medes who functioned as priests and diviners under the Achaemenian Persians (sixth–fourth

---

37. *The Life of Jesus Critically Examined* (trans. G. Eliot; 2d ed.; New York: Macmillan, 1902; repr. Philadelphia: Fortress, 1972) 173.

38. K. Ferrari d'Occhieppo, *Der Stern Der Weisen: Geschichte oder Legende?* (Vienna: Herold, 1969) 14, comments: "Hätte aber Matthäus, wie rationalistische Erklärer meinen, von dorther das 'Motiv' übernommen, dann wäre wohl wenn schon kein wörtliches Zitat, so doch ein deutlicherer Anklang zu erwarten gewesen, als er tatsächlich vorhanden ist." Christians welcomed Balaam's involuntary prophecy of the star, but as every explicit reference to Balaam himself in the New Testament is emphatically negative, as either a symbol of avarice (2 Pet 2:15, Jude 11) or of immorality (Rev 2:14), it should be doubted that the figure of Balaam himself could have provided a basis for developing the image of the Magi.

39. Strauss, *Life of Jesus*, 177.

centuries B.C.).[40] Herodotus (1:132) wrote that "no sacrifice can be offered without a Magian." They also interpreted dreams (Herodotus 1:107, 120, 128). Other classical writers knew that the magi served before fire altars (Strabo 15:3:15, 12:3:37; Xenophon, *Cyropedia* 4:5:14, 7:5:57) and offered libations (Strabo 15:3:14).[41]

Both Herodotus and Darius I in his famous Behistun Inscription report that a magos named Bardiya/Smerdis seized power for seven months, posing as the brother of Cambyses, before Darius gained power in the fall of 522 B.C.[42] The Old Persian version of the Behistun Inscription calls this imposter, also known as Gaumata, a *maguš*. The corresponding Elamite version calls him a *ma-ku-iš*, but the Akkadian version LU KUR *ma-da-[a-a]* 'Median man'.[43]

After the overthrow of Gaumata/Smerdis, Herodotus (3:79) reports the massacre of many magi, an event that was later commemorated by the festival of the *magophonia*. This tradition is also reported in other classical sources (Ctesias §46, Strabo 15:3:24, Josephus *Antiquities* 11:31). W. B. Henning believes that a Sogdian word in the Manichaean-Sogdian manuscript, *mwgzt* (**Magu-žati*), is support for Herodotus's *magophonia*.[44] In any case the suppression of the magi was neither universal nor long-

40. According to M. Boyce, *A History of Zoroastrianism 2: Under the Achaemenians* (Leiden: Brill, 1982) 19, "The original meaning of the term, it has been suggested, was perhaps 'member of the tribe' (as in Avestan *moghu*), given a special sense among the Medes as 'member of the priestly tribe.'" Herodotus's view that the magi were originally a Median tribe is supported by E. Benveniste, *Les mages dans l'ancien Iran* (Paris: G.-P. Maisonneuve, 1938) 11, but is questioned by G. Messina, *Der Ursprung der Magier und die zarathuštrische Religion* (Rome: Pontificio Instituto Biblico, 1930) 77.

41. On the role of the magi under the Achaemenians, see: M. A. Dandamaev, *Persien unter den ersten Achämeniden* (trans. H.-D. Pohl; Wiesbaden: Ludwig Reichert, 1976) 238–40; J. M. Cook, *The Persian Empire* (New York: Schocken, 1983) 154–55; R. N. Frye, *The History of Ancient Iran* (Munich: Beck, 1984) 120–24; M. Schwartz, "The Religion of Achaemenian Iran," *The Cambridge History of Iran 2: The Median and Achaemenian Periods* (ed. I. Gershevitch; Cambridge: Cambridge University, 1985) 696–97.

42. J. Wiesehöfer, *Der Aufstand Gaumātas und die Anfänge Dareios I* (Bonn: Rudolf Habelt, 1978).

43. For the Old Persian version see R. G. Kent, *Old Persian* (New Haven: American Oriental Society, 1953). For the Elamite version see G. Cameron, "The Elamite Version of the Bisitun Inscription," *JCS* 14 (1960) 59–68; W. Hinz, "Die Behistan-Inscrift des Darius in ihrer ursprünglichen Fassung," *Archäologische Mitteilungen aus Iran* 7 (1974) 121–34. For the Akkadian version see E. von Voigtlander, *The Bisitun Inscription of Darius the Great* (London: Lund Humphries, 1978); R. Schmitt, "Zur babylonischen Version der Bisitun Inschrift," *AfO* 27 (1980) 106–26. For the Aramaic version see J. C. Greenfield and B. Porten, *The Bisitun Inscription of Darius the Great: Aramaic Version* (London: Lund Humphries, 1982).

44. W. B. Henning, "The Murder of the Magi," *JRAS* (1943) 133–36.

lasting as the Elamite tablets from Darius's reign from Persepolis record grants of grain to various magi.[45]

The Persians continued to use derivations from the word *maguš* as a word for 'priest' down to the end of the Sasanian era, ca. A.D. 650. An ordinary priest was called *mog*, and the chief priest *magupat* 'master of the magi' or even *magupat magupatan* 'chief priest of the chief priests'.[46]

The relationship of the magi to Zoroaster and his teachings is a complex and controversial issue. The traditional dates of Zoroaster, which had been calculated as 628–551 B.C. on Arabic data, have now been placed back to 1000 B.C. and even earlier.[47] The only certain writings that can be attributed to Zoroaster himself are the Gathas. The magi are strikingly absent from these and the later Avesta.[48]

One may reasonably surmise that the Zoroastrians and the magi were probably initially in conflict for two reasons: (1) the magi appear to have been polytheistic (Xenophon, *Cyropedia* 3:3:22, 8:3:11–12), whereas Zoroaster's own teachings about Ahura Mazda were either monotheistic or dualistic;[49] (2) Zoroaster was from the northeast and the magi were established in northwestern Iran. According to Boyce, "It is reasonable, however, to suppose that the existence of this hereditary priesthood [i.e., the magi], with its own traditions and forms of worship, was a major factor in western Iranian resistance to Zoroastrian proselytizing."[50]

The religion of the Achaemenian kings is another area of controversy. Although Ahura Mazda, Zoroaster's god, is exalted in Darius's Behistun Inscription, the prophet himself is not named in the Old Persian texts and the Achaemenid kings are not honored in later

---

45. See R. T. Hallock, *Persepolis Fortification Tablets* (Chicago: University of Chicago, 1969).

46. On *magupat* see M. Boyce, *Zorastrians* (London: Routledge, 1979) 102; for *magupat magupatan* see V. G. Lukonin, "Political, Social, and Administrative Institutions: Taxes and Trade," *The Cambridge History of Iran 3: The Seleucid, Parthian, and Sasanid Periods* (ed. E. Yarshater; Cambridge: Cambridge University, 1983), 2:689.

47. Boyce, *A History of Zoroastrianism 1: The Early Period* (Leiden: Brill, 1975) 3, 189–91; A. S. Shahbazi, "The 'Traditional Date of Zoroaster' Explained," *BSOAS* 40 (1977) 25–35; G. Gnoli, *Zoroaster's Time and Homeland* (Naples: Instituto Universitario Orientale, 1980).

48. Boyce, *History of Zoroastrianism*, 1:10. For an overview, see my "Religions of the Biblical World: Persia," *International Standard Biblical Encyclopedia* (ed. G. W. Bromiley; Grand Rapids: Eerdmans, 1988), 4:123–29. On the Gathas see J. Duchesne-Guillemin, *The Hymns of Zarathustra* (Boston: Beacon, 1963); S. Insler, *The Gathas of Zarathustra* (Leiden: Brill, 1975).

49. J. W. Boyd and D. A. Crosby, "Is Zoroastrianism Dualistic or Monotheistic?" *JAAR* 47 (1979) 557–88.

50. Boyce, *History of Zoroastrianism*, 2:21.

Zoroastrian scriptures.[51] A. D. Nock's judgment on his matter is cautiously stated:

> The balance of probability seems to me to indicate that Zoroaster's *Gathas* had been accepted by *some* of the Magi as inspired and that their phraseology and ideas had exercised *some* influence on them and through them on the language of Xerxes at least.[52]

With the conquest of Asia Minor by the Persian army under Cyrus in 546 B.C. came the settlement of many Medes and Persians accompanied by their magi.[53] A famous relief from the satrapal capital of Dascylion in northwest Asia Minor depicts magi bringing animal sacrifices.[54] Franz Cumont hypothesized that it was probably through the agency of the magi in Asia Minor that Persian teachings were transmitted into western Mithraism.[55] Recently considerable criticisms have been raised against Cumont's thesis because of the lack of solid evidence to support it. For example,

> There are three chief objections to [Cumont's] theory of the origin of Mithraism: (1) that his arguments for the identification of some Mithraic gods with Magian gods are circular, not to say arbitrary; (2) that some claimed identities of function are of no such thing, or at least are undemonstrable; (3) that there is no Western evidence for some fundamental Magian beliefs.[56]

51. A. Jackson, "The Religion of the Achaemenian Kings," *JAOS* 21 (1900) 160–84; V. Strouve, "The Religion of the Achaemenids and Zoroastrianism," *Cahiers d'histoire mondiale* 5 (1959–60) 529–45; J. R. Hinnells, "Religion at Persepolis," *Religion* 3 (1973) 158–59; G. Gnoli, "Politique religieuse et conception de la royauté sous les Achéménides," *Commémoration Cyrus* (Leiden: Brill, 1974), 2:117–90; H. Koch, *Die religiösen Verhältnisse der Dariuszeit* (Wiesbaden: Harrassowitz, 1977); Boyce, *History of Zoroastrianism*, 2:49–131.

52. A. D. Nock, "The Problem of Zoroaster," *American Journal of Archaeology* 53 (1949) 277; repr. in his *Essays on Religion and the Ancient World* (ed. Z. Stewart; Cambridge: Harvard University 1972) 690.

53. J. Bidez and F. Cumont, *Les mages hellénisés* (Paris: "Les Belles Lettres", 1938), 1:90–91; F. Cumont, *Oriental Religions in Roman Paganism* (Chicago: Open Court, 1911; repr. New York: Dover, 1956) 139–41.

54. E. Akurgal, "Griechisch-persische Reliefs aus Daskyleion," *Iranica Antiqua* 6 (1966) 147–56.

55. F. Cumont, "Mithra en Asie Mineure," *Antolian Studies Presented to William Hepburn Buckler* (Manchester: Manchester University, 1939) 67–76; idem, *The Mysteries of Mithra* (Chicago: Open Court, 1903; repr. New York: Dover, 1956).

56. R. L. Gordon, "Franz Cumont and the Doctrines of Mithraism," *Mithraic Studies* (ed. J. R. Hinnells; Manchester: Manchester University, 1975), 1:242; see also Gordon, "Mithraism and Roman Society," *Religion* 2 (1972) 92–121. For the post-Christian development of Mithraism, see my *"The Apocalypse of Adam*, Mithraism, and Pre-Christian

In any case, from the fourth century B.C. classical writers (Plato, Pliny the Elder, Plutarch, and others) maintained that Zoroaster himself was a μάγος and that the magi were his followers.[57] For example, Plutarch (*Moralia* 5:369E) relates: "The Magian Zoroaster . . . called the one [god] Oromazes and the other Areimanius." When Apuleius was on trial for magic, he argued that *magus* meant 'priest' in Persia and cited Plato to indicate that the Persian princes studied the *"mageia* of Zoroaster, son of Oromazos"* (The Defense of Apuleius* § 26).

b. *The Magi and Magic*

The Greek word μάγος is first found in the fragments of the sixth-century B.C. pre-Socratics, Heraclitus and Pythagoras. Though the Medo-Persian magi were but rarely associated with spells (except at Herodotus 7:191), by the fifth century the word in some cases seems to have become synonymous with the Greek word *goētēs* 'wizard, sorcerer'.[58] In Sophocles' play, *Oedipus the King*, Oedipus berates the blind seer Teiresias:

> The trusty Creon, my familiar friend,
> Hath lain in wait to oust me and suborned
> This mountebank [μάγον], this juggling charlatan,
> This tricksy beggar-priest, for gain alone.[59]

By the Roman era (e.g., Tacitus, *Annals* 2:27; 12:22, 59) the magi and their arts were associated with sorcery. The English word "magic" is derived from the Latin *magicus* which in turn is a loan from the Greek μαγικός.[60] Because of the association of the magi with Zoroaster, Pliny the Elder asserted, "Without doubt magic arose in Persia with Zoroaster" (30:2).

It is in the sense of μάγος as 'magician' that one reads of the activities of Simon from Samaria, who 'practiced sorcery' μαγεύων (Acts 8:9) and amazed the people with his 'magic' μαγείαις (Acts 8:11). The Apocryphal *Acts of Peter* describes how Simon astounded the crowds at

Gnosticism," *Etudes Mithriaques, Textes et Mémoires* (ed. J. Duchesne-Guillemin; Teheran-Liège: Bibliothèque Pahlavi, 1978), 4:537–63.

57. Boyce, *History of Zoroastrianism*, 2:261; J. H. Moulton, *Early Zoroastrianism: The Origins, the Prophet, the Magi* (London: Williams and Norgate, 1913; repr. Amsterdam: Philo Press, 1972) 197.

58. See G. Delling on γόης, *TDNT* 1:737–38; idem on μάγος, *TDNT* 4:356–59.

59. *Sophocles* (trans. F. Storr; LCL; London: Heinemann, 1928), 1:38–39, lines 385–88.

60. On the definition of magic and its diffusion in the ancient world, see my *Mandiac Incantation Texts* (New Haven: American Oriental Society, 1967); idem, "Magic in the Biblical World," *Tyndale Bulletin* 34 (1983) 169–200.

Rome by his "magical" flights until Peer prayed that he might crash to the ground.[61] Although the book of Acts describes Simon simply as a magician, the early church fathers came to regard Simon as the fountainhead of all the Gnostic heresies.[62]

Elsewhere in Acts (13:6, 8) of a Jewish sorcerer, a μάγος named Elymas Bar-Jesus, who was influential at the court of Sergius Paulus, the proconsul of Cyprus. Josephus (*Antiquities* 20:142) records another Jewish μάγος from Cyprus named Atomus, through whose arts Felix, the governor of Judea, gained the hand of Drusilla (cf. Acts 24:24–25).

By the New Testament era most of the occurrences of the word μάγος were in the pejorative sense of 'magic'.[63] According to J. M. Hull, "The apostolic fathers always use the word μάγος in a bad sense. The apologists use μάγος and its cognates about sixteen times and always in the bad sense." H. Remus likewise states, "In the second century use of μάγος, μαγεία, and derivative or related words is almost uniformly negative in the extant Christian sources."[64] I would therefore argue that it is more credible to believe that Matthew's use of the word in a positive context was based on a historic episode than on a desire to develop a midrashic embroidering of the nativity event.

c. *The Magi and Astrology*

Among the functions of the Persian magi was their work as diviners. In the Hellenistic age magi in the west continued to have a reputation for foretelling the future. Cicero (*De Divinatione* 1:47; followed by Plutarch, *Alexander* 3:7) records that when Alexander was born the magi interpreted a spontaneous fire in the temple of Artemis at Ephesus as a sign that a great calamity for Asia had been born.[65]

From the fourth century B.C. on, the magi were increasingly associated with the Chaldeans as astrologers.[66] The name *Chaldean* assumed

61. Hennecke and Schneemelcher, *New Testament Apocrypha*, 2:289–316.

62. See R. P. Casey, "Simon Magus," *The Beginnings of Christianity* (ed. F. J. Foakes Jackson and K. Lake; London: Macmillan, 1933; repr. Grand Rapids: Baker, 1966), 5:151–63; E. Yamauchi, *Pre-Christian Gnosticism* (2d ed.; Grand Rapids: Baker, 1983) 58–65, 201–03; J. D. M. Derrett, "Simon Magus (Acts 8:9–24), *ZAW* 33 (1982) 52–68.

63. See A. F. Segal, "Hellenistic Magic: Some Questions of Definition," *Studies in Gnosticism and Hellenistic Religions* (ed. R. Van Den Broek and M. J. Vermaseren; Leiden: Brill, 1981) 349–75.

64. J. M. Hull, *Hellenistic Magic and the Synoptic Tradition* (Studies in Biblical Theology 2/28; London: SCM, 1974) 123; H. Remus, "'Magic or Miracle'? Some Second Century Instances," *The Second Century* 2 (1982) 130; see also my "Magic or Miracle?" *Gospel Perspective 6: The Miracles of Jesus* (ed. D. Wenham and C. Blomberg; Sheffield: JSOT Press, 1986) 89–91.

65. J. R. Hamilton, *Plutarch, Alexander, A Comentary* (Oxford: Clarendon, 1969) 8.

66. Bidez and Cumont, *Les mages hellénisés*, 1:33–36.

different meanings at different periods. (1) Originally in the Neo-
Assyrian and Neo-Babylonian periods it meant an inhabitant of lower
Mesopotamia.[67] (2) In the Hellenistic age it could mean a Babylonian
priest or scholar versed in astrology, or a Greek who had studied such
lore. (3) In the Roman and early Christian era it came to signify an
astrologer.

The development of *Chaldean* in a professional as well as an ethnic
sense derived from the interest in astronomy/astrology developed by
priestly scholars among the Chaldeans. An interesting Greek text of
Pseudo-Berossus asserts:

> From the time of Nabonassar [747–734 B.C.], the Chaldeans accurately
> recorded the times of the motion of the stars. The polymaths among the
> Greeks learned from the Chaldeans that—as Alexander (Polyhistor) and
> Berossus, men versed in Chaldean antiquities, say—Nabonassar gathered
> together (the accounts of) the deeds of the kings before him and did away
> with them so that the reckoning of the Chaldean kings would begin with
> him.[68]

Although there were considerable contacts between the Aegean
and the Near East before Alexander, it was only after his capture of the
area that a flood of Greeks visited and in some cases settled in Mesopotamia.[69] There some of them acquired a knowledge of Chaldean astrology.[70] According to Wilhelm Eilers:

> It is not for nothing that astrologers were called "Chaldeans," for their
> true home was in Aramaean southern Babylon, in Uruk which, especially

67. See my "Chaldea, Chaldeans," *The New International Dictionary of Biblical Archaeology* (ed. E. M. Blaiklock and R. K. Harrison; Grand Rapids: Zondervan, 1983) 123–25.
The use of "Chaldean" in Dan 2:10; 4:7 [4]; 5:7, 11 in the sense of "astrologer" has been
regarded as a clear case of anachronism. A. R. Millard, "Daniel 1–6 and History," *EvQ* 49
(1977) 70, however, points out that there is as yet no known example of "Chaldean" as
either an ethnic or professional term from Neo-Babylonian texts.

68. Cited by J. A. Brinkman, *A Political History of Post-Kassite Babylonia* 1158–722 B.C.
(Rome: Pontificium Institutum Biblicum, 1968) 227.

69. J. Oelsner, "Zur Bedeutung der 'Graeco-Babyloniaca' für die Überlieferung des
Sumerischen und Akkadischen," *Mitteilungen des Instituts für Orientforschung* 17 (1972) 356–
64; H. J. Nissen, "Sudbabylonien in parthischer und sasanidischer Zeit," *ZDMG*, supple-
ment 1 (1969) 1036–37; J. Boardman, *The Greeks Overseas* (2d ed.; London: Thames and
Hudson, 1980) 50–52; T. F. R. G. Braun, "The Greeks in the Near East," *The Cambridge
Ancient History* (ed. J. Boardman and N. G. L. Hammond; 2d ed.; Cambridge: Cambridge
University, 1982), 3/3:31–24. On the pre-Alexandrian contacts between the Aegean and
the Near East, see my *Greece and Babylon* (Grand Rapids: Baker, 1967).

70. J. Bidez, "Les écoles chaldéennes sous Alexandre et les séleucides," *Annuaire de
l'institut de philologie et d'histoire orientales* 3 (1935) 41–89.

in the Seleucid-Parthian period, was the center of ancient astronomy and interpretation of the stars. The latest dated cuneiform texts include clay tablets from this place containing astronomical observations; these texts come from the first century A.D.[71]

In the hellenistic age Chaldeans also travelled west, where they practiced their divinatory arts. The most famous example was Berossus, a Chaldean priest who left Babylon to teach astrology to the Greeks on the island of Cos some time after 281 B.C. His famous *Babyloniaca*, written in Greek, contains some invaluable traditions on astrological matters.[72]

A factor that may have contributed to the identification of the magi with the Chaldeans and astrologers is their association with Zoroaster. The Greek spelling of Zoroaster's name, *Zorōástēr* (Persian *Zarathuštra*), was first recorded in Xanthos of Lydia.[73] The Greeks saw in this name the word *astēr* 'star'. Hermodorus, a pupil of Plato, explained Zoroaster's name as *astrothútes* 'star worshipper'.[74] Because of these associations a mass of astrological matter circulated under the name of Zoroaster.[75]

4. The Development and Diffusion of Astrology

a. The Development of Astrology in Mesopotamia

Astronomy, the observation of celestial phenomena, was rarely separable in antiquity from astrology, the belief that a knowledge of such phenomena could be used to divine the future. The earliest develop-

71. W. Eilers, "Iran and Mesopotamia," *Cambridge History of Iran* 3: *The Seleucid, Parthian, and Sasanid Periods* (ed. E. Yarshater; Cambridge: Cambridge University, 1983) 1:501.

72. S. M. Burstein, *The Babyloniaca of Berossus* (Malibu: Undena, 1978) 31–32.

73. Boyce, *History of Zoroastrianism*, 2:183.

74. Ibid., 260.

75. W. Gundel and H. G. Gundel, *Astrologumena: Die astrologische Literatur in der Antike und ihre Geschichte* (Wiesbaden: Sudhoffs Archiv, 1966) 40–51, 60–66. Astrological lore is also found in the ninth-century A.D. Zoroastrian text, the Bundahišn; see D. N. MacKenzie, "Zoroastrian Astrology in the Bundahišn," *BSOAS* 27 (1964) 511–29. A. L. Oppenheim, "The Babylonian Evidence of Achaemenian Rule in Mesopotamia," *The Cambridge History of Iran* 3: *The Seleucid, Parthian, and Sasanid Periods* (ed. E. Yarshater; Cambridge: Cambridge University, 1983), 1:576, remarks: "the pseudo-Persian astrological literature of the Parthian period prepared the way for the influx of Greek astrology in the Sasanian period, and its incorporation into the Zoroastrian scriptures." D. Pingree, "Astronomy and Astrology in India and Iran," *Isis* 54 (1963) 241, concludes: "However, trustworthy knowledge of Iranian astronomy and astrology is non-existent before the reign of Shapur I (A.D. 240–270)." For the general dearth of evidence from the Parthian period (250 B.C.–A.D. 225), which is the most important period for the growth of Judaism and Christianity, see my review of *The Cambridge History of Iran* 3: *The Seleucid, Parthian, and Sasanid Period*, ed. E. Yarshater (1983), *AHR* 89 (1984) 1055–56.

ment of astrology in Mesopotamia consisted in the simple observation of astral omens, especially of the seven "planets" (including the sun and moon), which were also regarded as gods. English names for the observable celestial objects go ultimately back to the Babylonian by way of the Greeks and Romans:[76]

Babylonian	Greek	Roman
Shamash	Helios	Sol
Sin	Selene	Luna
Nebo	Hermes	Mercury
Ishtar	Aphrodite	Venus
Nergal	Ares	Mars
Marduk	Zeus	Jupiter
Ninib	Kronos	Saturn

The observation of a Venus cycle in the reign of Ammisaduqa of the Old Babylonian period (early second millennium B.C.) is a linchpin in ancient Mesopotamian chronology. By the end of the first millennium B.C. Babylonian astronomers had careful records of eclipses going back seven hundred years.[77]

Many of the texts from Ashurbanipal's (668-626 B.C.) famous library at Nineveh are reports of astral omens, including about 70 tablets of the important series *Enuma Anu Enlil*, which may go back to about 1000 B.C. Such omens were carefully recorded and studied by the *baru* priests, who reported their conclusions to the king.[78]

The development of astrology as we know it today was made possible by the discovery of the Zodiac, that is, the realization that the sun in passing through its path, the ecliptic, goes through twelve constellations, each "ruling" at 30-degree section of the circle. This made possible the casting of horoscopes based on the position of the planets and stars at the moment of one's birth. Otto Neugebauer points out the differences between the earlier astral omens and the later astrology:

The [Assyrian] predictions concern the king and the country as a whole and are based on observed astronomical appearances, not on computation

76. Cumont, "Les noms des planèts et astrolatrie chez les grecs," *L'antiquité classique* 4 (1935) 5–45.

77. G. L. Huxley, *The Interaction of Greek and Babylonian Astronomy* (Belfast: Queen's University, 1964) 12.

78. S. Parpola, *Letters from Assyrian Scholars to the Kings Esarhaddon and Assurbanipal* (Kevalaer: Butzon & Bercker, 1970).

and not on the moment of birth. . . . Hellenistic horoscopes, however, concern a specific person and depend upon the computed position of the seven celestial bodies and of the zodiacal signs in their relation to the given horizon, for a given moment, the moment of birth.[79]

The Zodiacal constellations are first mentioned about 700 B.C. according to B. L. Van der Waerden, but not until about 400 B.C. according to Neugebauer.[80] In any case the earliest known cuneiform horoscope comes from about the latter date.[81] Four examples are known from the third century B.C.

b. *The Diffusion of Astrology to the West*

According to G. L. Huxley the names of the zodiacal constellations were borrowed from Mesopotamia by the Greeks in the sixth century B.C.[82] Herodotus (1:73) reports that Thales of Miletus, the "Father of Science," predicted the eclipse of 585 B.C., possibly with the use of Mesopotamian lore.[83] A specific case of borrowing may be seen in the discovery of the so-called Metonic calendar in Babylonian in 481 B.C., a half century before its publication in Athens in 432 B.C.[84]

79. O. Neugebauer, *The Exact Sciences in Antiquity* (2d ed.; Providence: Brown University, 1962) 170. See also D. Pingree, "Mesopotamian Astronomy and Astral Omens in Other Civilizations," *Mesopotamien und seine Nachbaren* (ed. H.-J. Nissen and J. Renger; Berlin: Dietrich Reimer, 1982) 613–31.

80. B. L. Van der Waerden, "History of the Zodiac," *AfO* 16 (1953) 216–18. Neugebauer, *The Exact Sciences in Antiquity*, 102, 140, prefers to speak of such constellations as "ecliptical constellations" until we find evidence of their use in casting horoscopes. See D. R. Dicks, *Early Greek Astronomy to Aristotle* (Ithaca: Cornell University, 1970) 172; R. R. Newton, "Astronomy in Ancient Literate Societies," *The Place of Astronomy in the Ancient World* (ed. D. G. Kendall et al.; London: British Academy, 1974) 13.

81. The earliest known cuneiform horoscope is dated to 410 B.C.; see A. Sachs, "Babylonian Horoscopes," *JCS* 6 (1952) 49–75. For other examples see P. Hilaire de Wynghene, *Les présages astrologiques* (Rome: Pontificio Instituto Biblico, 1932). Cf. Neugebauer, "Demotic Horoscopes," *JAOS* 63 (1943) 115–26; O. Neugebauer and H. B. Van Hoesen, *Greek Horoscopes* (Philadelphia: American Philosophical Society, 1959). The six known Greek horoscopes are from the reign of Augustus.

82. *Interaction of Greek and Babylonian Astronomy* 3.

83. B. Farrington, *Greek Science* (Harmondsworth: Penguin, 1953) 36. On the other hand, Neugebauer, *The Exact Sciences in Antiquity*, 142, and Dicks, *Early Greek Astronomy to Aristotle*, 174, are sceptical of this tradition because of the unsatisfactory state of Babylonian sciences in regard to the prediction of eclipses.

84. B. Z. Wacholder and D. B. Weisberg, "Visibility of the New Moon in Cuneiform and Rabbinic Sources," *HUCA* 42 (1971) 227–41; and Pingree, "Mesopotamian Astronomy and Astral Omens," 619. Arguing for the possibility of an independent Greek discovery of the Metonic cycle are Dicks (*Early Greek Astronomy to Aristotle*, 172) and Neugebauer (*A History of Ancient Mathematical Astronomy* [New York: Springer-Verlag, 1975], 1:4).

The first depiction of the Zodiac in Egypt comes from a temple at Esna from the third of second century B.C.[85] The famous circular Zodiac from the Dendera temple dates from 30 B.C.[86] Its Mesopotamian origin is betrayed by the design of each sign.

While acknowledging key contributions of the Babylonians such as their sexagesimal reckoning and carefully recorded ephemeridae, Neugebauer would stress the independent hellenistic (Ptolemaic) contributions:

> The roots of astrology are undoubtedly to be found in Mesopotamia, emerging from the general omen literature. Yet, we known much less about the history of Babylonian astrology than is generally assumed. Only that much seems clear that it was a far less developed doctrine than we find in Greek astrological literature. The real center of ancient astrology from which it spread over the whole world, is undoubtedly Hellenistic Alexandria.[87]

Though the exact dates of the astrological Hermetic literature are disputed, its roots may reach back to Ptolemaic times.[88] One of the earliest manuals of astrological techniques was composed in Alexandria about 150 B.C. under the names of the sixth-century pharaoh, Nechepso, and his scribe, Petosiris.

With their victories over the Greeks in the second century B.C., the Romans were inundated with Greek influence in many fields, including philosophy and astrology. Astrology was given great prestige among the Romans by its support by Stoic philosophers. In the last century of the Roman Republic astrology was widely accepted by the elite as *the* scientific method of divination—with the exception of a few sceptics like Cicero. Cicero's two learned friends, Nigidius Figulus and Terentius Varro, were believers in astrology.[89]

85. R. A. Parker, "Ancient Egyptian Astronomy," *The Place of Astronomy in the Ancient World* (ed. D. G. Kendall et al.; London: British Academy, 1974) 61.

86. J. N. Lockyer, *The Dawn of Astronomy* (New York/London: Macmillan, 1894; repr. Cambridge: MIT, 1964) 134, 146.

87. Neugebauer, *Ancient Mathematical Astronomy*, 5; see also his article "On Some Aspects of Early Greek Astronomy," *Preceedings of the American Philosophical Society* 116 (1972) 251, and his edited set, *Astronomical Cuneiform Texts: Babylonian Ephemeridae of the Seleucid Period* (3 vols.; London: Lund Humphries, 1955). M. P. Nilsson, *The Rise of Astrology in the Hellenistic Age* (Lund: The Observatory, 1943) 5, also declares: "Because of this naive character of Babylonian astrology, it is permitted to doubt the correctness of the common opinion that the Babylonians created the great astrological system. . . . It can be proved that this is an achievement of the Greeks." F. Rochberg-Halton, "New Evidence for the History of Astrology," *JNES* 43 (1984) 115-40, while conceding the Greek innovations, points out new evidence for Babylonian antecedents of the later astrology.

88. E. Yamauchi, "Hermetic Literature," *IDBSup* 408.

89. F. H. Cramer, *Astrology in Roman Law and Politics* (Philadelphia: American Philosophical Society, 1954) 58-73.

But the growing influence of the astrologers was considered a danger to the state. In 139 B.C. Cornelius Scipio Hispalus expelled the astrologers from Rome. In the early Roman Empire such expulsions were ordered time and time again.

> Accordingly, first in 33 B.C. by action of the aedile Agrippa, later by senatorial decree, and about 52 by imperial edict, the city or all Italy was repeatedly cleared of *mathematici, Chaldaei, astrologi, magi,* γόητης, or however they were called, perhaps ten times over the period 33 B.C. to A.D. 93, and possibly once made under Marcus Aurelius.[90]

Though a satirist like Juvenal might poke fun at astrologers (*Satire* 6:585–86), historians like Suetonius and Dio Cassius were persuaded by the efficacy of astrology. Almost without exception the Julio-Claudian and Flavian emperors of the first century believed in the potency of astrology. S. Dill observes:

> It is not hard to see why the emperors at once believed in these black arts and profoundly distrusted their professors. They wished to keep a monopoly of that awful lore, lest it might excite dangerous hopes in possible pretenders. To consult a Chaldean seer on the fate of the prince, or to possess his horoscope, was always suspicious, and might often be fatal.[91]

On the day of Augustus's birth, Nigidius Figulus allegedly prophesied a notable destiny for the future ruler from a knowledge of the hour of his birth (Suetonius, *Augustus* 94:5; Dio Cassius 45:1:3–5). At Apollonia the astrologer Theogenes cast a horoscope for Augustus (Suetonius, *Augustus* 94:12): "From that time on Augustus had such faith in his destiny, that he made his horoscope public and issued a silver coin stamped with the sign of the constellation Capricornus, under which he was born." Manilius, a poet who lived during Augustus's reign, wrote an extant work on the stars, which is cited in the great *Mathesis* of Firmicus Maternus (4th cent. A.D.).[92] In A.D. 11 Augus-

90. R. MacMullen, *Enemies of the Roman Order* (Cambridge: Harvard University, 1966) 132–33.

91. S. Dill, *Roman Society from Nero to Marcus Aurelius* (London: Macmillan, 1904; repr. New York: Meridian, 1956) 447.

92. Manilius, *M. Manilii Astronomicon* (ed. A. E. Housman; 2d ed.; London: Cambridge University, 1937). See W. Hübner, "Manilius als Astrologe und Dichter," *Sprache und Literatur (Literatur der julisch-claudischen und der flavischen Zeit)* (ed. W. Haase; Aufstieg und Niedergang der römischen Welt: Principat 32; Berlin: de Gruyter, 1984), 1:126–320. Firmicus Maternus, *Ancient Astrology: Theory and Practice* (trans. J. R. Bram; Park Ridge, NJ: Noyes, 1975).

tus passed a law making it a crime to consult astrologers about the fate of the emperor.[93]

Suetonius's life of Tiberius (A.D. 14–37) is filled with numerous references to astrologers. Because he feared their potential for his enemies, "He banished the astrologers as well, but pardoned such as begged for indulgence and promised to give up their art" (*Tibierius* 36). Juvenal made fun of the emperor's "herd of Chaldean astrologers" surrounding him in his retirement at Capri (*Satire* 10:94).

Claudius (A.D. 41–54) tried to revive the ancient order of augurs, but banished astrologers (Tacitus, *Annals* 12:52). His wife, Agrippina the Younger, and her son Nero were devotees of astrology. Nero (A.D. 54–68) delayed his coronation at the advice of his Chaldeans.[94] To avert the dangers portended by a comet, Nero determined to put to death some distinguished men (Suetonius, *Nero* 36).

Though Vespasian (A.D. 69–79) banished astrologers, he retained the most skillful for his own guidance (Dio Cassius 66:10:9). According to Suetonius (*Titus* 9) Titus (A.D. 79–81) inquired into horoscopes. Domitian (A.D. 81–96) put Mettius Pompusianus to death because he had an imperial horoscope (Suetonius, *Domitian* 10). Just before his assassination Domitian put to death the astrologer Ascletarion, who had correctly predicted that dogs would attack his own corpse after his death (*Domitian* 15).

It is most likely that Herod the Great would not have been satisfied with the massacre of the babes, but would have also killed the bearers of the unwelcome tidings as well (Matt 2:12, 16) if he had been able to keep the Magi from escaping.

c. *Astrology among the Jews*

While there has never been a doubt about Jewish interest in astrology in the Middle Ages, as evidenced for example in the Kabbalah, there has been some question as to how widely and how early this interest extended.[95] Both in the Sasanian (A.D. 225–650) and Parthian (250 B.C.–A.D. 225) eras rabbis in Mesopotamia did not question the validity of astrology, but only whether it applied to Israel.[96] There are

93. MacMullen, *Enemies of the Roman Order*, 132.

94. Grant, *Nero: Emperior in Revolt*, 148. Astral influence was admitted by Seneca, Nero's Stoic tutor; see Cramer, *Astrology in Roman Law and Politics*, 118–21.

95. On astrology in the Kabbalah see S. Gandz, *Studies in Hebrew Astronomy* (ed. S. Sternberg; New York: Ktav, 1970); A. Altman, "Astrology," *Encyclopaedia Judaica* (Jerusalem: Encyclopaedia Judaica, 1971), 3:788–95; G. Scholem, *Kabbalah* (New York: New American Libary, 1974) 186–87.

96. J. Neusner, *A History of the Jews in Babylonia 2: The Early Sasanian Period* (Leiden: Brill, 1966) 84–85; idem, *A History of the Jews in Babylonia 1: The Parthian Period* (Leiden:

numerous references to astrology in the Talmud; for example, *b. Šabb.*
156a-b reports the teaching of Rabbi Ḥanina Bar Hama (early third
cent. A.D.), who thought that the constellation at the hour of one's birth
determined one's character. He disagreed with many rabbis who held
that "Israel is not subject to planetary influences" (literally "Israel has
no star").

The recently published Jewish magical text, the *Sepher Ha-Razim*
(third century A.D.), holds that Noah learned: "to master the investigation of the strata of the heavens, to go about in all that is in their seven
abodes, to observe all the astrological signs, to examine the course of
the sun, to explain the observations of the moon, and to know the
paths of the Great Bear, Orion, and the Pleiades. . . ."[97]

From the Byzantine era (fourth-sixth centuries A.D.) are four synagogues with zodiacal representations on their mosaic floors: at Beth
Alpha (sixth century), Naᶜaran (sixth century), Ḥusaifa (fifth century),
and Hammath-Tiberias (fourth century).[98] But what do these figures
mean? E. E. Urbach believes that these were innocuous decorations,
citing *Targum Pseudo-Jonathan* (on Lev 26:1): "You shall not set up a
figured stone in your land, to bow down to it, but a mosaic pavement of
designs and forms you may set in the floor of your places of worship, so
long as you do not do obeisance to it."[99] R. Hachlili maintains that
when the synagogue replaced the temple, synagogue art represented
the annual ritual acts symbolically in these mosaics.[100] The issue is still
very much open to debate.

Brill, 1969) 171; L. Wächter, "Astrologie und Schicksalsglaube im rabbinischen Juden-
tums," *Kairos* 11 (1969) 181-200; R. A. Rosenberg, "The 'Star of the Messiah' Reconsidered," *Bib* 53 (1972) 105-09; J. H. Charlesworth, "Jewish Astrology in the Talmud,
Pseudepigrapha, the Dead Sea Scrolls, and Early Palestinian Synagogues," *HTR* 70 (1977)
183-200; idem, "Jewish Interest in Astrology during the Hellenistic and Roman Period,"
Religion (Hellenistisches Judentum in römischer Zeit: Allgemeines) (ed. W. Haase; Aufstieg und
Niedergang der römischen Welt: Principat 20; Berlin: de Gruyter, 1987), 2:926-50.

97. M. A. Morgan, *Sepher Ha-Razim: The Book of Mysteries* (Chico: Scholars Press,
1983) 17. M. Margalioth, *Sepher Ha-Razim* (Jerusalem: American Academy for Jewish
Research, 1966), dated the work of the third century A.D.; Morgan (p. 8) also suggests
third or fourth century; I. Gruenwald, "Knowledge and Vision," *Israel Oriental Studies* 3
(1973) 71, prefers a fifth-sixth century date.

98. See E. R. Goodenough, *Jewish Symbols in the Greco-Roman Period* (Princeton:
Princeton University, 1969), 13:202; L. Levine, ed., *Ancient Synagogues Revealed* (Jerusalem:
Israel Exploration Society, 1981) 66-69, 136-37, 142-43; M. Dothan, *Hammath-Tiberias*
(Jerusalem: Israel Exploration Society, 1983).

99. Cited by E. E. Urbach, "The Rabbinical Laws of Idolatry in the Second and Third
Centuries in the Light of Archaeological and Historical Facts," *IEJ* 9 (1959) 237 n. 89. See
also W. B. Tatum, "The LXX Version of the Second Commandment (Ex 20:3-6 = Deut
5:7-10)," *JSJ* 17 (1986) 177-95.

100. R. Hachlili, "The Zodiac in Ancient Jewish Art: Representation and Significance," *BASOR* 228 (1977) 61-77. See also: I. Sonne, "The Zodiac Theme in Ancient

Jewish knowledge of the Zodiac is already attested in the first century A.D., for example, by Josephus when he makes the following comparison of the sacred elements in the temple: "The seven lamps . . . represented the planets; the loaves on the table, twelve in number, the circle of the Zodiac and the year" (*Jewish Wars* 5:217–18). Furthermore, a clay tablet with zodiacal signs was found in a hellenistic stratum at Gezer.[101]

Indisputable early evidence of Jewish interest in astrology has now been provided by the publication of two important documents from the Dead Sea Scrolls of Qumran. The first of these documents (4QCryptic; formerly 4Q186), published by J. M. Allegro in 1964, was written in a strange amalgam of proto-Hebrew, Greek, and cryptic signs:

> . . . and his thighs are long and thin, and his toes are thin and long, and he is of the Second Vault. He has six (parts) spirit in the House of Light, and three in the Pit of Darkness. And this is the time of birth on which he is brought forth—on the festival of Taurus. He will be poor; and this is his beast—Taurus (2:5–9).[102]

The text reflects the idea that the body and spirit are determined by the zodiacal sign of birth: the ratio of the man's spirit in light of darkness depends on the relative length of the days.

Another Aramaic text from Cave 4, originally published by Jean Starcky in 1964, seems to be the horoscope of a new Solomon, whose hair would be red and during his youth he would be like a lion.[103] Both of these texts have provoked considerable discussion.[104]

Synagogues and in Hebrew Printed Books," *Studies in Bibliography and Booklore* 1 (1953) 3–13; R. Wischnitzer, "The Beth Alpha Mosaic: A New Interpretation," *Jewish Social Studies* 17 (1955) 133–44; G. Stemberger, "Die Bedeutung des Tierkreises auf Mosaikfuss-böden spätantiker Synagogen," *Kairos* 17 (1975) 11–56. For Christian adaptations of the Zodiac motif, see W. Huebner, *Zodiacus Christianus* (Königstein: Hain, 1983). I owe many of these references to my doctoral student, Lester Ness, who is writing his dissertation on the subject of the Zodiac motif in Judaism.

101. M. Delcor, "Recherches sur un horoscope en langue hébraïque provenant de Qumran," *RevQ* 6 (1966) 536.

102. J. M. Allegro, "An Astrological Cryptic Document from Qumran," *JSS* 9 (1964) 291–94; idem, *Qumrân Cave IV*.1 (Discoveries in the Judaean Desert 5; Oxford: Clarendon, 1968) 88–91.

103. J. Carmignac, "Les Horoscopes de Qumran," *RevQ* 5 (1965) 216; J. Starcky, "Un texte messianique araméen de la grotte 4 de Qumrân," *Mémorial du cinquantenaire de l'Ecole des Langues Orientales Anciennes de l'Institut Catholique de Paris* (Paris: Bloud et Gay, 1964) 51–66.

104. Delcor, "Recherches sur un horoscope"; A. Dupont-Sommer, "Deux documents horoscopiques esséniens découverts à Qoumrân près de la Mer Morte," *CRAIBL* (1965) 239–53; F. Sen, "Los horóscopos de Qumrán," *Cultura bíblica* 23 (1966) 366–67; A.

Also from Cave 4 are fragments from an as yet unpublished brontologion, which gives the signs of the Zodiac and then makes predictions on the basis of thunder: "If it thunders in the sign of the Twins, terror and distress caused by foreigners. . . ." The closest parallel is the brontologion ascribed to Zoroaster in the *Geoponica* 1:1.[105]

Attitudes toward astrology are not uniformly represented in the Pseudepigrapha (200 B.C.–A.D. 200). On the one hand, astrology is condemned, as Charlesworth notes:

> According to the author of 1 *Enoch* 8:3 (probably early second century B.C.), astrology is an evil and demonic idea since it was taught to men by one of the fallen angels, Baraqiyal. The third book of the *Sibylline Oracles* (second century B.C.), in lines 220–36 praises righteous men who neither search the mystical meaning of the movements of the heavenly bodies nor are deceived by the predictions of Chaldean astrology.[106]

In a similar fashion, *Jubilees* 12:17 has Abraham coming to himself after sitting up at night to observe the stars: "And a word came into his heart, saying: 'All of the signs of the stars and the signs of the sun and the moon are all in the hand of the Lord. Why am I seeking?'"[107]

On the other hand, parts of 1 *Enoch* such as 72:1–37 incorporate numerous zodiacal ideas. 1 *Enoch* 80:2–8 attributes the disorders of the planets to the sons of men. 2 *Enoch*, which dates to the late first century A.D., has Enoch declaring: "And I saw the eighth heaven, which is called in the Hebrew language Muzaloth, the changer of the season, of dry and of wet, and the 12 zodiacs, which are above the seventh heaven. And I saw the ninth heaven, which in the Hebrew language is called

---

Dupont-Sommer, "La secte des Esséniens et les horoscopes de Qumran," *Archaeologia* 15 (1967) 24–31; J. Fitzmyer, "A Bibliographical Aid to the Study of the Qumran Cave IV Texts," *CBQ* 31 (1969) 70–71; M. Hengel, *Judaism and Hellenism* (Philadelphia: Fortress, 1974), 1:236–37, 2:158–59; M. R. Lehmann, "New Light on Astrology in Qumran and the Talmud," *RevQ* (1975) 599–602.

105. J. T. Milik, *Ten Years of Discovery in the Wilderness of Judaea* (Naperville: Alec R. Allenson, 1959) 42; Charlesworth, "Jewish Astrology," 192 n. 28 comments: "Unfortunately the two fragmentary columns of another scroll are unpublished, although J. T. Milik mentioned them twenty years ago." Divination by thunder and lightning was especially practiced by the Etruscans and Romans. See O.-W. Von Vacano, *The Etruscans in the Ancient World* (Bloomington: Indiana University, 1965) 19–23; R. Bloch, "La divination en Etrurie et à Rome," *La Divination* (ed. A. Caquot and M. Leibovici; Paris: Presses Universitaires de France, 1968), 1:197–232.

106. Charlesworth, "Jewish Astrology," 188.

107. J. H. Charlesworth, ed., *The Old Testament Pseudepigrapha* (Garden City: Doubleday, 1983–85), 2:81.

Kukhavim, where the heavenly houses of the 12 zodiacs are" (21:6, version J).[108]

J. H. Charlesworth has recently published a Syriac manuscript called the *Treatise of Shem* which is the only Jewish Pseudepigraphon that consistently advocates astrology.[109] It is a calendologion, that is, it seeks to determine the character of a year according to the zodiacal sign in which it begins. According to Charlesworth's analysis, the document was composed by an Alexandrian Jew shortly after the battle of Actium in 31 B.C.: "The recovery of the Treatise of Shem, coupled with the indisputable fact of a 'most unusual celestial display' near the time of Jesus' birth, by no means prove that Matthew ii preserves reliable historical information; but it is now more difficult to claim that Matthew's star was created purely out of a myth."[110]

Conclusion

The Magi in Matthew became elaborately developed in legend and in art. A number of scholars have considered the original story in Matthew to be a distorted reflection of the trip of Tiridates, a midrash on the adoration of the shepherds in Luke, or a midrash of Balaam's prophecy. But after tracing the background of the Magi and the diffusion of astrology from Mesopotamia to the west and noting the evidence of Jewish interest in astrology as demonstrated by the Treatise of Shem and the Qumran materials, I would conclude that we can best understand the story of the Magi in Matthew not as a literary creation but as based on a historical episode.

---

108. Ibid., 1:136. No fewer than eleven MSS of Enoch were found at Qumran. See J. T. Milik, *The Books of Enoch: Aramaic Fragments of Qumrân Cave 4* (Oxford: Clarendon, 1976).

109. Charlesworth, *Old Testament Pseudepigrapha*, 1:473-80.

110. Charlesworth, "Rylands Syriac MS 44 and a New Addition to the Pseudepigrapha: The Treatise of Shem," *BJRL* 60 (1977-78) 390. See also J. H. Charlesworth and J. R. Mueller, "Die 'Schrift des Sem': Einführung, Text und Übersetzung," *Religion (Hellenistisches Judentum in römischer Zeit: Allgemeines)* (ed. W. Haase; Aufstieg und Niedergang der römischen Welt: Principat 20; Berlin: de Gruyter, 1987), 2:951-87.

The Star of the Magi and Babylonian Astronomy

Konradin Ferrari-D'Occhieppo

Many of the earliest attempts at a scientific explanation of the celestial phenomena alluded to in Matt 2:1–12 fell short because almost nothing was known about Babylonian astronomy. Its rediscovery did not start before the last decades of the nineteenth century. In 1925 a small fragment of a clay tablet, dating from the year 7/6 B.C., presented the first indisputable evidence that contemporaneous Babylonian astronomers, at least in a rather crude manner, had either observed or perhaps calculated the great planetary conjunction of Jupiter and Saturn in the constellation of Pisces.[1] Such a conjunction, long before its epigraphic confirmation, had played an important role in the explanation of the "Star" of the Magi. The information derived from this tablet, however, did not add decisive details in favor of this hypothesis.

Hence, many quite different explanations have been proposed by astronomers, professionals as well as amateurs. Some of these authors have not only completely ignored Babylonian astronomy and its astrological implications, but sometimes have not even considered the original Greek text of the gospel, although translations may be misleading in critical cases, especially with respect to the precise meaning of astronomical statements. In short, it has seemed as if there were a great number of equally suitable celestial phenomena within but a dozen years to be considered. Of course, the disagreement among the astronomers about the proper solution of the problem confirmed the view of those theologians who assumed that the story of the Magi as a whole was nothing but a pious myth.

Konradin Ferrari-d'Ochieppo is Emeritus Professor in the Department of Theoretical Astronomy at the University of Vienna.

1. VAT 290 + 1836. See P. Schnabel, "Der jüngste datierbare Keilschrifttext," *ZA* 36 (1925) 66–70.

In the mid-1960s, I published a new approach to the problem, after having studied the original sources of Babylonian astronomy, which had been published and masterfully commented on by Otto Neugebauer and A. J. Sachs in the previous decade.[2] I arrived at the conclusion that a clear decision in favor of one certain solution was possible. It could be shown, on the basis of precise numerical data, in part derived from the Babylonian planetary theories and in part directly from clay tablets excavated in the ruins of Babylon, that two extremely rare planetary phenomena, calculated many decades in advance by those ancient astronomers, fitted in a unique manner the statements of the gospel about the star. Even the appearance of its standing still for about three hours after nightfall above an appropriate place on earth could be explained as a calculable natural phenomenon. Further researches resulted in some additional arguments in favor of this view of the matter.[3]

This paper presents, for the first time in English, a summary of my views on this problem.

Evidence from Ancient Astronomy

The question of whether a celestial phenomenon reported within an allegedly historical context actually happened within a given span of time often occurs to a historically engaged astronomer. In all such cases, one should start from the working hypothesis that the report under consideration is factual and should, tentatively, be taken as literally as possible. If, in positive cases, the reality of the phenomena alluded to in the given text has been actually proved, more precise dates of the historical facts of the context will be gained as a result.

Thus, if one takes the first chapters of Matthew's Gospel as essentially factual, one must suppose that the learned Christian author, who at about A.D. 80 (as is generally assumed) composed its final text, had

2. K. Ferrari-D'Occhieppo, "Jupiter und Saturn nach babylonischen Quellen," *Österreichische Akademie der Wissenschaften, math.-nat. Klasse, Sitzungsbericht* 173 (1965) 343–76; O. Neugebauer, *Astronomical Cuneiform Texts* (3 vols.; London: Lund Humphries, 1955); A. J. Sachs, *Late Babylonian Astronomical and Related Texts* (Providence: Brown University, 1955).

3. See my "Der Stern der Magier," *Österreichische Akademie der Wissenschaften, phil.-hist. Klasse, Anzeiger* 111 (1974) 319–45; "Zur Hypothese einer 854-jährigen Planetenperiode in der babylonischen Astronomie," *Österreichische Akademie der Wissenschaften, phil.-hist. Klasse, Anzeiger* 113 (1976) 231–34; and *Der Stern der Weisen: Geschichte oder Legende?* (2d ed.; Vienna: Herold, 1977). Also see the later works of Neugebauer, *History of Ancient Mathematical Astronomy* (3 vols.; Berlin/Heidelberg/New York: Springer, 1975).

some sources written at an earlier time at his disposal. Except for the enumeration of the early ancestors, evidently taken from the biblical book of Chronicles, the origin and the early youth of Jesus are told along a tradition preserved among the relatives of Joseph and written down in Aramaic. There is a more or less literal translation into Greek of some simple reports (such as Matt 1:18–25 and 2:13–23), but a large portion of Matt 2:1–12 appears stylistically at variance with the sections preceding and following it. One must suppose that they were originally connected by an equally simple record of the visit of the Magi—perhaps similar to (but certainly not identical with) that preserved in papyrus codex Bodmer V (see below).

On the other hand, it is known from recent researches that there existed connections between certain members of the "order of the Magi" (as one may call it) and some Jewish and early Christian communities. Thus, it was undoubtedly possible that the author of the final composition of Matthew's Gospel could have replaced the first simple record of the visit of the Magi with the present form of Matt 2:1–12, a more detailed and, in part, even technically written text originating from the Magi.

The statement that some expressions in the text under consideration must be understood as technical terms is justified by present knowledge of Babylonian astronomy, as restored by modern scientists from a systematic study of many hundreds of clay tablets found in the ruins of Babylon and Uruk. Evidently as a basis for long-term astrological predictions, the Babylonian astronomers of the last centuries B.C. continuously computed the dates and zodiacal longitudes of certain cyclically returning phases of the planets. As far as Saturn, Jupiter, and Mars are concerned, the following special phases were computed: (1) their first reappearance in the morning, (2 and 4) the two stationary points in the apparent motion relative to the fixed stars, preceding and following (3) their last observable rise in the evening, when the planet in question could be seen during the whole night at the climax of its brightness, and (5) their disappearance in the evening dusk.

Three of those special phases are mentioned unmistakably in Matthew's text. While it is said that the Magi came ἀπὸ ἀνατολῶν 'from the rising' (Matt 2:1)—the general direction of the rising stars being properly described in Greek by the plural without an article—they attributed the quality of a very important omen to the evening rise of a certain star observed ἐν τῇ ἀνατολῇ 'in the rising' (Matt 2:2) where the singular with the definite article is used. Equally stressed is another evening considerably later when the same star reached its (second) stationary point, ἐστάθη 'stopped' (Matt 2:9). But Herod inquired from the Magi τὸν χρόνον τοῦ φαινομένου ἀστέρος 'the exact time the star had appeared' (Matt 2:7), because he believed that this was the birth date of the royal child, as may be seen from Matt 2:16: κατὰ τὸν χρόνον ὃν ἠκρίβωσεν παρὰ τῶν μάγων 'in accordance with the time he had learned from the Magi'.

Hence, it is certain that the star was one of three planets—Jupiter, Saturn, or Mars—because the fixed stars are always stationary in relation to each other and the stationary points of Venus and Mercury, being scarcely observable without precise instruments, usually were ignored in the long-term computations of the Babylonian astronomers.

From the secrecy of Herod's inquiry one must conclude that the Magi had been summoned to their pilgrimage not by any unforeseen phenomenon in the sky, spectacular to common people, but by a planetary appearance, less impressive to people, yet recognized as a highly extraordinary event by the Magi from their computations.

In order to make the proper choice among the celestial phenomena between, say, 12 B.C. and A.D. 1 some astrological considerations will be helpful.[4]

The planet Mars had since early times been identified with Nergal, a deity of fatal influence similar to Ares in Greek mythology or Mars in Roman mythology. In political astrology it was considered as representative of hostile nations to the west of Babylon. Hence, one may safely exclude any possibility that it might have been the star alluded to in Matthew.

The planet Jupiter, in Babylonian astrology, was the "Bright Star of Marduk," the supreme male deity, comparable to Zeus and Jupiter in Greek and Roman mythology. Even if the Magi were adherents of the religion of Zoroaster, they would not have had any difficulty in considering this same planet as Ahuramazda's Star, announcing good fortune in every case.

With due regard to the fact that the Jewish nation did not play an important role in the ancient history of the Near East, except for some short periods, it is not surprising that in the Babylonian sources none of the five bright planets was exclusively held to represent the Jews in the sky. But a well-known saying of the prophet Amos (5:26), repeated with variations in the Damascus Document (7:14–15) and in the Acts of

4. Astronomy and astrology were inseparably intertwined in antiquity, and even though astrology must be acknowledged as a legitimate part of the philosophy of the ancient Magi, who on a high moral and intellectual level tried to understand God (or the gods) and humanity—heaven and earth—as one cosmos, I do not accept the validity of astrology as a science since it does not have an observable, repeatable base.

the Apostles (7:43), sufficiently proves that the alleged relation between Saturn and the Jews was a superstition of Akkadian origin, once condemned by the prophets, yet actually surviving not only until the beginning of the Christian era, but even in medieval astrology.

Additional astrological information can be deduced from the constellations of the zodiac where certain planetary phenomena appeared. Since within the span of time considered here Jupiter met Saturn only once (in the constellation of Pisces), I restrict my discussion to the latter, at present. In Babylonian astrology the zodiac was related to the curved chain of fertile countries from Mesopotamia to Egypt. Hence, a planetary phenomenon near the central part of that constellation was considered to be important to Palestine. (It is irrelevant to this issue whether the opinion of medieval astrologers, that the whole constellation of Pisces should be related to the Jews, was current already by the time of Jesus' birth.) At least the second stationary points of Jupiter and Saturn, in 7 B.C., lay in the very middle of the Fishes, although it was about the 350th degree of the zodiac (the 20th of Pisces) according to the Babylonian method of counting longitudes then in use.

One important remark is necessary here: in Babylonian astrology, the fixed star Regulus in the constellation of the Lion was always related to the King of Babylonia, never to any foreign ruler. Hence, whatever happened in that constellation about the beginning of the Christian era, would have been understood as an omen relative to the then Parthian rulers of Babylon, but not to Herod or to the expected Messiah.

Thus, Babylonian planetary theories show that on Ululu 21, Babylonian Seleucid Era 305 = 15 September 7 B.C. the planets Jupiter and Saturn, about one degree apart in longitude (the small latitudes were ignored in Babylonian long-term computations), were expected to rise at sunset, and thus, visible during the whole night, would draw their majestic arc over the sky. Two months later, Arahsamna 20/21 = 12/13 November, they were expected to reach their stationary points, differing only by three minutes of arc in longitude, in the central part of the constellation of Pisces.

Hence, according to the results of the Babylonian planetary theories, the significant planets in the appropriate part of the zodiac appeared extraordinarily close together in those phases, which I believe are alluded to in Matthew. The correctness of my restoration of the Babylonian calculation of longitudes can be proved by comparison with certain entries in almanacs of the Seleucid Era (S.E.) 300 and 301. The dates given above can be read directly from an almanac tablet of the year S.E.

305, except for the badly damaged date of Jupiter's station.[5] The preserved portion of the cipher indicates a day number of 19 rather than 20, but the difference of one unit may be explained by a rounding-off error in the (un-preserved) intermediate part of the original Babylonian calculations.

In the almanac tablets, the Babylonian astronomers used to assemble the results of the individual computational tables for each year in a strictly chronological order, and in a highly abbreviated form. From the extraordinary fact that there are fragments of at least four different copies of the almanac of S.E. 305 preserved, one may conclude that the celestial phenomena expected in that year had excited the curiosity of the Babylonians in an unusual degree. Indeed, such a close coincidence of the stationary points of Jupiter and Saturn is extremely rare. The Babylonian astronomers, from the periods used in their computations, were able to conclude that at least 854 years must elapse before a recurrence of such a coincidence in the Fishes might be possible (that is, twice the length of the great period of Jupiter).

The Philosophy of the Magi

I frankly admit that, even on the basis of the alleged relevance of the constellation and of the planets involved, the astrological evidence alone could not be sufficient to explain the pilgrimage of the Magi from their distant homeland to Jerusalem, nor their precise question about a newborn King of the Jews (Matt 2:2). One might imagine that, from the planetary phenomena given, they could have expected any other happy or important event among the Jews. But, in practice, astrologers always have made ample use of other sources of information and of analogies with more or less similar cases in the past.

Keeping this in mind, it is important to note that there was a numerous Jewish diaspora in Babylonia and Syria. Thus, the expectation—founded in Jewish prophecy—of a Savior-King, the Messiah, was well known in the pagan world. On the other hand, the Babylonian astronomers in their archive of tablets (preserved, in part, up to the present time) could find a vague analogy preceding the exceptional phenomena of 7 B.C. by about 119 years. In 126 B.C. Jupiter and Saturn, being also in the constellation of Pisces, had their last observable rises

---

5. BM 34614 = LBAT 1193; BM 34659 = LBAT 1194; BM 35429 = LBAT 1195; VAT 290 + 1836 = LBAT 1196. See A. J. Sachs and C. B. F. Walker, "Kepler's View of the Star of Bethlehem and the Babylonian Almanac for 7/6 B.C.," *Iraq* 46 (1984) 43–55.

on two successive evenings, while their longitudes, at the same time, had shown twice the difference that occurred in 7 B.C. Their second stationary points in 126 B.C. differed in longitude by 45 minutes of arc, a high multiple of the three-minute difference in 7 B.C., and additionally in the opposite direction.

About the same year, 126 B.C., Alexander Jannaeus was born, who was the first king of the Hasmonean dynasty to secure renown even in the chronicles of pagan historians. Hence, an astrologer might have argued as follows: When Alexander Jannaeus was born as a junior son of the High Priest John Hyrcanus, there existed no Jewish kingdom at all, whereas in 7 B.C. King Herod's royal power seemed to be firmly established. Now, if the "weak" planetary phenomena of 126 B.C. were able to produce a king of the Jews who, in spite of internal opposition and great external hostilities, maintained his throne for over 27 years, the much more exceptional conjunction in 7 B.C. might justify the expectation of an extraordinarily happy and glorious King of the Jews who might fulfill the ancient prophecies of a truly Messianic age.

There is no difficulty in understanding that, notwithstanding the fact that the coincidence of two equally named phases of *two* planets in the same constellation formed the basis for the astrological prediction, only Jupiter, the dominant planet, was particularly spoken of as "his star."

Unfortunately, there is no reliable information about the religious background of those Magi who worshiped the child Jesus. Yet, the following hypothesis may be proposed: The last descendants of Marduk's priests in Babylon persevered at the old and partially ruined sanctuary of that deity and devoted themselves to the study of the stars and their alleged relevance. But they no longer used any priestly titles (as the colophons of many astronomical tablets show), because they inclined to a sort of religious syncretism without sharp distinctions between Marduk or Ahuramazda or even Yahweh. Thus they were able to share the Messianic hope of the Jewish prophets, and at the same time look for that Savior-King's birthdate along their astrological rules—the unique evening when the star of the supreme god (Jupiter) would rise side by side with the planet of the Jewish people (Saturn).

Of course, among the small number of Babylonian astronomers of that late time, very few were able to undertake the long journey to Jerusalem. When they traversed the northern part of the vast Arabian territory (probably accompanied by a commercial caravan), some other Magi of a community living in Arabia could have joined the former. Thus, Justin's statement that the Magi had come from Arabia may be

correct (*Dialogue with Tryphon* 77, 78). Similarly, the report underlying
the final composition of Matthew might have been written by an
Arabian participant.

The Context of Matthew 2

Having demonstrated the consistency of the astronomical statements of the gospel with the results of the Babylonian planetary theory
and its astrological consequences, I now examine how the remaining
information of the biblical text fits this working hypothesis.

First of all, the Magi, from astrological computations made years in
advance, could have expected the birth of a royal child of extraordinary
destiny among the Jews. Of course, they hoped to find him in the royal
palace of his capital, and they did not need to have the star going before
them like a guide's lantern. And indeed, the text of the gospel does not
state anything of that sort before they arrived at Jerusalem.

Rather, the Magi receive Herod's command to search for the child
(given according to Micah's prophecy [5:2]), and it was only after their
audience with Herod, when they had already started toward Bethlehem
in the late afternoon of 12 November 7 B.C., that they are said to have
seen the star (apparently) going before them. That is, Jupiter appeared
approximately 50 degrees above the horizon in the very direction they
were riding. Just at this moment, perhaps one hour or so before they
could have reached their destiny, an outburst of exceedingly great joy—
unusual in the factual style of the gospels—is inserted into the report
(Matt 2:10). It may be understood in this way: In Jerusalem, the Magi
must have been deeply disappointed by the reactions produced by their
announcement of a newborn king. Herod, to whom they owed the
advice to go to Bethlehem, had not the air of trustworthiness. They had
to obey him, but they felt serious doubts as to whether they had been
deceived. In such a spirit of dejection, even intelligent people are liable
to feel encouraged by any promising circumstances that otherwise
might be considered insignificant. They must have recalled that in this
very night the two planets were to become stationary in the zodiac.

When the sky grew darker, Saturn became visible near Jupiter.
About half an hour later, the diffuse cone of the zodiacal light appeared,
with Jupiter being close to its top. One could imagine that it was the
star that sent a broad light beam toward the earth. Marvellously enough,
notwithstanding the sky's turning around its pole as usual, the bright
axis of the cone of light persistently pointed to the same place, the
northwestern hill of Bethlehem (which was seen in the direction of
southwest by the Magi, who approached it from Jerusalem). Thus, it

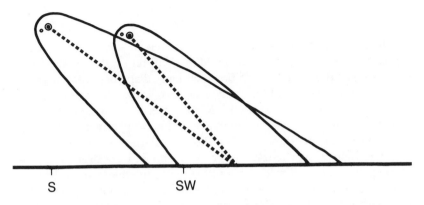

Fig. 1. Schematic diagram of the zodiacal light. On 12 November 7 B.C., between 7:45 and 9:45 P.M., Jupiter and Saturn are near the top of the zodiacal light, which appeared above the southwest horizon to the Magi riding toward Bethlehem from Jerusalem. The variation from one position to the other proceeded so slowly that (notwithstanding the rotation of the sky around its pole and the planets moving from left to right), in consequence of the setting point of the bright axis (dashed line) being practically immovable for more than three hours, the star (Jupiter) seemed to stand still above that same point. Note that, in reality, there are no sharp contours, but a gradual decrease of brightness along the axis, and from the latter toward both sides of the light cone. The brightness of the zodiacal light matches that of the Milky Way, but without any cloudy structure.

appeared as if the star stood still, not only with respect to the zodiac (as had been calculated by the Magi), but also above a certain place on the earth, which was (scientifically speaking, by mere chance) just that part of the village where the child was dwelling with his parents. Yet, it is not asserted in the gospel that the star pointed exactly to a certain house.

The apparition just described was neither a product of their imagination, nor a miracle. It can be astronomically explained in this way: At the date in question, 12 November 7 B.C., during the first three hours of darkness, the setting point of the bright axis of the zodiacal light moved slowly from the Archer to the Goat, where the change of declination, and consequently that of the azimuth too, is negligible in proportion to the broad and diffuse appearance of the light cone. This phenomenon must have been the more impressive to the Magi, since it had not been foreseen from their computations. (The zodiacal light is schematically illustrated in figure 1.)

Additional Evidence

In the papyrus codex Bodmer V, written in Egypt in the fourth century, the story of the Magi is told in a different but consistent way, yet without the fanciful additions of long dialogues and incredible exaggerations that appear in more recent copies of the so-called *Proto-evangelium of James* (cf. 21:2–3).[6] Most experts in ancient Christian literature will have serious doubts whether any historically reliable information may be found in this codex. Yet, I argue as follows.

The *Nativity*, as the codex is entitled, should have originally ended at the point when, after Joseph's return with two midwives, it becomes evident that the Virgin has already borne her son Jesus in a miraculous way without any human assistance (chap. 20). What follows, is a loose assembly of episodes compiled, apparently, from various and fragmentary sources. Thus, it is probable that, by a lucky chance, the report about the Magi, even within this otherwise unhistorical book, has been taken from a very old and reliable tradition, originating from a small group of faithful people who had formerly sheltered the holy family in Egypt.

Indeed, if according to Matthew's Gospel, the holy family spent some years in Egypt, it was quite natural that Joseph plainly spoke to his hosts about his experience with the Magi, who had become, unintentionally, the cause of his flight. A few sentences that are very similar in the papyrus text and in the gospel resulted probably from the fact that the author of the final composition of the gospel not only had before him the "technical" report of the Magi themselves, but a previous record originating from the tradition among Joseph's relations. But the papyrus text—without contradictions to the gospel—supplies some additional information. First, Joseph was already engaged in preparations for departure, when the Magi arrived at Bethlehem. Then, two sentences summarize the fact that they had been previously summoned by Herod's servants to inform him about the star. But, perhaps secretly, Joseph received additional information from the Magi that they saw two stars, in one and the same rising, that (apparently) went before them, until they arrived at the cave, the holy family's interim habitation: ειδον αστερας εν τη ανατολη και πφοηγαν αυτους εως εισηλθαν εν τω

---

6. M. Testuz, *Papyrus Bodmer V: Nativité de Marie* (Cologne/Geneva: Bibliotheca Bodmeriana, 1958) 110–14. For English translations of *Protoevangelium of James* see M. R. James, *The Apocryphal New Testament* (Oxford: Clarendon, 1924) 38–49; E. Hennecke and W. Schneemelcher, *New Testament Apocrypha* (Philadelphia: Westminster, 1963), 1:370–88. I have included the Greek text and an English translation of *Protoevangelium of James* 21:1–22:1 as an appendix to this essay.

σπηλαιω, 'They saw stars in the ascent and they [i.e., the stars] went before them until they entered the cave.'[7]

Although the copyist has omitted the number two (β' in Greek), the plural is warranted by the endings of both the substantive and the verb related to it. In my opinion, the consistency of that plural of "stars" with the main thesis of the present paper provides a reciprocal attestation, in favor of the former as well as in favor of the authenticity of that primary source about the visit of the Magi used by the writer of the papyrus codex.

At last, the Magi are said to have seen the child 'standing by his mother Mary's side': εστωτα μετα της μητρος αυτου Μαριας (21:3). If one takes the latter remark literally, it would be favorable to the old Christian tradition that January was the anniversary of Jesus' birthday. For in this case he would have been about ten months old and thus able to stand when the Magi saw him on 12 November 7 B.C.

The tradition just mentioned might have originated in this way: Perhaps in remembering the anniversary of Jesus' birth, nearly eight weeks after the visit of the Magi, Joseph realized that the Hebrew date of Tebeth 15 was identical with Tybi 15 in the then popular Old Egyptian calendar (but Tybi 11 in the reformed Alexandrian calendar [Julian: January 6]): Since neither Joseph nor his illiterate hosts knew that this apparent conformity of their national calendars in 6 B.C. resulted from a rare chance, they did not notice the difference between the respective lengths of the preceding Jewish lunar year (the calendar by which Joseph reckoned the anniversary) and the Egyptian solar year. But the twin date Tybi 15/Tybi 11 as the anniversary of Jesus' birth survived in the Egyptian tradition.[8]

In fact, this Egyptian tradition, already somewhat obscured toward the end of the second century when the Old Egyptian calendar had become obsolete, is found in *Stomateis*, a work by Clement of Alexandria (A.D. 150–211[?]). Clement assumed that Jesus was exactly 30 years old when he was baptized in the 15th year of Tiberius (1:21:145; cf. Luke

7. *Protoevangelium of James* 21:2–3 (*Papyrus Bodmer V*, 112). The Greek text is here written without accents as in Bodmer V.

8. The equation Tebeth 15 (Hebrew) = Tybi 15 (Old Egyptian) = Tybi 11 (Alexandrian) was valid uniquely in 6 B.C. because of the different rules governing those calendars. Note that Joseph *without* any written calendar, and without having counted days, could realize the date of Tebeth 15, since he was certainly able to see that in the preceding night the moon had just begun to wane, and in the morning remained visible for a short time after sunrise (as has been proved by modern astronomical computation). Hence, this day, by reason of its following immediately the second full moon after the holy family's departure from Bethlehem in the month of Arahsamna (Hebrew: Marcheshwan), had to be counted as the 15th of Tebeth.

3:23). Consequently, Jesus was born in the 28th year of Augustus, or 194 years 1 month 13 days before the death of Commodus (= 70,853 days, figuring on 365 days per year). Computing backward from Commodus's death, 1 January 193, gives a result of Tybi 11 (Alexandrian).[9] A few lines later (1:21:146), Clement writes that there was a controversy between several Christian (or Gnostic) communities as to whether Tybi 15 or Tybi 11 was the accurate date of Jesus' baptism. Evidently, people had forgotten that originally both those dates (but in different calendar systems) denoted the same day, 6 January 6 B.C., which was also Tebeth 15 in the Jewish calendar—the first anniversary of Jesus' birth. It was, of course, by mere (Gnostic?) speculation that afterward both Alexandrian dates were chosen for the annual celebration of his baptism. The essential point of my investigation proves that a genuine Egyptian tradition of the first anniversary of Jesus' birth was not improbable. This result is perfectly compatible with the astronomically determined date of the Magi's visit, and equally valid whether or not the very year of Jesus' birth included a twin Adar.

APPENDIX

Greek text of *Protoevangelium of James* 21:1–22:1 (taken from M. Testuz, *Papyrus Bodmer V: Nativité de Marie* [Cologne/Geneva: Bibliotheca Bodmeriana, 1958] 110, 112).

και ειδου Ιωσηφ ητυμασθη του εξελθειν εν τη Ιουδεα. και θυρυβοσ εγενετο μεγασ εν βηθλεμ τησ Ιουδεασ. ηλθωσαν γαρ μαγοι λεγοντεσ· που εστιν ο βασιλευσ των Ιουδεων; ιδομεν γαρ τον αστερα αυτου εν τη ανατολη και ηλθαμεν προσκυνησε αυτω. και ακουσασ ο Ηρωδησ εταραχθη. και επεμψεν υπερετασ και μετεπεμψατο αυτουσ. και διεσαφησαν αυτω περι του αστεροσ. και ειδου ειδον αστερασ εν τη ανατολη και προηγαν αυτουσ εωσ εισηλθαν εν τω σπηλαιω. και εστη επι την κεφαλην του παιδιου. και ιδοντεσ οι μαγοι εστωτα μετα τησ μητροσ αυτου Μαριασ εξεβαλλον απο τησ πηρασ αυτων δωρα χρυσον και λιβανον και σμυρναν. και χρηματισθεντεσ υπο του

9. Evidently, Clement of Alexandria was acquainted with the chronological method of his elder countryman Claudius Ptolemy, the famous astronomer (100–160) who, notwithstanding precise knolwedge of the natural lengths of years and months, used "Egyptian Years" of 365 days each (without any exceptions) and round months of 30 days each as invariable units in calculating long intervals of time. In the present case, in order to get correctly the result, Tybi 11 (Alexandrian), one must also take account of the fact that Commodus had been murdered in the night of 31 December 192/1 January 193 which, according to the Egyptian use, had to be reckoned as the night of the *former* date.

αγγελου δια αλλησ οδου ανεχωρησαν εισ την χωραν. τοτε Ηρωδησ ειδων οτι
ενεπεχθη υπο των μαγων . . .

English translation of *Protoevangelium of James* 21:1–22:1 (following, in-
tentionally, as literally as possible the rather clumsy Greek text).

> And behold, Joseph prepared for departure in Judea. And a great
> uproar arose at Bethlehem in Judea. For Magi had arrived who said:
> "Where is the King of the Jews? We have seen his star in the ascent and
> we have come to worship him." And Herod, as he heard it, was terrified.
> And he sent servants and summoned them. And they informed him about
> the star. And behold, they saw stars[a] in the [same] ascent and they [i.e.,
> the stars] went before them until they entered the cave. And (he/she/it)[b]
> stood at the head of the child. And as the Magi saw him standing by the
> side of his mother Mary, they threw out of their bag gifts, gold and
> francincense and myrrh. And after having gotten a revelation by the angel
> they traveled by another way into their homeland. Then Herod, as he saw
> that he has been deluded by the Magi . . .

[a] By courtesy of the Bodmer Foundation, Geneva, I have collated a photograph of
the important page numbered $\overline{\text{MB}}$(Greek capitals, = 42) of the papyrus codex in question.
Thanks to the excellent state of preservation of this page it could be read letter by letter
with absolute certainty. Thus, there is no doubt about the remarkable plural of "stars"
and the verb related to it, nor about the singular of "ascent," emphasized by the addition
of the word "same" in brackets.

[b] From the Greek verb "stood" alone, one cannot decide the gender of its subject.
But it is not improbable that the author of that primary source, which the writer of the
codex has more or less correctly copied, meant to say that either *Joseph* or *Mary* took his
or her place behind the child Jesus, thus standing "at the head" of their little son, when
the foreign Magi appeared at the entrance of the poor habitation. But other copyists, a
few centuries later, did not hesitate to declare that it was the *star* which entered the cave
and stood above the child's head.

Jesus' Life: A New Chronology

Jerry Vardaman

The word chronology means a study of time. All scientific research about the past demands an application of chronology to the span of history under investigation. The Bible is grounded in history, and chronology must be dealt with by students of both the Old Testament and the New Testament. One of the greatest contributions that archaeology makes to the study of the Bible comes at the point of chronology. This article will deal primarily with the chronology of the life of Jesus, where archaeological investigations have yielded helpful information on key historical facts that relate to the time of our Lord. Much has been learned; there is still much to learn. And a large part of what we learn in the future will be a result of continuing investigations, particularly with written (and numismatic) materials supplied by archaeological discovery.

The present state of New Testament chronology is one of un-certainty. The goal of chronology is to attain the greatest certainty possible concerning the times when specific events occurred. In the life of Jesus, for example, it would be of the greatest value to know:

1. What was the day, month, and year in which Jesus was born?
2. When did Jesus' family go to Egypt and when did they return?
3. When did Jesus begin his public ministry?[1]
4. When was Jesus crucified?

Jerry Vardaman is Director of Special Programs of the Cobb Institute of Archaeology at Mississipi State University, and Professor of Religion.

I wish to thank Bob Wolverton, Professor of Classics at Mississippi State University, who greatly assisted in editing and revising the second part of my article on microletters.

1. When the Nativity Conference was held in December 1983, I suggested A.D. 17 as the year when Jesus began his ministry. I now believe that A.D. 15 is more accurate, and have made some changes throughout this essay accordingly.

It is impossible in the present state of affairs to know the answers to any of the above questions. It is even hazardous to try to reach any consensus among New Testament scholars as to when any of these events took place. Perhaps it is possible to say, however, that the prevailing view is that Jesus was born between 8 and 2 B.C., and that he died around A.D. 30–33. It is my opinion that this standard chronology, especially with reference to his death, is approximately a decade too late. In the first part of this paper I set forth briefly those considerations that have entered into my judgment that Jesus was born in late 12 B.C., and that he was crucified around A.D. 21, at the beginning of Passover.

Evidence That Jesus Was Born in 12 B.C. and Died in A.D. 21

Josephus

Josephus refers to Jesus in *Antiquities* 18:63–64, mentioning that Jesus was wise, won over many Jews and Greeks, was crucified by Pilate; however, his followers testified that he rose from the dead, and the tribe of Christians had not died out, even in the last years of the first century A.D., when Josephus wrote. The authenticity of this passage is disputed by many, but I believe that Josephus is referring to the biblical Jesus. Granted, some of Josephus's statements could have been expanded by Christian scribes, but the core of what is reported about Jesus by Josephus is fully authentic and Josephus's testimony is located at the right place historically. Unnoticed by most students of Josephus is the fact that Josephus places Jesus in a time frame for beginning his ministry *no later than A.D.* 15–19 (and possibly slightly earlier).

It is true that Josephus is not always arranged chronologically. Nevertheless, it is just as true, demonstrably, that Josephus is *sometimes* chronological in his arrangement of material—certainly in his general arrangement of material. For example, Moses is not reported in the later part of his *Antiquities*, but in the earlier part. In Josephus's account of Jesus, it is strange that Jesus would be dated to the approximate time he was (A.D. 15–19) unless that is indeed when Jesus was carrying on his ministry. Note the context of historical events in which Jesus is mentioned:

1. Parthians request, then reject, Vonones (*Antiquities* 18:46ff.) = A.D. 14–17
2. Silanus removed and Piso becomes governor of Syria (*Antiquities* 18:52, 54) = A.D. 17
3. Orodes rules in Armenia (*Antiquities* 18:52) = A.D. 15–18

4. Germanicus sent to East; poisoned by Piso(?) (*Antiquities* 18:54) = A.D. 17–19
5. Josephus's reference to Jesus (*Antiquities* 18:63–64)
6. Mundus seduces Paulina; Tiberius overthrows Isis cult (*Antiquities* 18:65ff.) = A.D. 19
7. Fulvia cheated; Tiberius expels Jews from Rome (*Antiquities* 18:81–83) = A.D. 19

Thus, Josephus turns out to be even more important in his testimony to Jesus' ministry when one recognizes that this event is placed within a historical context dating around A.D. 15–19. And it is not possible to remove the passage as inauthentic and to solve the problem of this early setting by that denial. Josephus just as certainly places Pilate, who crucified Jesus, in this same historical context, even if one denies the value of Josephus's testimony to Jesus (see *Antiquities* 18:55–62).

If one accepts the historical value of Josephus's testimony to Jesus and to Pilate, and the time frame in which these testimonies occur, then one is at once presented with a problem in the chronology that dates the death of Jesus around A.D. 30–33. On the other hand, it would be natural for Jesus to be involved in his public ministry around A.D. 15–19 if he were born, as I believe, around the fall of 12 B.C. Thus, in the fall of A.D. 15, for example, Jesus would have been *arriving* at thirty years of age, just as Luke 3:23 mentions: "And Jesus was starting to be about thirty years of age."

Jesus as Starting to be Thirty Years of Age (Luke 3:23)

Luke 3:23 strongly implies that at the time of beginning his public ministry Jesus was not quite thirty years of age. It is impossible, it seems, to make sense of a chronology that places the beginning of Jesus' public ministry after A.D. 25 and still give any meaning to Luke's statement that he was *almost* thirty when he began his ministry.

Most students of the New Testament accept the fact that King Herod died in 4 B.C. (*Jewish War* 1:661–64, *Antiquities* 17:188–92). Herod was certainly alive when Jesus was born, and enough information is available from the New Testament writers to know that Herod lived for several months after the birth of Jesus before he died (Matt 2:1–20). Under no circumstance, therefore, is it safe to date Jesus' birth after 5 B.C. (Information will be presented below to show that Jesus must have been born several years before Herod's death, and not just months.) In any event, table 1 shows when Jesus was about to become thirty if he was born by 5 B.C.

TABLE 1.   *When Jesus Was about to Become Thirty (Luke 3:23) if Born by 5 B.C.*

Year	Age of Jesus	Year	Age of Jesus	Year	Age of Jesus	
5 B.C.	1	A.D. 6	11	A.D. 16	21	
4	2	7	12	17	22	
3	3	8	13	18	23	
2	4	9	14	19	24	
1	5	10	15	20	25	
A.D. 1	6	11	16	21	26	
2	7	12	17	22	27	⎫
3	8	13	18	23	28	Any year at
4	9	14	19	24	29	this point qualifies
5	10	15	20	25	30	⎭

John the Baptist and the Fifteenth Year of Tiberius (Luke 3:1)

Luke 3:1 mentions that John the Baptist came preaching in the fifteenth year of Tiberius's rule (probably about six months before the beginning of Jesus' ministry). The difficulty with this statement is knowing by what starting point Luke counted fifteen years. It seems likely that Luke was not counting from the death of Augustus on 19 August A.D. 14, since this would yield a date of A.D. 28 (19 August A.D. 14 = year 1; A.D. 15 = year 2; . . . and A.D. 28 = year 15). If this were the case, then Luke contradicted himself in saying that Jesus began his ministry when almost thirty (Luke 3:23), which could have occurred no later than A.D. 25, as seen above. Thus, given this date for the beginning of Jesus' ministry and the possible date for Paul's conversion (not later than A.D. 26) and his second post-conversion journey to Jerusalem about the time of the death of Agrippa I, it is necessary to look for some other method of reckoning by Luke, of which there seem to be two possibilities.

It might be possible to begin the fifteen years in A.D. 4, following the death of Gaius. Tiberius went into voluntary exile on the Island of Rhodes for almost eight years (6 B.C.–A.D. 2), following his realization that Augustus was going to adopt his two grandsons, Lucius and Gaius, to succeed him in power (Vellius Paterculus, *History of Rome* 99–103). These two grandsons of Augustus died prematurely (Lucius in A.D. 2, Gaius in A.D. 4), and Augustus was forced to make another choice for his successor. Soon after the death of Gaius, Augustus adopted Tiberius as his successor, and the star of Tiberius's political power began to rise. Tiberius had already returned to Rome in A.D. 2, but may not have enjoyed Augustus's full favor at that time. When Gaius died, however,

TABLE 2. *Year Fifteen of Tiberius's Rule, Dating from the Death of Gaius in* A.D. 4

Year	Tiberius's Rule	Year	Tiberius's Rule
February A.D. 4[a]	1	A.D. 11	9
April A.D. 4[b]	2	12	10
A.D. 5	3	13	11
6	4	14	12
7	5	15	13
8	6	16	14
9	7	17	15 [after April]
10	8		

[a] Death of Gaius.
[b] Change in year of kings.

Augustus decisively turned to his stepson Tiberius, and Marcus Vipsanius, Agrippa's son by the same name (the latter was soon dropped from consideration as a successor). Tiberius was also given a proconsular *imperium* (decree of power) in A.D. 4—exactly the same title held by Augustus when he was alive. This year could possibly be the date from which Luke reckoned the fifteenth year of Tiberius; if so, one would arrive at the year A.D. 17 (see table 2).

Formerly, I preferred this explanation for the fifteenth year of Tiberius in Luke 3:1; I now propose that Luke originally wrote "in the second year of Tiberius," which was later corrupted to the present reading of fifteenth year. I am not aware of any manuscript tradition with such a reading; my proposal instead rests on evidence from coins and papyri on which scribes wrote "B" (= "EI" = 2) with an appearance of "EI" (= 15).

A coin from Antioch-in-Syria shows this possibility arising. The legend reads: "Under Flaccus, belonging to the people of Antioch, [year] 82" (see fig. 1).[2] Note how easily the letter *B* could be mistaken for *EI*, due to the way that *B* was sometimes written with gaps in its lower loop, not an uncommon feature in Greek epigraphy of the first century A.D.[3] Thus Luke might have originally written B L TIBEPIOY, where the first *B* (= 2) could have been misunderstood by a later scribe to be

2. Warwick Wroth, *Catalogue of the Greek Coins of Galatia, Cappadocia, and Syria* (London: British Museum, 1899) 170, nos. 161–62.
3. See *Catalogue of the Greek Papyri in the John Rylands Library*, vol. 2: *Documents of the Ptolemaic and Roman Periods* (ed. J. deM. Johnson, V. Martin, and A. S. Hunt; Manchester: University Press, 1915), no. 178, line 9 (cf. pl. 4), for similar forms of B in the word βλάβος.

Fig. 1. Coin from Antioch-in-Syria showing possible confusion between B (= 2) and EI (= 15); Greek legend: "Under Flaccus, belonging to the people of Antioch, [year] 82."

EI (= 15), thus confusing the true reading. If year two is the correct reading in Luke 3:1, then any time after April (and perhaps as late as August) might suit the time of John's call. And before the end of the same year, A.D. 15, the ministry of Jesus began in Judea.

Strengthening this possibility is the fact that A.D. 13/14 was a Jubilee year.[4] If this were true, then Jesus' sermon in the synagogue of

4. This is based on extrapolating backward in cycles of forty-nine years from A.D. 1190 (a Jubilee year). Cf. Benedict Zuckermann, *A Treatise on the Sabbatical Cycle and the*

Nazareth would have had extra significance: the people were *not* set at liberty, but were still in the servitude that had fallen upon them in the previous Jubilee year (37/36 B.C.) when Herod had enslaved them. Jesus' "freedom" was not the kind that pleased the people of Nazareth, who, with their nationalistic hopes left empty, plotted his death. This Jubilee cycle fits the year he began his work, and is in agreement with the dates found on the coins of Damascus and Caesarea-on-the-Sea (see below).

This discussion is intended to solve the chronological problem of Luke 3:1 by showing how a copying error could have taken place. Other possibilities exist, but my proposed solution has the advantage of meshing with the other chronological evidence for Jesus' life. (See below, Postscript: The Chronology of Pilate.)

The Census of Quirinius (Luke 2:2)

Luke 2:2 mentions that when Jesus was born in Bethlehem, Quirinius was serving as governor of Syria, and that he was apparently carrying out a census of the entire area by the authority of Augustus at the same time. The knotty question of Quirinius is the major historical problem of the New Testament. I summarize here some of the results of my forthcoming investigation of Quirinius.

It is necessary to return to Lucius and Gaius, the two grandsons of Augustus who died early. When their father Marcus Vipsanius Agrippa died in 12 B.C., Augustus was left without an associate in supreme command (Agrippa had been in charge of the east, and Augustus of the west). Until Lucius and Gaius were mature enough to rule, it seems that Augustus appointed Quirinius, among others, to serve on an interim basis. Agrippa died in March, 12 B.C., and it is my opinion that Quirinius took his place in the region of Syria (at least between 12 and 10 B.C.). He was serving as consul in Rome when Agrippa died—consul being the normal post held before appointment as governor of Syria. As governor of Syria, he would have controlled vast provinces, with the right of traveling all over Asia, as far east as the Euphrates and the Parthian empire, and as far south as Arabia, which at this time was only a Roman client state. He could have carried out a census of all the area under his control. It is my considered opinion that an inscription found over three hundred years ago mentions this census conducted under Quirinius in 12/11 B.C. A translation of the inscription of Aemilius Secundus (Lapis Venetus) reads as follows:

Jubilee (trans. A. Lowy; London: Chronological Institute, 1866; repr. New York: Hermon, 1974) 55. See also under the year 1190 in Matthew Paris, *Chronica major*, vol. 2 (ed. H. R. Luard; London: Longmans, 1874).

Quintus Aemilius Secundus, son of Quintus, of the gens Palatina, in military field service of the Divine Augustus under P(ublius) Sulpi(c)ius Quirinius [Year two of Quirinius(?): Legate(?): Proconsul(?)]: by Caesar, in Syria, he was decorated with military honors; Prefect of the First Augustan Band (Cohort): Prefect of the II Cohort Classica.

By order of Quirinius, I made a census of the city of Apamea, which had 117,000 citizens; the same was sent by Quirinius against the Ituraeans. I seized one of their strongholds on Mount Lebanon; and at the beginning of my military career I was Prefect of the Engineers, but was appointed to the Aerarium [the senatorial treasury] by the two consuls; and in the colony [of Beirut] I was Questor-Aedile [treasurer] two times; I was Duumvir [one of the two chief magistrates] two times; (I was also) Pontifex.

This was placed here by Q. Aemilius Secundus, son of the above Quintus, of the gens Palatina, and by Aemilia Chia, slave woman set free. This monument [tomb] does not pass on to any heir.[5]

There is considerable evidence that under Augustus various provincial censuses were conducted throughout the Roman world. Dio Cassius (*Roman History* 54:28:4) mentions that when Agrippa died, Augustus would not look on his corpse; the reason that some used to explain this strange action was that in the year of a census (= 12/11 B.C.) if such a sight were seen by the censor (= Augustus), then the whole undertaking had to be done again. Dio further mentions that Augustus himself rendered his own census returns in 11 B.C. (*Roman History* 54:35:1ff.).[6] The same word that Luke (2:2) used to describe the census of Quirinius in the east (ἀπογραφή) is used by Dio to describe the census of Augustus in 12/11 B.C. From an examination of over two hundred Roman-period census returns recovered by archaeological investigations, it is possible to reconstruct the normal course of a census. About May or June an edict was posted by the provincial governors informing the populace that the time of the periodic Roman census was near. The people then had one year to file their returns. Normally,

---

5. On this inscription, consult Hermann Dessau, *Inscriptiones latinae selectae* (Berlin: Weidemann, 1892–1916), no. 2683; and William M. Ramsay, *Was Christ Born at Bethlehem?* (London: Hodder and Stoughton, 1898) 274. See also *Corpus inscriptionum latinarum* (Berlin: Reimer, 1862–), 5:136; and *Ephemeris epigraphica* (Berlin: Reimer, 1872–1913), 4:538. The upper portion of the text is now missing, and one is left to guesswork about some points of S. Orsato's posthumous interpretation of the complete text (*Marmi eruditi overo lettere sopra alcune antiche inscrizioni* [Padova: G. Comino, 1719] 276–77). Microletters show that the text dates to 10 B.C., that the fortress Secundus took on Mount Lebanon was Baitokiki, and that the colony mentioned was Beirut (Berytus). On microletters see below.

6. Cf. E. G. Hardy, *The Monumentum Ancyranum* (Oxford: Clarendon, 1923) 57ff., who discounts the value of Dio's history here. It is, however, Hardy's theory that must be discounted.

TABLE 3. *Roman Censuses in the Late First Century B.C. (until A.D. 6),*
Showing Seventeen-year Cycle

Year of Census Declaration (= end)	Year of Census Decree (= start)	
↓	↓	⎰ Roman censuses
1 2 3 4 5 6 7 8 9 10 11 12 13 14 15 16 17		⎱ in seventeen-year cycles

28 27 26 25 24 23 22 21 20 19 18 17 16 15 14 13 12
B.C.

11 10 9 8 7 6 5 4 3 2 1 1 2 3 4 5 6
                                    B.C. A.D.

people would wait until the last weeks to file (like modern income tax!), but there are indications that some filed at once. So, applied to the census of Quirinius in 12 B.C., the citizens of Bethlehem could have filed their census returns any time between May/June 12 B.C. and May/June 11 B.C. Scholars who do not opt for 12 B.C., if they are consistent with New Testament evidence, must then go to A.D. 6 to fit their theories of Jesus' birth *into a census year.*

There are other indications that 12/11 B.C. was a census year. Livy (*Epitomes* 138–39) mentions that Drusus conducted a census in Gaul in 12 B.C. Drusus was the father of Claudius, the later Roman Emperor (A.D. 41–54), and Claudius also mentioned that his father conducted a census in Gaul in 12 B.C. (alluded to in Tacitus, *Annals* 11:23:1–25:1, but described at length in a famous inscription now called the *Tablets of Lyons*).[7] Other sources indicate that Gaul experienced another census in 29/28 B.C. (Livy, *Epitomes* 134). And Josephus tells of a second(?) census conducted in A.D. 6/7 by Quirinius in the east (*Antiquities* 18:1–10). Putting all of this information together, one sees that 12/11 B.C. was exactly the halfway point between a Roman census in 29/28 B.C. and the Roman census in A.D. 6/7. This fact seems to indicate that the Roman census periods in the first century B.C. fell seventeen years apart, but after A.D. 6, such events fell fourteen years apart (see table 3). Various classical sources seem to support 46 B.C., also, as a census year, and if this is so, it may have been Julius Caesar who instituted this seventeen-year cycle.

It must be granted that it was not the usual pattern for a Roman governor of Syria to serve two terms in office, as Luke implies of

7. *Corpus inscriptionum latinarum,* vol. 13: no. 1668; for convenience see N. Lewis and M. Reinhold, *Roman Civilization* (New York: Columbia University, 1955), 2:131–34.

Quirinius by saying that Jesus was born during the *first* census that
Quirinius conducted (Luke 2:2). Luke's statement strongly suggests
that Quirinius conducted a second census (cf. Acts 5:36, 37), which I
hold is the one that Josephus mentions that Quirinius carried out in
A.D. 6/7 (*Antiquities* 18:1–10). One should not forget that in A.D. 2
Quirinius married Amelia Lepida, the widow of Lucius (the adopted
grandson of and potential successor to Augustus). Quirinius's marriage
with Amelia Lepida must have raised his prestige with Augustus considerably and made him now, for all practical purposes, a member of the
imperial house. In due time (A.D. 21–23, shortly before his death),
Quirinius's marriage with Lepida fell apart and ended in divorce (Tacitus, *Annals* 3:48; Suetonius, *Tiberius* 49), but it is now easy to see how
Quirinius would have enjoyed intimate friendship with Augustus while
the emperor lived (until A.D. 14). Thus, because of Quirinius's marriage
with Lepida, all rules would have been set aside in granting to him
another term as governor of Syria.

Other Considerations That Jesus Was Born in 12 B.C.

Many other evidences point to 12 B.C. as the true date of Jesus'
birth. Space permits only the briefest mention of a few of these, but
each of these can be expanded greatly.

The Time of Paul's Conversion.   Paul mentions in Galatians that after
he was converted he was gone from Jerusalem for a period of three
years (Gal 1:18). A second time, he was gone from Jerusalem for a
period of fourteen years (Gal 2:1). Acts 11:30 says that Paul visited
Jerusalem before the death of Herod Agrippa I (mentioned in Acts 12),
most likely in late A.D. 44 (or possibly January A.D. 45). Assuming that
the fourteen-year interval that Paul was away from Jerusalem is to be
fitted with this visit of Paul before Herod Agrippa's death in A.D. 44,
one must reach back to at least A.D. 30 for Paul's visit with Peter (Gal
1:18). And one must allow at least three years before that for his
conversion (= A.D. 27). Paul was converted some years after the death
of Jesus, so Jesus must have died well before A.D. 26. My position here
is quite contrary to that of many New Testament scholars, especially
those who have been influenced by John Knox in his work, *Chapters in a
Life of Paul.*[8]

Indications that the Death Year of Jesus Fell during a Census.   It has
already been pointed out that after A.D. 6/7, the periodic Roman cen-

8. John Knox, *Chapters in a Life of Paul* (rev. ed.; Macon, GA: Mercer University,
1987).

suses fell fourteen years apart. This means that A.D. 20/21 was a census year and that A.D. 34 was the following one. The evidence for Paul's time of conversion (contra Knox) rules out that Jesus was put to death as late as A.D. 34 (or that Paul was converted then, as Knox now holds).[9] In any event, Matt 22:17 and Mark 12:14 both state that when Jesus' enemies sought to trap him in the incident of the tribute money, they asked Jesus if it was right to render the "census tax" (κῆνσος) to Caesar. This event seems to signify that the year of Jesus' death was related to a census year.

Evidence shows that while Germanicus was in the east between A.D. 17 and 19, he changed the Roman fiscal policies. He forced subject nations to pay taxes in *Roman* money, and not in the coinage of the individual cities or states.[10] The reason for this is that the coinages of other nations were greatly debased at this time, and Germanicus was possibly trying to protect Roman currency from being debased as well. But to the Jews this action was drastic. It meant that they had to handle Roman money when paying their census dues or any other payment to their overlords. If this regulation was new, and had to be applied in the forthcoming census of A.D. 20/21, then it would have caused anger and much discussion among the Jews, who tried to use coins without images or pictures of temples or emperors.[11] This clue would seem to indicate that Jesus died around A.D. 21, at the beginning of Passover. The census that year would not have closed until May/June, but Jesus died several weeks before that, on Nisan 14, which fell on April 14 or April 16, depending on the calendar (Julian/Gregorian) used.[12]

---

9. Ibid., xix, and esp. p. 46; cf. chart and discussion on p. 68. In his 1950 ed. he argued for A.D. 35 as the year of Paul's conversion. See also R. Jewett, *Dating Paul's Life* (London: SCM, 1979) 162, 30–33; J. Murphy-O'Connor, *St. Paul's Corinth: Texts and Archaeology* (Wilmington, DE: Glazier, 1983) 140 (quite unsatisfactory conclusions); G. W. Bowersock, *Roman Arabia* (Cambridge: Harvard University, 1983) 68–69, who assigns Paul's escape from Damascus to the last days of Tiberius (A.D. 37) and before the death of Arctas (A.D. 40).

10. See the famous document known as the Palmyra Tariff (especially lines 153–58), published in *Orientis graeci inscriptiones selectae* (ed. W. Dittenberger; Leipzig: Hirzel, 1903–5) 336 (no. 629). For an alternate edition see G. A. Cooke, *A Text-Book of North-Semitic Inscriptions* (Oxford: Clarendon, 1903) 313–40 (no. 147).

11. However, Jews did use Tyrian shekels to pay annual temple dues each year to redeem Israelite males, and such coins did have images of pagan nature on them. This is why Jesus scorned their hypocrisy in this matter. These Tyrian shekels were used since, up to their end around the time of Jerusalem's fall, they were made of pure silver (90%+). Y. Meshorer, *Ancient Jewish Coinage*, vol. 2: *Herod the Great through Bar Cochba* (Dix Hills, NY: Amphora, 1982) 7–9, is wrong to assign these coins to Jerusalem after 20 B.C.

12. See F. Wünschmann, review of *The Messiah Jesus and John the Baptist*, by R. Eisler, *Astronomische Nachrichten* 1930–33: 405–6.

Halley's Comet as the Christmas Star. Between August 24 and October 17 of 12 B.C., a brilliant comet passed near the earth. It is now known as Halley's Comet. It arose in the due east but after September 9/10, it was seen only in the west. This comet made an extremely close (15 million miles) pass near the earth, and attained a brightness as bright as any star in the heavens at that time. Many of the things that Matthew mentions about the star that appeared at Jesus' birth fit this comet perfectly and cannot be made to agree with any other known heavenly phenomena of that period. This would give the general period of late 12 B.C. or spring 11 B.C. when Jesus was born—likely around the Tabernacle season in 12 B.C. This could explain why Mary went with Joseph to Bethlehem: it was customary for wives to attend festivals (cf. Luke 2:43), but not necessary for them to attend or be involved in census returns. The Old Testament tells us that the festival of Tabernacles was the most joyous one the Jews observed (Deut 16:14; cf. Josephus *Antiquities* 4:206 [where women are to be included]; cf. the joy that accompanies it, in *Antiquities* 8:124 and 11:156), and, in my view, God chose to make the Tabernacle season of 12 B.C. the most joyous one of all—in which Jesus "became flesh and *tabernacled* among us" (John 1:14–18).

New Light from Microletters

After the Nativity Conference, at which I presented the foregoing portion of this paper, I made what I consider new and significant discoveries. These discoveries resulted from research done in the coin room of the British Museum in the summer of 1984, when Nikos Kokkinos was working with me. Since Kokkinos and I have not formally discussed the following conclusions, I alone must be held accountable for them, even though we do agree on at least two basic points: the existence of microletters on ancient coins and the date of Jesus' birth. The findings discussed below yield information on the chronology of the life, public ministry, and death of Jesus, and the date of conversion of the apostle Paul. On both subjects I present evidence found on coins of the period, coins that are literally covered with microletters.

Before taking up these subjects, however, I wish to say something about microletters and their use in antiquity. As I continued to study coins, the presence of microletters on them became clearer and clearer; at last, I had to accept the fact that microletters existed on ancient coins, from the earliest times up through the Hellenistic and Roman periods, and beyond. How and why were such letters placed on coins? I determined at least four reasons for their appearance:

1. Some microletters might have been placed on ancient dies to serve as guide letters. Light tracings could have been made on a die before the final, bolder lettering or art work was completed. Apparently these letters were cut with a diamond (see Jer 17:1).

2. Some letters could have been placed on coins or seals or inscriptions (for I find such letters on more objects of the past than just coins) to attest to the authenticity of the object. If small microletters were added to the die, undetectable without the magnifying glass used by ancient artisans,[13] then it becomes more difficult to copy all of the information, thus protecting the coin from counterfeiting. The multitude of microletters on the genuine coins made it practically impossible to make a second copy of the die exactly as the original engraver designed it.

3. Microletters eliminated the need for crowding all vital information on coins in the main legends. In other words, the mintmasters were not as concerned as we might demand today to place date, place minted, etc., on the coin's bold legend. They had their own way of doing this—by placing at least some of the information in the microletters.

4. Some microletters were not placed on the original dies, but in rare instances were scratched individually on the surface of coins as they were issued from the mints. I do not fully understand why, but these could have been used to indicate some kind of control in certain instances—such as a payment for something, or so much money allocated to a city. Sometimes, as well, rulers were mentioned in these types of microletters. This kind of graffiti has been noticed already by E. T. Newell.[14]

Whatever their original purpose(s), the use of microletters was spread over so many civilizations for so many centuries that their presence cannot be denied or ignored.

Microletters on a Coin Minted by Aretas IV

With only this much introduction to the subject of microletters, let me turn to one of the coins studied and indicate the presence and

---

13. For information on magnifying glasses in antiquity, see Pliny, *Natural History* 36:199, 37:28; Anton Bammer, "Recent Excavations at the Altar of Artemis in Ephesus," *Archaeology* 27 (1974) 203–4; R. J. Forbes, *Studies in Ancient Technology* (2d ed.; Leiden: Brill, 1966), 5:189–91, with references; and G. Sines and Y. A. Sakellarakis, "Lenses in Antiquity," *AJA* 91 (1987) 191–96.

14. E. T. Newell, "Reattribution of Certain Tetradrachms of Alexander the Great," *American Journal of Numismatics* 46 (1912) 112.

Fig. 2. (*obverse*). Coin from Damascus, dated to year 328 (LHKT) of the Seleucid era, struck under Aretas IV (A.D. 16); the monogram (LAH) behind Tyche's head is interpreted as "Year 1 of Aretas."

importance of its microletters (see fig. 2). According to the British Museum catalogue, this coin was struck at Damascus in "the time of Tiberius," that is, A.D. 14–37.[15] From microletters on the coin itself, we can date its minting much more precisely and demonstrate, as well, that it was struck under the authority of King Aretas IV.

15. Wroth, *Catalogue of the Greek Coins of Galatia, Cappadocia, and Syria*, 283 (no. 4; cf. pl. 34.6).

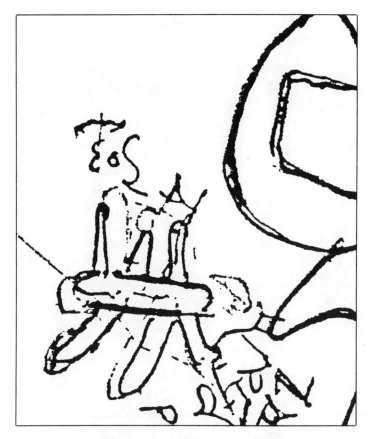

Fig. 2. (*obverse, inset*). Monogram reading "Year 1 of Aretas."

Description of the Coin.   The obverse of the coin shows the turreted Tyche of the city of Damascus looking to the right. The object behind Tyche is not a star (contra the British Museum catalogue), but rather a monogram meaning 'year one of Aretas'. Aretas's full name, as the microletters show, was Gaius Julius Aretas. The reverse features Nike, the goddess of victory, wearing a chiton and holding a wreath in her right hand; a palm branch shows behind her. In the left field, LHKT = 328 of the Seleucid era = A.D. 16; in the right field, ΔAMACKHNωN = 'of the people of Damascus'. Nike was frequently shown on coins of Damascus (for example, Aretas III[16] and Cleopatra), so the present

16. See Y. Meshorer, *Nabatean Coins* (Qedem 3; Jerusalem: Institute of Archaeology, Hebrew University, 1975), pl. 1–1a.

Fig. 2 (*reverse*). Coin from Damascus, dated to year 328 (LHKT) of the Seleucid era, struck under Aretas IV (A.D. 16); reference to REX JESVS in lower left.

example is not unusual. The reason for her appearance on this particular coin must stem from the victories that Germanicus had just gained over the Germans in A.D. 15–16, which led to his appointment to the eastern provinces and his installation in Antioch-in-Syria as supreme Roman commander of the area in A.D. 18. Had his appointment been determined, for Syria, as early as A.D. 15 or 16?

Microletters in the lower left reverse of this coin very clearly show the words "REX JESVS." Many other coins of Damascus, including one with a date of LZKT (= A.D. 15), also mention Jesus in microletters.

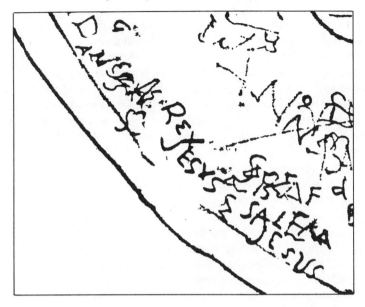

Fig. 2. (*reverse, inset*). Microletters reading REX JESVS.

Usually Jesus is called "King Jesus," a title frequently given him in the New Testament (but not always in a favorable way).

Aretas IV. Aretas IV, under whose authority this coin was most probably made, is the only king—other than members of the Herodian family (Herod I, Agrippa I, and Agrippa II)—to be mentioned in the New Testament. He was the father-in-law of Herod Antipas, according to Josephus (*Antiquities* 18:109), who also reports that war came about between Herod Antipas and Aretas, when Antipas divorced Aretas's daughter (Phaselis?) in order to marry Herodias (*Antiquities* 18:110). I would date Antipas's divorce from Phaselis around A.D. 17/18 and his marriage to Herodias in the same year: so, Antipas and Phaselis were likely still married when this coin was struck.

A major conclusion obtained from the microletters on this coin, then, is that it was struck under the authority of Aretas IV, while Tiberius was emperor but not still in control of the city of Damascus. Aretas ruled from 11 B.C. to A.D. 37 (although some scholars assign to him the years 9 B.C.–A.D. 39). Since various Nabatean coins (especially those minted under Aretas IV) show an abbreviation system similar to the monogram behind Tyche's head, the diemaker of this coin well understood what the symbol meant, as did the owners of the coin. It is clear that previous studies of Aretas and his career simply have not recognized the importance of this coin for determining when he controlled Damascus. When Philip died, around A.D. 33/34, Aretas and Antipas again warred over questions of boundary disputes; but, since Antipas and Tiberius were apparently close friends, Tiberius likely sided with Antipas, and consequently Aretas lost Damascus. In any case, on the basis of later coins of Damascus, Tiberius clearly seems to have had possession of the city after A.D. 33/34[17] and to the end of his career in A.D. 37.

This evidence refutes a commonly held view that Aretas's control over Damascus came from the Emperor Gaius (Caligula) (A.D. 37–41) who, it has been asserted, returned Damascus to Nabatean hands. There is also an earlier Aretas, known as Aretas III, who controlled Damascus between ca. 85 and 62 B.C.; interestingly, some coins of his reign also show Nike extending a crown of victory in her hand. Thus, coins of Damascus displaying Nike to commemorate some victory were rather common, and the coin under discussion, celebrating the victories of Germanicus in A.D. 14–16, was in a long tradition.

Implications for New Testament Chronology. What do the microletters on this coin reveal about the dates of Jesus and the conversion of Paul? While the information contained in the microletters reveals much about the political history of this period, the most important references on this coin are to "Jesus of Nazareth." He is mentioned frequently, often in titles and phrases found in the New Testament, for example, "Jesus, King of the Jews," "King," "the Righteous One," and "Messiah." Reference to the first year of his "reign" is repeated often, although not always with the same degree of fullness; for example, "Year one of Jesus of Nazareth in Galalee [*sic*]." What seems quite clear, then, is that the first year of the ministry of Jesus began in late A.D. 15 and extended into the next year. On the basis of this evidence, therefore, all the dates of the life, career, and death of Jesus will have to be reexamined.

Paul's conversion had to take place between A.D. 16 (the date of the issuance of this coin) and A.D. 33/34 (the year in which the control of Damascus passed from Aretas IV to Tiberius). Other evidence, such as Gal 1:17 and 2:1 and Luke's account of Paul's second return to Jerusalem before the death of Agrippa I (Acts 11:28, 12:19–23) suggests a conversion date of no later than A.D. 26; and possibly Paul's conversion

---

17. E. Schürer, *The History of the Jewish People in the Age of Jesus Christ* (rev. and ed. G. Vermes and F. Millar; Edinburgh: Clark, 1973), 1:582 n. 25.

took place as early as A.D. 24/25.[18] Note also that Paul mentions Aretas in 2 Cor 11:32–33: "In Damascus the governor [ethnarch] under King Aretas had the city of the Damascenes guarded in order to arrest me. But I was lowered in a basket from a window in the wall and slipped through his hands."

Microletters on a Coin Minted by Agrippa I

I now present evidence of microletters that mention Jesus on another coin, this one minted by Agrippa I in A.D. 44 at Caesarea-on-the-Sea (fig. 3).[19] Y. Meshorer dates this coin immediately upon the return of Agrippa from Rome, after Claudius became emperor, and thus assigns the date of A.D. 41/42.[20] However, the coin repeatedly bears the date LZ ('year seven') in microletters, which persuades me that this rare coin is to be assigned to A.D. 43/44.

The obverse of the coin shows Agrippa I standing between two figures. The figure on the right, according to the microletters, is the emperor Claudius (A.D. 41–54), who is crowning Agrippa with a wreath. Agrippa holds a *patera* (*mesomphalos*) in his right hand and wears a long veil on his head. On an unpublished seal from Machaerus, now in the possession of Southwestern Baptist Seminary (Fort Worth, Texas), Agrippa is shown with a similar veil on his head, holding a *patera*, and

18. Assuming that Paul was converted about A.D. 26 (see my essay, "New Chronology of Paul," *Biblical Illustrator* [Winter 1991]), his return to Jerusalem three years later could have been motivated, in part, by his desire to help poor Christians during the sabbatical year of A.D. 26/27. (Poor Christians were especially vulnerable during sabbatical years and could not rely on their Jewish neighbors for food if they failed to observe the sabbatical years.) Paul's next return, fourteen years later (Gal. 1:18, 2:1; Acts 11:28), thus could have fallen during the sabbatical year of A.D. 40/41. And his third missionary journey terminated just at the start of the sabbatical year in Tishri A.D. 54. Paul had distinguished himself by his spirit to help the distressed during the sabbatical years (Acts 11:30 [learning some of his kindness from Barnabas]; cf. Acts 4:36–37; Gal 2:10; 1 Cor 16:1–4; Acts 20:35; Rom 15:25–31; 2 Cor 8:1–9:15; Gal 6:7–10; Acts 24:17, 26). But, while Paul commands generosity in his later writings (for example, 1 Tim 6:17–19), he gives no indication of contributing to the poor saints of Jerusalem. It is likely that the distasteful experiences stemming from his arrest at the close of his third missionary journey led him to avoid Jerusalem until the end of his life. The chronology just outlined could also explain the revelation of 2 Cor 12:2: he would have received some revelation at Antioch (just as Agabus received one about the same time [Acts 11:28]) approving his visit to Jerusalem, and urging, among other things, the contribution to the poor of Jerusalem, of which he was not to speak.

19. F. W. Madden, *History of Jewish Coinage, and of Money in the Old and New Testaments* (London: Bernard Quaritch, 1864) 109–10; Meshorer, *Ancient Jewish Coinage*, 2:55–57; A. Kindler, *Bulletin, Museum Ha'aretz* 11 (1969) 10–16 [Hebrew], with references.

20. Meshorer, *Ancient Jewish Coinage*, 2:55.

Fig. 3. Obverse of a coin from Caesarea-on-the-Sea, struck in year 7 (LZ) of Agrippa I (=A.D. 43/44), with many microletters referring to Jesus.

pouring a libation over an altar (detectable only with the most careful photographic procedures). The Greek legend reads, "King Agrippa, Friend of Caesar."

The figure on the left is more problematic, but a close inspection suggests that the figure is a personification of the Roman Senate—often portrayed in this time period as a female. (The poor condition of this coin makes it virtually impossible to determine the figure's sex, and the hair is long enough to allow the figure to be male or female.) In any

Fig. 3. (*inset*). Microletters reading JESVS LKΓ MORTV^S_M.

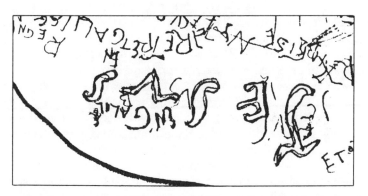

Fig. 3. (*inset*). Microletters showing that Jesus' REGNVM started in the 327th year (LZKT) of the Seleucid era.

case, the figure of the Senate, if understood properly, raises a palm branch, which symbolizes the establishment of the peace treaty between Agrippa and Rome in A.D. 41.

Within a circle of dots, the reverse shows clasped hands, signifying the formation of the treaty. The Greek legend, fully spelled out and translated, reads, "The vow of the Great King Agrippa with Augustus Caesar [T. Claudius?] and the Roman people and the treaty of friendship with him." The countermark contains a portrait of Vespasian, showing that the coin circulated for at least thirty years. Note the mention of Jesus in large microletters between the Greek word "Romans" and the clasped hands.

Microletters on the obverse provide the date of the minting. At Agrippa's left elbow is the date LZ = year seven = A.D. 44. At the top of his head are the words, JESVS LKΓ MORTV$\frac{S}{M}$, 'year twenty-three of Jesus' death', which would mean that Jesus died in A.D. 21. At Agrippa's feet and upside down, one reads that Jesus' REGNVM started in the 327th year (LZKT) of the Seleucid era, thus giving a date of A.D. 15 for the beginning of his "reign."

The careful reader will note many other references to Jesus in the microletters besides those mentioned above. Even though Agrippa is the main personality being honored by the coin's bold letters on both sides, in the microletters Jesus is mentioned more frequently than Agrippa! Caesarea certainly had a large Jewish element,[21] many of whom, just as at Damascus, could have been employed in the mint. Since Jesus died in A.D. 21, by the year A.D. 44 his life and deeds were well known in Caesarea and throughout the entire Levant. Paul himself came to Caesarea only ten years after this coin was struck (A.D. 54) and reminded the son of Agrippa I that the events connected with Jesus and his gospel were not done in a corner, but on the center stage of history at that time (Acts 26:26). Paul was tried before Agrippa II in A.D. 56 after being imprisoned in Caesarea for two years (Acts 24:27). Thus, Jesus was well known at Caesarea before A.D. 44, either through Gentile contacts (such as Cornelius, Acts 10) or through Jews; clearly, both groups had a basic understanding of his deeds by that time, and they helped to spread knowledge about him, especially with people like Philip the evangelist living in the city (Acts 8:40, 21:8–15).

These and other coins (which now can be more accurately dated) and their microletters provide the earliest nonbiblical, nonliterary testimonies of Jesus. Although conventional texts claim that the letter of Pliny to the Emperor Trajan (A.D. 110–11) constitutes the earliest non-Christian reference to Jesus, coins antedate this and even earlier references, thus demonstrating that non-Christian references to Jesus were widespread in geography and time. What must be emphasized, however, is the point that coins with microletters appear before any literary evidences presently known that mention Jesus. At this time, I am aware of no coin earlier than ones from Damascus, such as the above, citing Jesus and facts about his career.

---

21. Josephus reports that twenty thousand Jews were slaughtered in Caesarea at the outbreak of the first Jewish revolt *Jewish War* 2:457). For other references to Jews in Caesarea, see the index in vol. 10 of the Loeb Classical Library edition of Josephus.

Conclusions

As the result of my discoveries to date, these conclusions are, I believe, warranted:

1. The proposed dates of the birth, ministry, and death of Jesus agree well with Luke's statement (3:23) that "Jesus himself began to be about thirty years of age" at the time of his baptism by John. If Jesus had been born in 12 B.C., as I believe he was, by the fall of A.D. 15 he would have been at least twenty-seven, thereby fitting well Luke's assertion that he was about thirty years old.

2. The first year of the ministry of Jesus included late A.D. 15 and early-to-middle A.D. 16, at which time coins from Damascus were struck referring to the first year of Jesus' "reign."

3. The possibility of a simple error in copying the text of Luke 3:1 (reading year two instead of year fifteen) could tie other bits of evidence together and force a reevaluation of all the dates related to Jesus and his ministry.

4. The conversion of Paul should be dated earlier than most scholars have argued. This event, normally dated A.D. 34–36, could not have happened later than A.D. 27 and could have been as early as A.D. 24/25. Again, the new evidence would agree well with the words of both Paul and Luke.

5. Finally, the above conclusions call for a reexamination of the lives and careers of many others who lived, worked, and taught in the days and years contemporaneous with Jesus and the early Christians. For example, the works of Josephus, whose accuracy has been seriously questioned by many modern historians and biblical scholars, accurately places Jesus' career (A.D. 15–19) in the same approximate historical context that the microletters point to—around A.D. 15–21 (see *Antiquities* 18:48–83).

All these conclusions (summarized in table 4) point to one exciting prospect, that more scholars will pursue the subject of microletters on coins and will, eventually, add to or change the pages of history from which we are still learning today.

Postscript: The Chronology of Pilate

Problems of chronology relating to Pontius Pilate are complex. The majority of New Testament and classical scholars date Pilate's rule as procurator/prefect of Judea between A.D. 26 and 36.[22] My contention is that the case for this traditional date of Pontius Pilate is not as airtight

---

22. E.g., Schürer, *History of the Jewish People in the Age of Jesus Christ*, 1:383.

TABLE 4.   Suggested New Chronology of Jesus' Life

Event	Date
Birth (Halley's Comet = Bethlehem Star)	August–October 12 B.C.
Flight to Egypt	12/11 B.C.
Return from Egypt (after Herod's death in March/April	4 B.C.
Start of ministry (thus his ministry is six years long)	After midyear A.D. 15
Death	Passover A.D. 21

as its defenders believe, and that more and more scholars will reject this older chronology of Pilate for a better system as they study the problem more carefully. Daniel Schwartz of the history department of the Hebrew University of Jerusalem has already arrived at an earlier date for the start of Pilate's career (A.D. 14/15), although he leaves Pilate in office as late as A.D. 37.[23] I would end Pilate's career earlier than Schwartz. It must be stressed that the year of Pilate's dismissal is not as critical as the date of the beginning of his career.

If Jesus started his career as early as A.D. 14, as I have argued above, Pilate had to appear on the scene in Judea no later than A.D. 21, the time of Jesus' death. Of course, other New Testament references to Pilate must be accommodated by an earlier chronology than A.D. 21.[24] I believe that the evidence for Pilate's service in Judea prior to A.D. 21 is sufficiently strong to demonstrate that he could indeed have put Jesus to death as early as A.D. 21. I feel, moreover, that Pilate was dismissed from his post in Judea by A.D. 25/26 but will not insist on the date for his dismissal as strongly as the beginning of his service.

It seems possible that Pilate was dismissed about the time that Tiberius moved from Rome to the island of Capri. Pilate could have

23. D. Schwartz, "The Appointment of Pontius Pilate and the Chronology of *Antiquities of the Jews, Books 18–20," Zion* 48 (1983) 325–45 [Hebrew]. I would agree with Schwartz's early date for Pilate, although I am not indebted to him for this early date, having arrived in my position earlier and holding an earlier date than he does. See pp. 342ff. for Schwartz's views on the beginning of Pilate's career (A.D. 18/19) and final year (A.D. 37). See also D. Schwartz, "Josephus and Philo on Pontius Pilate," *Jerusalem Cathedra* (Detroit: Wayne State University, 1983), 3:26–45.

24. Since I accept Luke 3:1 as referring to Tiberius's second year (= A.D. 15), I necessarily would date Pilate no later than that year, since he is related in the same verse to the same year that John the Baptist starts his ministry. Significantly many scholars question whether the New Testament writers or Josephus (in *Antiquities* 18–20) concerned themselves with chronology in the presentation of their materials. My contention is that a recognizable chronology, though loose in places due to material sometimes being presented topically, is generally suggested.

been dismissed even a few months before Tiberius's transfer to his island retreat, to which occasionally Tiberius had already taken himself, at least as early as A.D. 21. After A.D. 26, Tiberius took up permanent residence at Capri, and visited the Italian mainland rarely after that date. When Josephus describes Pilate's dismissal in *Antiquities* 18:89 he states that before Pilate could get to Rome, Tiberius had already μεταστάς (translated 'died' or 'passed away' by modern translators; I take the idea to mean that before Pilate got to Italy Tiberius had already *moved* to Capri). The natural place for Pilate to be sent, if he were dismissed as late as A.D. 36 or 37, as most scholars assert, was not to Rome but to Capri, since that was Tiberius's main residence by that time. Quite often μετατίθημι bears the meaning of 'moved'. In approximately one-half of the usages in Josephus and the New Testament μετατίθημι has the meaning of 'moved'; thus, 'moved' is not a rare meaning and should be so understood in *Antiquities* 18:89.

On the other hand, real problems arise if one translates μεταστάς as 'died' in this passage. For one thing, Tiberius did not die in Rome but in Misenum (Tacitus, *Annals* 6:50). Moreover, 'moved' as the sense of μεταστάς seems more natural since Josephus lists numerous actions in *Antiquities* 18 of Tiberius after his "death," if that is the way the word is to be understood:

18:96	writes Vitellius
18:97	intrigues with friends to make war against Artabanus
18:101	seeks treaty with Artabanus
18:103	receives Darius, Artabanus's son, as hostage
18:104	receives report from Antipas about victory over Artabanus
18:105	receives similar report from Vitellius and replies to him
18:108	annexes territory of Herod Philip to Syria (A.D. 33/34)
18:115	receives report from Herod Antipas; orders Vitellius against Aretas IV

Some of these actions are clearly earlier than A.D. 37, the supposed date of Pilate's dismissal. For example, Philip's death is clearly stated to have been in the twentieth year of Tiberius (= A.D. 33/34). Since Pilate's dismissal is recorded at an earlier point in Josephus (*Antiquities* 18:89) than Philip's death (*Antiquities* 18:108) one could just as well argue that Pilate was dismissed earlier than Philip's death, which I believe to be the case. If Pilate was dismissed in A.D. 25/26 or thereabouts, it would be natural to record Philip's death at a later point in Josephus's account, and this is exactly what one finds. Finally, Josephus relates the death of Tiberius at a much later point, so that one can be sure that Josephus is not relating the death of Tiberius in *Antiquities* 18:89:

18:124   Tiberius died while Vitellius on way to Nabatea
18:179   Tiberius visited briefly at Tusculum, 12 miles from Rome
18:205   Tiberius returned to Capri and sickened
18:225   full account of Tiberius's death; power transferred to Gaius

Be all of this as it may, many clues point to Pilate assuming the office of governor of Judea well before A.D. 26. Not only does Josephus place Jesus within a historical context of A.D. 14–19 (see the early part of my study and *Antiquities* 18:43–86), but Pilate is placed by Josephus within this same period of time. Josephus clearly states that Jesus was put to death by Pilate, and lists various activities of Pilate in Judea and Samaria before he mentions Pilate's crucifixion of Jesus. Josephus mentions that Pilate was appointed before Tiberias was built (*Antiquities* 18:36; cf. *Jewish War* 2:168, where he mentions Tiberias's construction just before Pilate's appointment).[25] Also, before Pilate is said to have taken standards with busts of Tiberius into Jerusalem, Josephus mentions the death of Antiochus of Commagene, which is to be dated to A.D. 17 (*Antiquities* 18:53). Evidence like this is simply too strong to ignore.

One is not to insist, therefore, on the basis of Josephus's statement about Vitellius removing Pilate near the "death" of Tiberius that Pilate was removed in A.D. 36/37. When one carefully reviews Josephus's statement in *Antiquities* 18:89 and its context at first glance one might be drawn to this traditional opinion. Vitellius is called (18:88) a consul, which office he did not hold before A.D. 34 (his second consulate was in A.D. 43). My contention is that the text of Josephus is not free of great ambiguities in this passage. Was Josephus describing an earlier service of Vitellius in Syria, who only later attained the consulship? Was there another Vitellius whom Josephus here describes? One is even more confused in trying to understand John Malalas who mentions (9:226) a Vitellius who served as governor of Syria in 12 B.C., during the consulship of Quirinius. Has Josephus confused L. Vitellius with the consul L. Visellius who served in A.D. 24? At present we have no certain record of L. Vitellius serving in Syria following his consulship. We are simply at a loss, in our present ignorance, to know fully how to understand Josephus and his remarks about Vitellius the consul and the time of his dismissal of Pontius Pilate.

---

25. For the foundation of Tiberias, see M. Avi-Yonah, "The Foundation of Tiberias," *IEJ* 1 (1950/51) 160–69; A. Spijkerman, "Some Rare Jewish Coins," *Liber Annuus* 13 (1963) 298ff. If Spijkerman is correct, Tiberias was founded no later than A.D. 20, with A.D. 17 being possible.

Enough information presents itself, however, to question that Pilate was dismissed as late as A.D. 36/37. If Pilate served as early as A.D. 14/15, then Josephus's statement that he served ten years also demands careful study (*Antiquities* 18:89; cf. 18:177). If Pilate began his governorship as early as A.D. 14/15, a date for his dismissal around A.D. 25/26 well accords with a ten-year term related by Josephus. This date for the removal of Pilate agrees with the time of Paul's conversion, and in the absence of Pilate from the scene, the high priest used the occasion of a power vacuum to dispatch Paul to arrest the Christians of Damascus, and bring them bound to Jerusalem (Acts 9:2ff., 22:5ff., 26:10ff.; cf. Gal 1:13).

Unfortunately, great gaps exist in our knowledge of the Roman governors of Syria in the first century B.C., such as Quirinius's career, as well as in the first century A.D., such as the full careers of Flaccus and L. Vitellius. We are likewise ignorant of much of the careers of their military associates. If more knowledge of all these backgrounds were made available, some misunderstandings of Josephus's statements would disappear. Even though Josephus mentions the successor of Pilate, for example, one still is puzzled to know whether his name was Marullus (*Antiquities* 18:237) or Marcellus (*Antiquities* 18:89), or whether both individuals served separate terms.[26] To me it seems better to confess considerable ignorance of matters relating to Vitellius's dismissal of Pilate, as well, in the light of many uncertainties about this event.

When one firmly places Jesus within a historical context of A.D. 15–21, certain statements of the New Testament harmonize beautifully with known events of that period. For example, John the Baptist admonished the soldiers who heard him to be "content with your wages" (Luke 3:14). To me, John the Baptist's words can only be understood within the context of the mutinies and uprisings of Roman troops at that time (after the death of Augustus and the following months). In late A.D. 14 and the following months of A.D. 15, Roman troops in Pannonia and lower Germany mutinied due to their low rewards and the dangers to which they were exposed at the time. Moreover, Augustus in his will gave greater rewards to the pretorians (consisting of Germans and Gauls) than to his own loyal troops. Roman troops resented their long years of service, and the poor rewards they received when their service terminated. This situation reached such a tense state of affairs that Germanicus had to make concessions to his troops in Germany, which Tiberius, in the give and take of later Roman politics,

26. See the literature on this question gathered by L. H. Feldman, *Josephus and Modern Scholarship* (Berlin: de Gruyter, 1984) 320–23, nos. 1416–29d.

withdrew. All of this activity, which is unparalleled at other times in the
first half of the first century A.D., doubtless spilled over beyond Germany
and Pannonia, and made its own impact on Roman troops stationed
elsewhere, including the regions around Judea at this time (see Tacitus,
Annals 1:16ff., 1:31ff.). This background affords the perfect time for
John the Baptist's words to soldiers who listened to him to be peaceable,
fair, and content with their wages. Interestingly, John Malalas (10:236)
dates the death of John the Baptist in A.D. 17, during the consulship of
Flaccus and Rufus, even though in the same context he had just dated
his work as beginning in the consulship of Silanus and Nerva (= A.D. 28)!

One is therefore led to the conclusion to change the date of
Tiberius's year when John the Baptist began his ministry. My suggestion is that the correct reading in Luke 3:1 is not year "fifteen" but
"two" (= A.D. 15). Does the spelling of the word "fifteen" (πεντεκαιδεκάτῳ) in Luke 3:1 provide a clue to the textual error behind this
reading? I suggest that it is possible. Perhaps Luke's spelling of πεντεκαιδεκάτῳ arose in the manner I suggested above (p. 59).[27]

27. Elsewhere in the New Testament fifteen is uniformly spelled as δεκαπέντε even
by Luke himself (see John 11:18, Acts 27:28, Gal 1:18). The reader could be suspicious of
Luke's spelling in 3:1 on this basis, as well.

Herod's Death and Jesus' Birth

The Nativity and Herod's Death

Ernest L. Martin

The chronology associated with the birth of Jesus is most important not only in determining the reliability of the New Testament narratives but in solving some chronological aspects of Roman history during the "dark decade" from 6 B.C. to A.D. 4.[1] This paper is a survey of the problems regarding the historical occurrences of that critical decade; and some new suggestions are presented for solving those major chronological difficulties.[2]

It should be stated at the outset that I accept the view that the 15th year of Tiberius occurred in A.D. 28.[3] Since Jesus was "about 30 years" at the time, his birth would fit within a period that all the early fathers of the church believed that Jesus was born—between late 4 B.C and late 1 B.C. (This includes Irenaeus, even though on one occasion he wrote that Christ was near 50 years of age in order to confound his Gnostic adversaries on other matters; *Adversus haereses* 2:22, § 6.) The fact that the fathers place the nativity after the middle of 4 B.C. (and most within the period 3–2 B.C.) is a significant witness that deserves serious consideration as being factual, but has only received scant attention until now. The new historical information now becoming available suggests strongly that the early fathers were right.

The crux of the chronological problems associated with the nativity is fixing the time for Herod's death. To determine the terminus ad quem for his death would reveal the latest time for Jesus' birth because

Ernest Martin is Director of the Academy for Scriptural Knowledge in Alahambra, California.
    1. R. Syme, *The Crisis of 2 B.C.* (Munich: Bayerischen Akademie der Wissenschaften, 1974) 30.
    2. A fuller explanation is given in my *The Birth of Christ Recalculated* (2d ed.; Pasadena, CA: Foundation for Biblical Research, 1980), and *Inconsistencies in Josephus and Herodian Co-Regencies* (Pasadena, CA: Foundation for Biblical Research, 1982).
    3. See H. Hoehner, *Chronological Aspects of the Life of Christ* (Grand Rapids: Zondervan, 1977) 29–36 for a discussion of the fifteenth year of Tiberius.

Herod was still alive when Jesus was born (Matt 2:1). Josephus helps in this matter by stating that a lunar eclipse occurred not long before Herod's death and that Herod died before a Passover (*Antiquities* 17: 167, 213). Unfortunately, he does not say if the eclipse was partial or full, what time of night, or what calendar date or day of the week it occurred. Without one or more of these factors the modern astronomer is at a loss to identify the eclipse in a historical sense. Four lunar eclipses would have been observed at Jericho from 7 to early 1 B.C.: 23 March 5 B.C. (total, central at 8:30 P.M.), 15 September 5 B.C. (total, central at 10:30 P.M.), 13 March 4 B.C. (partial, central at 2:20 A.M.), and 10 January 1 B.C. (total, central at 1:00 A.M.). Since Josephus said that Passover occurred not too long after Herold's death, and that he died about two or three weeks after the eclipse, the 15 September 5 B.C. eclipse is not possible (the next Jewish feast was Tabernacles not Passover, and there are other problems as well). The other three eclipses are all possible. However, only thirty days occurred between both the 23 March 5 B.C. and 13 March 4 B.C. eclipses and the Passovers that followed, which is not long enough to accommodate the events that Josephus said took place in this time period. The most cogent reason is that Herod was given a *sheloshim* (Hebrew, šĕlōšîm 'thirty') mourning period after his death before the following Passover, and this alone took thirty days to accomplish.[4]

The only eclipse that fits the data is that of 10 January 1 B.C. This one has the best historical vouchers associated with it and it vindicates the majority of the early Christian fathers who said that Jesus was born in 3 or 2 B.C. I believe that there are seven historical and biblical factors that show the reasonableness of a 3 or 2 B.C. birth for Jesus.

First, it is known that Herod died sometime before a springtime Passover. But when that holy season arrived, the Jewish people in Palestine began a major revolt against Herod's son Archelaus (the new ruler). Within two months the affair developed into a full-scale war so serious that Quintilius Varus, the Roman governor of the province of Syria (who had control over Judea), mustered all the Roman forces in the area (three legions plus auxiliary forces) to subdue the Jewish revolutionaries. Josephus said this war occurred within an environment of Messianic expectation among the Jews (*Antiquities* 17:41–45). The Romans viewed such concepts with apprehension since they were aware that a Messiah was anticipated near that time who was expected to overthrow all the governments on earth and establish a Jewish world

---

4. A full explanation of this factor is given in my *New Historical Evidence Proving Herod Did Not Die in* 4 *B.C.* (Pasadena, CA: Foundation for Biblical Research, 1982).

kingdom with its capital at Jerusalem. Since approximately ten percent of the population of the Roman Empire was Jewish, and there were probably about one million Jews resident in Parthia (Rome's arch enemy on its eastern frontier), the occasion of this Jewish/Roman war was no time for Rome to relax its armed forces. But if this war took place in the summer of 4 B.C (which is the year commonly accepted today). a historical problem emerges: there is not one Roman record that indicates a major war taking place in Judea in 4 B.C. On the contrary, Augustus states that he was discharging many of his soldiers within the years 7 to 2 B.C. and giving them generous bonuses (*Res Gestae* 16). Such demobilization would have been unlikely if a serious war were raging during this period in one of the most strategic areas of the empire. On the other hand, if the eclipse associated with Herod's death were that of 10 January 1 B.C., then the Jewish/Roman war took place in the summer of 1 B.C. This makes the account of Augustus completely understandable and forges Roman and Jewish historical records into compatibility.

There is a second reason that validates this Jewish/Roman war as occurring in 1 B.C. When significant wars took place outside the official boundaries of the empire (such as this war), it was customary for the emperor to be awarded an "imperial acclamation" if victory were achieved by Rome. Roman records show that Augustus received an acclamation back in 8 B.C., but not another until A.D. 1.[5] If this significant Jewish/Roman war occurred in 4 B.C. why was there not an acclamation in 4 or 3 B.C.? Such a victory would have had all the necessary earmarks for gaining an acclamation. But if the war and victory were in 1 B.C., an award in the following year of A.D. 1 becomes reasonable.

Third, a new archaeological discovery substantiates the conclusion that a Jewish/Roman war occurred in the summer of 1 B.C. In 1960 an inscription was found in Greece describing a major victory secured by Gaius Caesar, the grandson and heir of Augustus. Pliny, a first-century Roman writer, said that Gaius accomplished important conquests in an Arabian area north of the Gulf of Aqaba. The new inscription shows these triumphs of Gaius were so significant that annual feasts were ordained as far away as Greece to honor his achievements—it was no minor war! The inscription shows that the battles were conducted "for the safety of all mankind."[6] Surely, this description indicates that some victory of distinction was being honored. Interestingly, the last military actions in the Jewish/ Roman war after the death of Herod took place in

5. Syme, *The Crisis of 2 B.C.*, 3.

6. J. E. G. Zetzel, "New Light on Gaius Caesar's Eastern Campaign," *Greek, Roman, and Byzantine Studies* 11 (1970) 259ff.

Idumaea, an Arabian area located south of Judea toward the Gulf of Aqaba. This region corresponds exactly with Pliny's account of Gaius's campaigns in Arabia. It is also known that Gaius's war happened in 1 B.C.—the year the Jewish/Roman war occurred as shown by new chronological indications. In addition, there is an eyewitness account of the war and the participation of Gaius in it. The author of the *Testament of Moses*, a Jewish writer who lived in Judea, said it was conducted by a "king" who had come from the west to gain the victory (6:8). And true enough, Gaius arrived directly from the west in 1 B.C. to end the war and he had all the credentials to be called a king.

There is a fourth reason that invalidates the supposition that Herod died in early 4 B.C. If the eclipse related to Herod's death were the earlier one of 13 March 4 B.C., an impossible situation is evident: the many events Josephus said happened between that eclipse and the next springtime Passover cannot be squeezed into the limited period of 30 days from 13 March to 11 April 4 B.C. A minimum of two months is necessary for the events Josephus narrates. Herod was sick when the eclipse took place and his condition then worsened and he travelled from Jericho to Callirrhoe for treatments and returned (about 50 miles round trip; allow approximately one week). Herod subsequently summoned Jewish leaders from all parts of the country to Jericho. For messengers to travel 130 miles or so, and then for the elders themselves to journey to Jericho took at least one week. Permission to execute Herod's rebellious son Antipater then arrived from Augustus. Herod had him killed and died himself five days later. Preparations for the funeral procession were then made and these included bringing the crown jewels and spices from Jerusalem, and relatives and military officers from all over the country (taking another week). The funeral procession travelled 200 stades or 23 miles from Jericho to the Herodium at a rate of 8 stades (0.9 miles) daily, taking approximately four weeks. A thirty-day *sheloshim* mourning period, conducted simultaneously with the funeral procession, was also consummated.[7] Archelaus, the new king, then took up his duties by changing ranks in the armed forces and hearing several lawsuits in the courts prior to the Passover (requiring approximately one more week).

The estimate of total time elapsed from Herod's death to the following Passover is approximately ten weeks. Timothy Barnes has noted that it is hardly possible to place all the events mentioned by Josephus into the single month between the eclipse of 13 March 4 B.C. and the following Passover on 11 April.[8] However, if Herod died

7. Martin, *New Historical Evidence*, 1–3.
8. T. Barnes, "The Date of Herod's Death," *JTS* 19 (1968) 209.

shortly after the eclipse of 10 January 1 B.C., everything that Josephus narrates fits the 89-day period up to the next Passover.

Fifth, the most important argument that Herod died in 1 B.C. is the record of the New Testament itself. John the Baptist began teaching in the fifteenth year of Tiberius (Luke 3:1). A short time later, Jesus commenced his own ministry when "about thirty" (Luke 3:23). It is known from coins, inscriptions, and documentary evidence that Tiberius's fifteenth year of rule was reckoned from 19 August A.D. 28 (or perhaps reaching back to January 1 if whole years were reckoned according to the Roman calendar) and it ended on 18 August A.D. 29. (or 31 December A.D. 28 if his regnal years were reckoned in whole years). Various regions of the empire had different ways of reckoning the regnal years of rulers. Whatever way one reckons the beginning of Tiberius's fifteenth year, thirty years prior to that year still points to the period of 3 to 2 B.C.

A sixth reason for placing the nativity of Jesus in 3 or 2 B.C. is the coincidence of this date with the New Testament account that Jesus was born at the time when a Roman census was being conducted: "There went out a decree from Caesar Augustus, that all the [Roman] world should be registered" (Luke 2:1). Historians have not been able to find any empire-wide census or registration in the years 7–5 B.C., but there is a reference to such a registration of all the Roman people not long before 5 February 2 B.C. written by Caesar Augustus himself: "While I was administering my thirteenth consulship [2 B.C.] the senate and the equestrian order *and the entire Roman people* gave me the title Father of my Country" (*Res Gestae* 35, italics added). This award was given to Augustus on 5 February 2 B.C., therefore the registration of citizen approval must have taken place in 3 B.C. Orosius, in the fifth century, also said that Roman records of his time revealed that a census was indeed held when Augustus was made "the first of men"—an apt description of his award "Father of the Country"—at a time when all the great nations gave an oath of obedience to Augustus (6:22, 7:2). Orosius dated the census to 3 B.C. And besides that, Josephus substantiates that an oath of obedience to Augustus was required in Judea not long before the death of Herod (*Antiquities* 17:41–45). This agrees nicely in a chronological sense with what Luke records. But more than that, an inscription found in Paphlagonia (eastern Turkey), also dated to 3 B.C., mentions an "oath sworn by all the people in the land at the altars of Augustus in the temples of Augustus in the various districts."[9] And dovetailing precisely with this inscription, the early (fifth century)

9. N. Lewis and M. Reinhold, *Roman Civilization* (New York: Columbia University, 1955; repr. New York: Harper Torchbooks, 1966), 2:34–35.

Armenian historian, Moses of Khoren, said the census that brought Joseph and Mary to Bethlehem was conducted by Roman agents in Armenia where they set up "the image of Augustus Caesar in every temple."[10] The similarity of this language is strikingly akin to the wording on the Paphlagonian inscription describing the oath taken in 3 B.C. These indications can allow us to reasonably conclude that the oath (of Josephus, the Paphlagonian inscription, and Orosius) and the census (mentioned by Luke, Orosius, and Moses of Khoren) were one and the same. All of these things happened in 3 B.C.

A final historical argument bolsters this reasoning. A Latin inscription found in 1764 about one-half mile south of the ancient villa of Quintilius Varus (at Tivoli, 20 miles east of Rome) states that the subject of the inscription had twice been governor of Syria. This can only refer to Quintilius Varus, who was Syrian governor at two different times. Numismatic evidence shows he ruled Syria from 6 to 4 B.C., and other historical evidence indicates that Varus was again governor from 2 B.C. to A.D. 1. Between his two governorships was Sentius Saturninus, whose tenure lasted from 4 to 2 B.C. Significantly, Tertullian (third century) said the imperial records showed that censuses were conducted in Judea during the time of Sentius Saturninus. (*Against Marcion* 4:7). Tertullian also placed the birth of Jesus in 3 or 2 B.C. This is precisely when Saturninus would have been governor according to my new interpretation. That the Gospel of Luke says Quirinius was governor of Syria when the census was taken is resolved by Justin Martyr's statement (second century) that Quirinius was only a procurator (not governor) of the province (*Apology* 1:34). In other words, he was simply an assistant to Saturninus, who was the actual governor as Tertullian stated.[11]

Altogether, these seven historical indications are powerful evidence that a 3 or 2 B.C. birth for Jesus has now become possible.

One problem remains. If Herod died in early 1 B.C. (and Jesus was born a year or two earlier), why did the sons of Herod who succeeded him in his kingdom seemingly reckon the beginning of their reigns as being 4 B.C.—not 1 B.C. as one would expect? This is not difficult to explain. It was common among rulers in eastern areas of the Roman Empire to add fictitious years to their own reigns if the political situation demanded it. Interestingly, the legitimate heirs to Herod's kingdom (Aristobulus and Alexander) were killed by Herod in 4 B.C., three years

---

10. R. W. Thomson, *History of the Armenians* (Cambridge: Harvard University, 1978) 163–64.

11. Martin, *Birth of Christ Recalculated*, 65–75.

before his death. But the successors to Herod, in order to legitimatize their right to rule in the eyes of their Jewish subjects, may have antedated the reckoning of their reigns to the deaths of the proper heirs—a normal practice then. E. J. Bickerman has shown that the rulers of the eastern areas of the Roman Empire (and Parthia) often predated their years of rule.[12] Some coins of the successors of King Herod show dates of reign *before* they actually took office.[13] Additionally, Herod let his son Antipater rule jointly with him during the last years of his rule, and Archelaus, the chief successor of Herod was reckoned as one who "had long exercised royal authority," not long after Herod's death (Josephus, *Jewish War* 2:26). All of this gives good evidence that antedating the rule of Herod's sons to 4 B.C. (to the time when the two legitimate sons of Herod were executed) is a reasonable proposition.

This could indicate that Herod's three sons ruled jointly with him in the last year or two of his reign. This was certainly true with Antipater. Josephus used the eyewitness account of Nicolas of Damascus that Antipater was "at least co-ruler with his father and in no different from a king" (*Antiquities* 17:2). Josephus mentions other co-rulerships in first-century Judea; for example, Hyrcanus II assumed power in 70/69 B.C. (*Antiquities* 14:4), but for the first two years he ruled jointly with his mother Queen Alexandra (*Jewish Wars* 1:120). Emil Schürer suggested that Josephus followed a chronographic handbook that gave the prince more years than he actually ruled.[14]

While all of the above gives evidence for joint rule in first-century Judea, one may not have to resort to this explanation to prove that the death of Herod occurred in 1 B.C. Ormund Edwards, independently of my work, has also argued that Herod died in early 1 B.C.[15] He believes that Josephus used two dating systems in determining the times for the ending years of Herod, and if he is correct there would be no need to resort to a belief in coregencies as I have suggested. "It is proposed," Edwards writes, "to rectify the inconsistencies in Herodian chronology by making a single, simple change: all the coins of the earlier Herods be dated according to the Hellenistic or civil (rather than the ecclesiastical)

12. E. J. Bickerman, "Notes on Seleucid and Parthian Chronology," *Berytus* 8 (1944) 77.

13. W. R. Thompson, "Chronology of the New Testament," *Zondervan Pictorial Encyclopedia of the Bible* (ed. M. C. Tenney; Grand Rapids: Zondervan, 1975), 1:822.

14. The editors of the new Schürer point out that Josephus may have followed a chronographic handbook in some of his synchronizations; see E. Schürer, *The History of the Jewish People in the Age of Jesus Christ* (rev. and ed. G. Vermes and F. Millar; Edinburgh: Clark, 1973), 1:201 n. 1.

15. O. Edwards, "Herodian Chronology," *PEQ* 114 (1982) 29-42.

Ernest L. Martin

calendar. The impression of coregencies in 4–1 B.C. is then an illusion created by the interplay of the two calendars, with their new year's days six months apart, exaggerated by antedating."[16]

Thus Edwards shows that it is not necessary to resort to co-regencies. Rather, the use of two calendrical systems and antedating of regencies, a common practice in the Hellenistic kingdoms (as Bickerman proves), would show that Herod died in the ecclesiastical year beginning in spring of 2 B.C. and his successors dated the beginning of their reigns (in a *de jure* sense) back to 3 B.C.[17] Thus, no matter what chronological method one uses to establish the regnal years of Herod, we are left with the conclusion that Herod died not long after the lunar eclipse of 10 January 1 B.C. and that Jesus was born in 3 or 2 B.C.

16. Edwards, ibid., 29. E. M. Smallwood, *The Jews under Roman Rule: From Pompey to Diocletian* (Leiden: Brill, 1976) 72 n. 37 and 77 n. 55, maintains that T. Corbishley ("The Chronology of Herod's Reign," *JTS* 36 [1935] 22–32) solved some of the chronological problems of Herod's middle years by reference to a dual dating system used by Josephus.

17. Edwards, "Herodian Chronology," 38.

"And They Went Eight Stades toward Herodeion"

Douglas Johnson

It is my position that Jesus Christ was born not long before 4 B.C., the year of Herod's death.[1] Ernest L. Martin disagrees with this position by maintaining that Herod the Great died in 1 B.C. and that Jesus was therefore born in 2 B.C.[2] Thus the pivotal issue of debate concerning the Nativity is the year of Herod's death.

The weakness of Martin's case for dating Herod's death in 1 B.C. causes his whole theory of "recalculating" Christ's birth to collapse. Taking his cue from W. E. Filmer's theory (1966), Martin first set forth his arguments for a 1 B.C. date for Herod's death in 1976.[3] He did this in spite of the fact that Filmer's theory had already been thoroughly discredited by T. D. Barnes in 1968.[4] In a 1983 follow-up article to Barnes, P. M. Bernegger further undermined the position of Filmer and Martin by proving that, according to Josephus's narrative concerning Herod's regnal years, the death of Herod must have occurred no later than 4 B.C.[5]

Undaunted by these criticisms against his theory, Martin still argues that Herod died in 1 B.C.

Douglas Johnson is Senior Process Expediter for Seagate Technology in Santa Cruz, California.

1. Douglas Johnson, "The Star of Bethlehem Reconsidered: A Refutation of the Mosley/Martin Historical Approach," *Planetarian* 10 (May 1981) 14-16; idem, "When the Star of Bethlehem Appeared," *Planetarian* 10 (March 1982) 20-23, 16; idem, "Letters," *Planetarian* 14 (September 1985) 5, 23.

2. See the previous essay in this volume, and Martin's "The Celestial Pageantry Dating Christ's Birth," *Christianity Today* 21 (3 December 1976) 16-18, 21-22; see also John Mosley, "When Was That Christmas Star?" *Griffith Observer* 44 (December 1980) 3.

3. W. E. Filmer, "The Chronology of the Reign of Herod the Great," *JTS* 17 (1966) 283-98. See n. 2 for Martin's works.

4. T. D. Barnes, "The Date of Herod's Death," *JTS* 19 (1968) 204-9.

5. P. M. Bernegger, "Affirmation of Herod's Death in 4 B.C.," *JTS* 34 (1983) 526-31.

Herod Died in 4 B.C.

The evidence for Herod's death in 4 B.C. is straightforward, but it is necessary to keep in mind that Josephus, the first-century A.D. historian who provides this evidence, used inclusive reckoning of years. Herod the Great was named king of Judea by the Roman Senate in 40 B.C. and died in the 37th year of his reign. Josephus also records that Herod captured Jerusalem and possessed the land of Judea in 37 B.C. and died 34 years after that date (*Antiquities* 17:191).

According to Josephus, Archelaus, Herod's son who succeeded him, was banished from the throne of Judea 37 years after Augustus Caesar defeated the naval forces of Antony and Cleopatra at the Battle of Actium in 31 B.C. (*Antiquities* 18:26). Thus, he was banished in A.D. 6. Elsewhere, Josephus reports that Archelaus was banished in the tenth year of his rule (*Antiquities* 17:342–44), thus giving a date of 4 B.C. as the beginning of his reign as ethnarch.

Herod's two other sons also began reigning about 4 B.C. Antipas lost his tetrarchy in A.D. 38/39 (coins minted in the 43d year of his rule have been found). Philip's reign ended in the 20th year of Tiberius Caesar (A.D. 33/34), after Philip had ruled his tetrarchy for 37 years.[6]

While the succession of Herod's three sons was being confirmed by Augustus in Rome according to Herod's will, a revolt in Judea was suppressed by Varus, the governor of Syria, who ruled from 7/6 to 5/4 B.C.[7] It is likely that Varus ended the Jerusalem revolt in the summer of 4 B.C.

Thus, the historical evidence points to 4 B.C. as the date of Herod's death. And, according to Paul L. Maier, it is "the problem of Herod's successors [that] forever condemns Martin's work . . . all arguments should focus here."[8]

Coregents with Herod?

How then does Martin deal with the fact that Herod's sons began their reigns in 4 B.C.? He offers the imaginative suggestions that (1) Antipater, another son of Herod, coreigned with Herod from 4 to 1 B.C., (2) Antipater and Herod died in 1 B.C., and (3) Herod's three succeeding sons "backdated" the commencement of their reigns to

6. See Barnes, "The Date of Herod's Death," 205, for evidence on both Antipas and Philip.

7. *Antiquities* 17:250–51; Barnes, ibid., 207.

8. Letter from Paul L. Maier, 20 June 1985.

4 B.C. to blot out the record of Antipater's rule.[9] These elaborate conjectures collapse under the weight of the following evidence.

Augustus Caesar, the Roman Emperor overseeing Herod's "client kingdom," commanded Herod never to relinquish his kingship. Such a transfer of power was to occur only upon the death of Herod (*Antiquities* 16:92). According to Josephus, Herod received the following order from Augustus concerning Herod's eventual choice of successor to the throne of Judea: "And when Herod was disposed to make such a settlement at once, Augustus said that he would not give him leave to deprive himself, while he was alive, of the power over his kingdom, or over his sons" (*Antiquities* 16:129). That is, as long as Herod was alive, there would be no coregents with Herod—only heirs to the throne (as listed in Herod's last will and testament) to rule *after* Herod's death and *after* their confirmation by the emperor.

Second, after receiving this order from Augustus, Herod made a speech to the people of Judea and told them that his sons were to reign "after him." At that time, Herod named Antipater first among the three sons he chose to succeed him. Then Herod reminded the people that "he desired that they should all pay court to himself, and esteem him king and lord of all." (*Antiquities* 16:133–34). Herod's position as king and Antipater's position as favored heir are clearly described by Josephus in his record of Herod's speech: "I must require these persons ... to rest their hopes on me *alone*; for it is not the kingdom, but the *mere honours of royalty*, which I am now delivering over to my sons. They will enjoy the pleasures of power, *as if actual rulers*, but upon me, however unwilling, will fall the burden of office" (*Jewish War* 1:461, emphasis added).

Third, Josephus offers additional evidence that Antipater was *not* a coregent or king when he writes that Antipater found it "hopeless to obtain the throne" because he was hated by the people and the army (*Antiquities* 17:1). The paradoxical statement (*Antiquities* 17:2) that, in spite of Antipater's "hopeless" condition, Antipater was "at least co-ruler with his father and in no way different from a king" refers to the honors of royalty allowed to Antipater by "concession" from King Herod. Josephus is not referring to a change in Antipater's legal status from favored heir to coregent. If Antipater had been a coregent, surely Josephus would have said so explicitly. Because Antipater was not a coregent (but a favored heir), Josephus described Antipater as "at least co-ruler" in an effort to measure his honors of royalty. Antipater had *de facto* influence, not *de jure* power.

9. Mosley, "When Was That Christmas Star?" 3.

T. D. Barnes translates this passage as, "Nevertheless [Antipater] ruled with his father *just as if* he were king." This description of Antipater as merely an heir to the throne (who acted as if he were king because of Herod's favor toward him) is identical in both passages in Josephus (*Antiquities* 17:1 and *Jewish War* 1:461).

A fourth argument that Antipater was not coregent with his father revolves around his conspiracy to kill Herod. After being named heir to the throne in his father's will, Antipater left Jerusalem with the will and lived in Rome with his friends (*Antiquities* 17:52–53). While living in Rome (for at least seven months) Antipater continually sought to have his father murdered.[10] Aside from the fact that Antipater could not have ruled Judea as king or coregent while he was living in Rome; I ask, If Antipater were already king, why did he continually try to have his father murdered? Obviously, he was merely an anxious heir who was trying to speed up his inheritance. In fact, Antipater lamented Herod's long life and complained that if he ever gained the throne of Judea, he would be too old to enjoy it (*Antiquities* 17:66). Antipater's plan was to have Herod murdered by others, while he remained free of suspicion through his absence from Jerusalem. But Herod learned of Antipater's plot and had him executed five days before his own death (*Antiquities* 17:83, 133, 187, 190–91).

Simply put, Herod was the sole king until his death and nobody reigned with him. In his efforts to rearrange history, Martin stretches the historical evidence to the breaking point. As Maier observed, "Martin's resort to coregencies for the Herodian sons just doesn't work at all, no matter how hard he clubs the evidence in order to try to make it fit."[11]

Eight Stades

In an uncorroborated report, Josephus mentions that a lunar eclipse immediately preceded Herod's death (*Antiquities* 17:167). Herod's funeral and its attendant events were then accomplished before the following Passover. Because of the evidence establishing the date of Herod's death in 4 B.C., the lunar eclipse of 13 March 4 B.C. is the logical choice to fit Josephus's account.

Although other evidence speaks against his theory, Martin thinks he has compelling evidence when he arrives at the subject of Herod's

---

10. *Antiquities* 17:79–88; see also 17:1–5 for Antipater's motives behind his conspiracy against Herod.

11. Letter from Paul L. Maier, 21 March 1985.

funeral. Martin claims that there is just not enough time between March 13 (the eclipse) and April 11 (the beginning of Passover) for the funeral of Herod and its related events. He bases his claim on his belief that Herod's funeral procession traveled only eight stades each day to cover a total of 200 stades (Greek, στάδιον; one stade is about 200 meters). On this point, Martin takes his cue from two misleading translations of Josephus.

In 1737 William Whiston suggested that Herod's funeral procession traveled eight stades (about one mile) each day for 25 days to cover the 200 stades between Jericho (where Herod died) and Herodeion (or Herodium, Herod's burial site). The Loeb Classical Library edition of Josephus's works (1963) also contains the suggestion that Herod's funeral procession traveled 8 stades each day.[12] If these two sources were correct, there would have been insufficient time between the eclipse and Passover in 4 B.C. for the events described by Josephus. However, they are not correct and Martin's reliance upon them is unfortunate.

The Greek text of Josephus's *Jewish Antiquities* 17:199 reads, ἤεσαν δὲ ἐπὶ Ἡρωδείου στάδια ὀκτώ, 'and they went eight stades toward Herodeion'. The phrase "each day" does not exist in any of the Greek texts of Josephus's accounts of Herod's funeral. Josephus recorded eight stades as the *total extent* of travel, not as a *rate* of travel. Martin's continued dependence on the Whiston and Loeb translations is unsupportable since Josephus only wrote, "And they went eight stades toward Herodeion." The phrase "each day" is a totally unfounded inference embraced by Martin.[13]

Harvard University Press now recognizes that this footnote is wrong. Zeph Stewart, executive trustee of the Loeb Classical Library, replied to me in a letter dated 5 April 1985 concerning this account:

Thank you very much for pointing out this error (as it clearly is). . . . I imagine that the writer of the note was merely following Whiston's attempt to reconcile the two passages in question. It was a mistaken

12. William Whiston, *The Works of Flavius Josephus* (London: W. Bowyer, 1737; repr. Grand Rapids: Baker, 1974), 367 n. reads, "At eight *stadia* or furlongs a-day, as here, Herod's funeral, conducted to Herodium (which lay at the distance from Jericho, where he died, of 200 *stadia* or furlongs [*Jewish War* 1:673]), must have taken up no less than twenty-five days." The Loeb Classical Library edition says, "The parallel in [Jewish War] 1:673 says that they travelled eight stades (one mile) each day until they had covered the 200 stades between Jericho and Herodeion" (*Josephus* [trans. R. Marcus and A. Wikgren; Cambridge: Harvard University, 1963], 8:463).

13. See his denouncement of my view in "New Historical Evidence Proving Herod Did Not Die in 4 B.C.," *Planetarian* 11 (December 1982) 5.

attempt, and I am sure that Professor Goold, present general editor of The Loeb Classical Library, will delete or correct the sentence in the next printing.

Whiston's attempt to reconcile the funeral accounts in *Jewish War* and *Jewish Antiquities* by inferring eight stades each day is also to be corrected by Baker Book House in future printings of *The Works of Flavius Josephus*.

One of the foremost scholars on the works of Josephus, Louis H. Feldman, offers the following comments on this crucial text:

> There is no mention of how long Herod's funeral took or how many stades were traveled each day. The phrase "each day" does not, in fact, occur in the text. The note in the Loeb edition on *AJ* [*Antiquities*] 17:199 is definitely an inference which has no basis in the Greek text.
>
> *AJ*'s use of *epi* with the genitive means 'in the direction toward'. The meaning would be that "they went 8 stades in the direction toward Herodeion." This does not, however, necessarily mean at all that they went 8 stades each day or that they traveled in units of 8 stades, although I admit that the verb *eiesan* is in the imperfect tense and hence might well mean 'they kept on going' or 'they used to go'. Inasmuch as this verb 'to go' in Greek does not have an aorist tense, the imperfect does not necessarily imply repeated action. The meaning is, then, that they went 8 stades in the direction of Herodeion. What happened after that is not stated. It is perfectly possible that thereafter the task of conveying the body was given to a group who could travel faster.
>
> The statement in *BJ* [*Jewish War*] clearly says that the body was conveyed 200 stades into Herodeion, but it does not tell us how. It is perfectly possible that after the initial 8 stades, it was conveyed the rest of the distance by another group without stating the number of days that this took.[14]

In addition, there are practical and logical reasons why Herod's funeral procession did not travel eight stades each day: (1) If the processional party had only marched eight stades each day through the wilderness, they would have spent the remainder of the day baking in the sun. (2) The procession would have required a large caravan loaded with provisions for food and lodging for 25 days. (3) With a large portion of the army off-duty for almost a month to walk in the procession, the kingdom's security would have been weakened. (4) There would have been no audience in the wilderness, as there was in Jericho, to appreciate the jeweled splendor of the procession. (5) If Lazarus

14. Letters from Louis H. Feldman, 14 March and 28 May 1985.

stank after being interred only four days in a cave (John 11:39), imagine the condition of the deceased king after 25 days of exposure to the warm Judean climate. Predatory birds would have likely annoyed the procession. (6) Jewish law requires prompt burial as a matter of respect for the dead. (7) The Jews did not embalm their dead, making prompt burial a necessity.[15]

After the pomp and ceremony of the first eight stades of the funeral procession for the benefit of the onlookers from Jericho, Herod was probably conveyed more expeditiously to Jerusalem by day's end. Then on the next day, he was conveyed from Jerusalem to Herodeion for burial.

Sheloshim

In another futile attempt to overturn the evidence for Herod's death in 4 B.C., Martin has introduced the issue of *sheloshim*. He is, unfortunately, confused about this Jewish practice, which cannot be used to argue successfully for a lengthy funeral or mourning period for Herod. Martin is in error when he says, "The twenty-five or so days it required to carry the bier to the Herodian would have taken up most of *Sheloshim*."[16] Rather, *sheloshim* is a thirty-day period of mourning for the dead observed by Jews, containing an initial seven-day period called *shivah*, "counted from the time of the burial"—not death.[17]

Does this then mean that thirty days of mourning must be fitted between Herod's burial and the following Passover? Not at all, since Passover always cancels a sheloshim period. "If the *shivah* had been completed, then the incoming festival canceled the entire *sheloshim* period."[18] Josephus's funeral accounts fit this practice, for he records that Archelaus mourned Herod seven days (*shivah*), then put an end to mourning (*Antiquities* 17:200; *Jewish War* 2:1). Passover immediately followed. Thus, *sheloshim* is not an issue at all.

Martin's attempt to place the death of Herod in 1 B.C. has failed to overcome the historical evidence establishing Herod's death in 4 B.C. Anyone seeking to identify the Star of Bethlehem or the time of Christ's birth should disregard Martin's theory and look at celestial events shortly before 4 B.C.

15. On points 6 and 7 see D. R. Hillers, "Burial," *Encyclopaedia Judaica* (Jerusalem: Keter, 1971), 4:1516–17. Jacob and Joseph were exceptions to point 7 because they died in Egypt where embalming was practiced.
16. Martin, "New Historical Evidence," 6.
17. Editorial Staff, "Sheloshim," *Encyclopaedia Judaica*, 14:1357–58.
18. A. Rothkoff, "Mourning," *Encyclopaedia Judaica*, 12:490.

The Date of the Death of Herod the Great

Harold W. Hoehner

According to Matt 2:1 and Luke 1:5 the terminus ad quem for the birth of Christ was before Herod the Great's death. Most scholars have accepted the death of Herod the Great as having occurred in 4 B.C.[1] This date was challenged in 1966 by W. E. Filmer who suggested that Herod died in 1 B.C. and is recently supported by E. L. Martin.[2] However, this later date has been questioned by D. Barnes and Douglas Johnson who think that the 4 B.C. date is the most viable.[3] Most recently Ormond Edwards, in discussing the chronology of Herod's life, suggested that his death was in 3 or 2 B.C.[4]

Consequently, there is currently much debate regarding the date of Herod's death. In my previous works I have accepted the 4 B.C. date, but this date is not necessary in my chronological reconstruction of the life of Christ.[5] In fact, in some ways a later date would be easier in explaining certain statements such as Jesus' ministry beginning when he was about thirty years old (Luke 3:23). However one must look at

Harold W. Hoehner is Professor of New Testament at Dallas Theological Seminary.

1. For example, Emil Schürer, *The History of the Jewish People in the Age of Jesus Christ* (rev. and ed. Geza Vermes and Fergus Millar; (Edinburgh: Clark, 1973), 1:326–28 n. 165; Jack Finegan, *Handbook of Biblical Chronology* (Princeton: 1964) 231; M. Stern, "Appendix: Chronology," and "The Reign of Herod and the Herodian Dynasty," *The Jewish People in the First Century* (ed. S. Safrai and M. Stern; Philadelphia: Fortress, 1974), 1:68, 270; Bo Reicke, *New Testament Era* (Philadelphia: Fortress, 1968) 104; F. F. Bruce, *New Testament History* (Garden City: Doubleday, 1971) 23.

2. Filmer, "The Chronology of the Reign of Herod the Great," *JTS* 17 (1966) 283–98; Martin, *The Birth of Christ Recalculated* (2d ed.; Pasadena: Foundation for Biblical Research, 1980). See Martin's essay in this volume.

3. Barnes, "The Date of Herod's Death," *JTS* 19 (1968) 204–9; Johnson, "The Star of Bethlehem Reconsidered: A Refutation of the Mosley/Martin Historical Approach," *Planetarian* 10 (May 1981) 14–16. See also Johnson's essay in this volume.

4. Edwards, "Herodian Chronology," *PEQ* 114 (1982) 29–42.

5. See my *Herod Antipas* (Cambridge: Cambridge University, 1972) 10 n. 5; *Chronological Aspects of the Life of Christ* (Grand Rapids: Zondervan, 1977) 13.

the historical data and determine the best date. This is the purpose of this paper.

The Beginning of the Reign of Herod the Great

Before one can establish the date of Herod the Great's death, it is necessary to determine when his reign began and to understand Josephus' method of counting years.

The Commencement of Herod's Reign

The beginning of Herod's reign of the Jews is explicitly mentioned in Josephus as occurring in the 184th Olympiad—the consuls being Gnaeus Domitius Calvinus (for the second time) and Gaius Asinius Pollio (*Antiquities* 14:389)—toward the end of 40 B.C.[6] However, to possess the kingdom is quite different from receiving the title of king, which Herod obtained in 40 B.C. while the country was still under the control of his enemy, the Parthian king Antigonus. Soon after Herod received his nomination as king, he returned to Palestine in order to gain his kingdom. Finally, in the summer of 37 B.C. Herod gained possession of his domain when, with the help of the Roman army, Jerusalem was captured.[7]

The date of Jerusalem's capture is disputed on two grounds. First, Dio Cassius places the capture in 38 B.C. during the consulship of Claudius and Norbanus (49:23:1). But this is too early for two reasons. First, Herod was not able to receive troops before the autumn of 38 B.C., shortly after Antony had captured Samosata (*Antiquities* 14:439–47; cf. Plutarch 34:2–4). Furthermore, Josephus makes it clear that after the Roman troops arrived, the winter weather came before the final capture of the city (*Antiquities* 14:453, 461, 465, 473), and thus could not be before 37 B.C. Second, Josephus mentions that the final siege was in the third year after Herod had been appointed king (*Antiquities* 14:465).[8] Therefore, Jerusalem could not have been captured before 37 B.C.

The second contention regarding the date of Jerusalem's capture is due to Josephus's statement (*Antiquities* 14:488) that it occurred twenty-seven years to the day after Pompey's capture of Jerusalem, and hence

6. Because of the narrative in Josephus, it is necessary for Herod's appointment to be at the end of 40 B.C. This makes Josephus slightly inaccurate because the 184th Olympiad ended on 30 June 40 B.C.

7. *Antiquities* 14:470–80 and *Jewish War* 1:349–52. This is confirmed by Tacitus *Histories* 5:9 and Dio Cassius 49:22:6.

8. Actually it was nearly two and one-half years after his appointment in late 40 B.C. for this siege began in the spring of 37 B.C.

Filmer would date it on the Day of Atonement 36 B.C.[9] But Jerusalem's defeat could not have been as late as 36 B.C., for in the spring of that year Antony led a large campaign against Parthia (*Dio Cassius* 49:24–31) with approximately 100,000 soldiers and it seems highly unlikely that Antony would have a large contingent of soldiers for the capture of Jerusalem in the same year.[10] That it occurred on the Day of Atonement has been greatly discussed.[11] Although Josephus does state that it happened twenty-seven years to the day after Pompey's capture of Jerusalem (*Antiquities* 14:488), he seems to contradict himself by saying that Jerusalem was defeated either three (*Antiquities* 14:487) or five months (*Jewish War* 1:351) after the siege began, which would date Jerusalem's defeat in the summer of 37 B.C.

Josephus notes that a famine (due to a sabbatical year) occurred during the final siege (*Antiquities* 14:475). It is difficult, however, to determine whether this was Tishri 38, Tishri 37, or Tishri 36, and it is impossible to know if it is referring to the beginning, middle, or end of the sabbatical year.[12] It is better to stay with more concrete data.

In conclusion, it seems best to reckon that Herod was proclaimed king in late 40 B.C. and that he became king *de facto* when he captured Jerusalem in the summer of 37. Hence, in calculating twenty-seven years from the time of Pompey's capture of Jerusalem in 63 B.C. to Herod's defeat of that city in 37, Josephus reckons the twenty-seven years inclusively.

Josephus's Reckoning of Years

There are three issues that need discussion here, namely, the calendar Josephus used, the method of counting regnal years, and inclusive reckoning.

The Calendar Josephus Used. Josephus states that the Jews used two calendars. The civil calendar began in the fall with Tishri 1 for selling and buying, and for the ordinary things of life. The religious calendar began in the spring with Nisan 1 for things that pertained to religious worship (*Antiquities* 1:80–81, Josephus places this near the beginning of his work in order to inform the Romans regarding the custom of the Jews). The use of two calendars can be readily seen in the Old Testament and Edwards presumes that this was the case in Josephus's day;

9. Filmer, "The Chronology of the Reign of Herod," 285–89.
10. N. C. Debevoise, *A Political History of Parthia* (Chicago: University of Chicago, 1938; repr. 1969) 124–25; cf. Stern, "Appendix: Chronology," 67.
11. See the lengthy note in Schürer, *The History of the Jewish People*, 1:284–86 n. 11.
12. Stern, "Appendix: Chronology," 67–68.

yet he goes on to show that after the Babylonian and Persian domina-
tion the Jews used the religious calendar for ecclesiastical and internal
purposes but the Seleucid calendar for political and external purposes.[13]
However, during the Roman period the Jews no longer used the Macedonian calendar. The discontinuance of the Macedonian calendar seems
to be the case, but to state that the Jews reverted back to the two
calendar system of ancient Israel may be overlooking one other option.
It is very possible that since Josephus is writing for the Roman audience
he may have used the Julian calendar, which begins with January 1 and
ends with December 31, for counting regnal years. It is necessary to
consider all three systems.

The Reckoning of Regnal Years.   Edwin Thiele has discussed the issue
of how regnal years were counted in the Old Testament and concluded
that two systems were used: the *accession-year system*, where the first
year of reign is not counted until the first day of the next new year, and
the *nonaccession-year system*, where the first year of the reign is counted
with the first day of rule and the second year begins on the first day of
the next new year.[14] This means that the first year of reign cold
conceivably be only a few days of the remaining old calendar year. It
seems that Josephus consistently uses the nonaccession-year system
and thus parts of years are counted as whole years.[15]

Inclusive reckoning.   Filmer and Martin think that it is invalid to
reckon inclusively.[16] Edwards points out that the new edition of Schürer
rejects inclusive reckoning during the Hasmonean era, but he overlooks
the fact that Herod's reign is counted this way by Josephus.[17] However,
the new edition of Schürer carefully states that the inclusive system
may not be viable for the Hasmonean period, although Josephus does
use it for Herod's reign.[18] Two things need to be considered. First, in
Schürer the reigns of Hyrcanus, Aristobulus I, Alexander Jannaeus, and
Alexandra are added together to see if they can be reckoned inclusively.
However, totaling the reigns of several kings is not the same as giving
the total years of one king. This is especially difficult when it is stated,

13. Edwards, "Herodian Chronology," 32–33.
14. E. Thiele, *The Mysterious Numbers of the Hebrew Kings* (3d ed.; Grand Rapids:
Zondervan, 1983) 43–60.
15. Cf. Schürer, *The History of the Jewish People*, 1:200–201 n. 1, 326–28 n. 165.
16. Filmer, "The Chronology of the Reign of Herod," 293–94; Martin, *The Birth of
Christ Recalculated*, 114.
17. Edwards, "Herodian Chronology," 35.
18. Schürer, *The History of the Jewish People*, 1:200–201 n. 1.

for example, that Aristobulus I reigns for only one year (*Antiquities* 13:318) with no indication of whether it was the tag end of a non-accession year or if it was almost twelve months. Second, Josephus records what he obtained from sources of the Hasmonean period, and it may be that during the Seleucid era inclusive reckoning was not used. But this does not in any way prove that the inclusive system was not used during the Roman period. For the Hasmonean period Josephus had to depend on sources long before his time, whereas for the Herodian period he could examine recent material that could be substantiated, in some cases, by living witnesses.

Furthermore, inclusive reckoning is used in Roman times, as seen in Josephus's discusssion of Herod's establishment of the athletic contest in Caesar's honor: Josephus says they occurred every fifth year (*Antiquities* 15:268, 16:138), when actually it occurred every fourth year. Also, Schürer points out that inclusive reckoning is seen, as mentioned above, in Josephus's reckoning (*Antiquities* 14:488) of twenty-seven years between the defeat of Jerusalem in 63 B.C. by Pompey and its defeat in 37 B.C. by Herod.[19] Again, Josephus states that the period of time between Herod's conquest in 37 B.C. and Titus's conquest in A.D. 70 is 107 years (*Antiquities* 20:250), when actually it is only 106 years. The same thing is seen in his reckoning of the Battle of Actium in the spring of 31 B.C. as being Herod's seventh year of reign (*Antiquities* 15:121, *Jewish War* 1:370), when it was only the sixth. Therefore, inclusive reckoning during the Roman times seems to have been readily used by Josephus.

In conclusion, it seems reasonable that in computing Herod's reign one needs to consider that it was reckoned in accordance with the Julian calendar, the nonaccession-year system, and inclusive reckoning.

The Death of Herod the Great

The date of the death of Herod must take into account Josephus's statement of Herod's death, the length of the reign of his successors, and whether or not there were coregencies.

Herod's Death

Despite Josephus's lengthy discussion of Herod's last days, the main concern of this article is the statement that he reigned for thirty-four years after he executed Antigonus and thirty-seven years from the time the Romans proclaimed him king (*Antiquities* 17:191, *Jewish War*

19. Ibid., 1:326–27 n. 165.

1:665). Having concluded above that he was proclaimed king in 40 B.C. and captured Jerusalem in 37 B.C., the result of late 5 B.C. or early 4 B.C. is obtained when reckoning according to the Julian calendar and inclusively. Before a more specific date is suggested one needs to consider other factors.

Herod's Successors

Not only is the beginning and the end of Herod's reign important in determining the date of his death, but also, one needs to see if chronological statements regarding his successors' reigns will fit. Although there was considerable dispute about who would succeed Herod it is necessary to reckon the beginning of that person's reign immediately after Herod's death.[20]

Archelaus. Josephus contradicts himself in stating the length of Archelaus's reign. In the *Antiquities* (17:342) he state that Archelaus was deposed in his tenth year and in *Jewish War* (2:111) he claims that Archelaus was deposed in his ninth year. In a previous publication I have discussed the possible reasons for Josephus's inconsistency.[21] It may well be that in the *Jewish War* Josephus is counting from the time Archelaus returned to his domain in 3 B.C. after the long dispute over Herod's will in Rome, whereas, in the context of *Antiquities* he may be reckoning from the time of Herod's death. However, the ten-year length of reign is more accurate because Josephus confirms it in his *Life* (5). If this be the case, then reckoning the tenth year from 4 B.C. would result in Archelaus's deposition in A.D. 6. This is further substantiated by Dio Cassius who explicitly states (55:27:6) that Archelaus was banished during the consulship of Aemilius Lepidus and Lucius Arruntius, or in A.D. 6. Therefore, the 4 B.C. date for Herod's death fits well.

Herod Antipas. According to Josephus and other historians, it can be deduced that Herod Antipas was deposed in the summer of A.D. 39.[22] This is substantiated by numismatic evidence, which shows the last coins of Herod Antipas were minted in his forty-third year.[23] Calculat-

---

20. Hoehner, *Herod Antipas*, 18–39.

21. Ibid., 301–2.

22. *Antiquities* 18:252; cf. 18:238, 256; 19:351. It is beyond the scope of this article to go into the details of calculating this date. Instead, see my *Herod Antipas*, 262–73.

23. F. W. Madden, *History of Jewish Coinage and of Money in the Old and New Testament* (London: Quaritch, 1864; repr. New York: Ktav, 1967) 99; F. de Saulcy and A. de Barthélemy, *Mélanges de numismatique* (Paris; Rollin et Feuardent, 1877), 2:93; F. W. Madden, *Coins of the Jews* (London: Trübner, 1881; repr. Hildesheim: Olms, 1976) 121–22;

ing backward yields a result of 4 B.C. for Antipas's accession and Herod the Great's death.

Philip the Tetrarch. Philip the Tetrarch died in the twentieth year of Tiberius's reign (19 August 33 to 18 August 34) and after thirty-seven years of rule over Trachonitis, Gaulanitis, and Batanaea (*Antiquities* 18:106). Since Philip reigned thirty-seven years, that is, he was in his thirty-eighth year (his last coin was minted in his thirty-seventh year),[24] and reckoning backward from the Julian year that ended 31 December A.D. 34, Philip would have begun his reign in 4 B.C. Again this would demonstrate that Herod the Great died in the same year.

Herod Agrippa I. The grandson of Herod the Great, Herod Agrippa I, is mentioned here because of the chronological link with Philip the Tetrarch and Herod Antipas. Herod Agrippa died when he was fifty-four years old and in the seventh year of his reign. Josephus goes on to say that Agrippa reigned for four years under Gaius, ruling during three of them over the tetrarchy of Philip and having Antipas's territory added in his fourth year. He reigned for another three years under Claudius, during which time he received the territories of Judea and Samaria (*Antiquities* 19:351). In calculating all these figures one comes to the conclusion that he reigned during Gaius's four years as emperor, from 18 March A.D. 37 to 24 January A.D. 41. Although Gaius conferred on Agrippa the tetrarchy of Philip shortly after he became emperor, it was not until Gaius's second year (summer 38) that Agrippa went to secure his territory (*Antiquities* 18:238).

The more important problem in the scope of this paper is Agrippa's acquisition of Antipas's territory. It occurred in the fourth year of Agrippa's rule (A.D. 40)—a year after Antipas's banishment. This is reasonable, for some time was needed between Antipas's deposition and Agrippa's acquisition of his lands.[25] Therefore, Agrippa I's rule fits well within the chronological scheme of acquiring the territories of Herod's sons.

Thus, a careful look at the dates of the succession of Herod the Great's sons and grandson, one can only conclude that the 4 B.C. date is the best date for Herod's death.

G. F. Hill, *Catalogue of the Greek Coins of Palestine* (London: British Museum, 1914; repr. Bologna: Forni, 1965) 230; A. Reifenberg, *Ancient Jewis Coins* (2d ed.; Jerusalem: Mass., 1947) 45; Y. Meshorer, *Jewish Coins of the Second Temple Period* (trans. I. H. Levine; Tel-Aviv: Am Hassefer, 1967), no. 75.

24. Meshorer, *Jewish Coins of the Second Temple Period*, no. 84.

25. For further details see my *Herod Antipas*, 262–63 n. 4.

Coregencies

Because the historical data point to the 4 B.C. date for the succession of Herod's sons, Filmer suggests that Archelaus and Antipas were corulers with Herod until his death in 1 B.C.[26] However, there is no indication whatever from the sources that this was so. Moreover, Herod was not the type to share or delegate his authority. Martin, realizing Filmer's dilemma, suggests another alternative. He proposes that Herod had fallen out of favor with the Emperor Augustus in 4 B.C. and that Antipater (i.e., Antipas) became coregent with Herod until his death.[27] The two things that need to be addressed here are the time of Herod's disgrace and the plausibiltiy of Antipater's coregency with Herod.

Time of Herod's disgrace.   The time when Herod came into disfavor with Augustus and was treated as a subject rather than a friend was in 8/7 B.C. and not during 4 to 1 B.C. The context of the disgrace (*Antiquities* 16:290) was right after his war with the Arabs around 10/9 B.C. (*Antiquities* 16:282-85) and before he executed his sons Alexander and Aristobulus in 7 B.C. (*Antiquities* 16:361-94, *Jewish War,* 1:538-51). In fact the reconciliation of Herod and Augustus came before the execution of Alexander and Aristobulus (*Antiquities* 16:352). There is no way that the time of Herod's disgrace can come after 7 B.C. Furthermore, at the time of Herod's disgrace there is no indication that Antipater was ruling with Herod. Also, Martin places the execution of Alexander and Aristobulus in 4 B.C.[28] This is impossible for as Schürer has pointed out, their execution cannot come later than 7 B.C.[29] Therefore, Martin takes the time of Herod's disgrace out of its proper context and forces it into a later context in order to fit his scheme of chronology.

Antipater's coregency with Herod.   Martin attempts to make a case for a two-year joint rule of Antipater with Herod.[30] However, the only time Josephus even hinted that Antipater was coregent is in Herod's defensive rhetoric against Antipater in order to show the court that he had given Antipater all the privileges and yet was betrayed by him in an

26. Filmer, "The Chronology of the Reign of Herod," 297.

27. Martin, *The Birth of Christ Recalculated,* 115-22.

28. Ibid., 117-20.

29. Schürer, *The History of the Jewish People,* 1:294 n. 18 states: "Since Saturninus was governor of Syria at the time of the condemnation [*Antiquities* 16:368], and indeed for some times afterwards [*Antiquities* 17:6, 24, 57], it must have taken place in 7 B.C., for he left Syria not later than the first half of 6 B.C."

30. Martin, *The Birth of Christ Recalculated,* 120-22.

assassination plot (*Antiquities* 17:115, *Jewish War* 1:625–31). But this speech is just rhetorical hyperbole.[31] The actual facts of the case are seen in Herod's speech when he declared that Antipater was heir to the throne (*Jewish War* 1:623) and that he (Herod) had written a contract that would assure him of future succession (*Antiquities* 17:116). This indicates that Antipater was not on the throne as coregent. Barnes considers Josephus's statement that Antipater was "at least co-ruler with his father and in no way different from a king" (*Antiquities* 17:3) as a clear indication that he was not a coregent.[32] This certainly seems to be the case, for how could he be coregent and still not be considered a king? Furthermore, as Johnson points out, how could Antipater be coregent when he was living in Rome and why would he continually try to murder his father in order to obtain the power of the throne?[33] Thus, there seems to be no indication that Antipater was ever a coregent with his father.

It is impossible to place the disgrace of Herod and the coregency of Herod with Antipater into Martin's chronological framework. It makes havoc of Josephus's description of events. The 4 B.C. date for Herod's death seems to be the best solution to the problem.

Integration with Roman History

There is a need to discuss Gaius's part in the debate of Herod's will and the date of Varus's involvement with the Jews.

Gaius and Herod's Will

Herod's sons went to Rome to determine which will of their father was valid and who would rule his domain. Augustus appointed his grandson Gaius to serve with him in the deliberation of Herod's will (*Antiquities* 17:229). Barnes states that Gaius's participation in the deliberation necessitates that it was done before the summer of 2 B.C.[34] Barnes carefully traces the steps of Gaius. Beginning in the later part of 2 B.C., Gaius went on military expeditions on the Danube frontier and then went east to Chios, Egypt, and Arabia. He passed through Palestine and began his governorship in Antioch of Syria in 1 B.C. or A.D. 1. Therefore, the deliberation of Herod's will was done before Gaius left Rome in 2 B.C. Hence, Herod must have died before that time. This

---

31. Barnes, "The Date of Herod's Death," 206.
32. Ibid., 206 n. 7.
33. Johnson, "The Star of Bethlehem Reconsidered," 14.
34. Barnes, "The Date of Herod's Death," 208.

supports the 4 B.C. date for Herod's death. The deliberation over the will most likely was during the summer and autumn of 4 B.C.[35]

Varus's Battle with the Jews

While the dispute over Herod's will was proceeding, a Jewish revolt occurred at Jerusalem during the feast of Pentecost (*Antiquities* 17:250–98, *Jewish War* 2:39–79). Sabinus, who had taken charge of Herod's palace in Jerusalem, sent the news of the revolt to Varus, the legate of Syria, who then dispatched the news to Rome. Because Sabinus was besieged, Varus sent three legions to quell the revolt. Martin poses the problem that since this was the most serious military operation between Pompey's invasion (63 B.C.) and the Roman war against the Jews in A.D. 66–70, how could this have occurred in 4 B.C. which is right in the middle of the period from 7 to 2 B.C. when Augustus was discharging legions?

The problem posed by Martin is not as great as it first appears. Certainly the revolt was widespread, but to place it on the level that Martin does is going beyond the evidence. Josephus does mention this revolt along with the Roman invasion in 63 B.C. and A.D. 66–70 (*Against Apion* 1:34), but he is not comparing this revolt with the other two. He is just listing the revolts, but does not denote how serious they were. Also, it seems that Varus quelled the revolt within six to ten weeks.[36] It could be done this rapidly because of Varus's large military contingent and because of his efficiency as a military leader.

Second, the extent of military discharges is not known from *Res Gestae* (16), the source, that Martin quotes. It was mainly concerned with the disbursment of funds for the retired soldiers rather than how many soldiers were discharged.

Third, although this may have been a time of peace in the Roman Empire, one must remember revolts are usually surprises. Varus handled the situation because Rome's security was threatened. On the other hand, the best time for a rebellion is when the military is disarming and is unprepared.

In conclusion, it seems that Varus's battle with the Jews can easily be fitted into the summer or autumn of 4 B.C. This battle does not raise an insurmountable problem for those who hold the 4 B.C. date for Herod's death.[37]

---

35. Hoehner, *Herod Antipas*, 33–39.

36. Ibid.

37. Jerry Vardaman has pointed out to me that microletters on a coin of Achulla, depicting Varus, demonstrate that he was transfered there after departing from Antioch

Conclusion

In examining the evidence for the year of Herod's death, I find the 4 B.C. date the most satisfactory. In agreement with this conclusion, Barnes also mentions that, according to Josephus, Herod died before he was seventy (*Antiquities* 17:148, *Jewish War* 1:647). If he were twenty-five when he was appointed governor of Galilee in 47 B.C. (*Antiquities* 14:158), then his death needs to fall before 2 B.C., which accords well with the 4 B.C. date.[38] Because of the scope of this article, I am not able to discuss the exact date of his death. The problem of the eclipse mentioned by Josephus that occurred before Herod's death (*Antiquities* 17:167) needs further studying but this detail does not seem insurmountable.

---

in Syria about 4 B.C. This coin dates to 2 B.C., making it unlikely at all that he could have been in Palestine when Martin's theory demands that he be there. For the coin, see L. Müller, *Numismatique de l'ancienne Africa* (Copenhagen: Luno, 1860–74; repr. Chicago: Argonaut, 1967), 2:43–46, 54; 4:39.

38. Barnes, "The Date of Herod's Death," 209. *Antiquities* 14:158 reads πεντεκαίδεκα γὰρ αὐτῷ ἐγεγόνει μόνον ἔτη, 'he was, in fact, only fifteen years old.' It appears that the text is corrupt or that Josephus was mistaken on this point, as this would place Herod's death (when he was seventy) in A.D. 9, a date much too late. Jerry Vardaman has communicated to me that the Zenon papyri assist in understanding how 15 and 25 could be confused in the original Greek text of Josephus. Perhaps the abbreviation for 25, L Ҟ , was confused with the abbreviation for 15, L Ιϵ .

The Date of the Nativity and the Chronology of Jesus' Life

Paul L. Maier

In 1968 I published an article that offered fresh evidence in support of Friday, 3 April A.D. 33, as the date of the Crucifixion.[1] Since then, much attention has focused on the other terminus of Jesus' life in response to recent recalculations of dates for the death of Herod the Great and the birth of Christ. Although a precise date, as in the case of the Crucifixion, still seems unattainable for the Nativity, some further refinement within the usual range of 7 to 4 B.C. is possible, which would suggest late 5 B.C. as the most probable time for the first Christmas. This time frame, along with 3 April A.D. 33 for the Crucifixion, provides a very balanced correlation of all surviving chronological clues in the New Testament, as well as the extrabiblical sources. Earlier or later dates, in either case, tend to disregard or manipulate at least one or more of the sources. Using the form of a running commentary on the relevant chronological *sedes* in the New Testament, I will respond briefly to the current status of research on each.

Paul L. Maier is Professor of History at Western Michigan University.

1. P. Maier, "Sejanus, Pilate, and the Date of the Crucifixion," *CH* 37 (1968) 3-13. Previously, A.D. 33 had been advocated by J. K. Fotheringham, "The Evidence of Astronomy and Technical Chronology for the Date of the Crucifixion," *JTS* 35 (1934) 146-62; G. Ogg, *The Chronology of the Public Ministry of Jesus* (Cambridge: Cambridge University, 1940) 244ff.; and B. Reicke, *New Testament Era* (Philadelphia: Fortress, 1968) 183-84. Since then, this date has also been endorsed by H. W. Hoehner, *Herod Antipas* (Cambridge: Cambridge University, 1972) 183, and *Chronological Aspects of the Life of Christ* (Grand Rapids: Zondervan, 1977) 95ff. For the most recent support, by C. J. Humphreys and W. G. Waddington, see n. 27 below and their essay in this volume.

The Nativity

The Decree of Caesar Augustus (Luke 2:1)

The claim that no non-Christian record exists of a universal Roman census ordered by Augustus is still valid.[2] The three celebrated censuses conducted by Augustus in 28 B.C., 8 B.C., and A.D. 14—Achievement No. 8 in his *Res Gestae*—are apparently enrollments of Roman citizens only, although they *may* have involved censuses in the provinces also, since some Roman citizens certainly lived outside Italy. Luke rather intends here a provincial census of noncitizens for purposes of taxation, and many records of such provincial registrations under Augustus have survived, including Gaul, Sicily, Cilicia, Cyrene, and Egypt. Among these were client kingdoms such as that of Herod the Great; for example, Archelaus (unrelated to Herod), client king of Cappadocia, instructed a subject tribe "to render in Roman fashion an account of their revenue and submit to tribute."[3] Provincial enrollments are also well attested in Dio Cassius (53:22) and Livy (*Epistles* 134ff.; *Annals* 1:31, 2:6). There is also an epigraphic mention of a census by Quirinius at Apamea in Syria (an autonomous "client" city-state).[4]

In view of such provincial enrollments, Mason Hammond concludes that Augustus began "a general census of the whole Empire for purposes of taxation" in 27 B.C.[5] This is congruent with Luke 2:1, but the only chronological clue for a Nativity enrollment would have to be some relationship with the middle census of Augustus in 8 B.C. Perhaps this citizens' census had a provincial counterpart instituted months later, although evidence is lacking.

Quirinius and the Census of Judea (Luke 2:2)

A bibliography on the vexed issue of which census and when Quirinius governed would fill pages, and the problem itself shows little hope of present solution. None of the proposed chronologies of the life of Jesus can resolve it, since the one recorded tenure of P. Sulpicius

2. See, for example, T. Mommsen, *Römisches Staatsrecht* (Leipzig: Hirzel, 1888), 2/3:417; L. R. Taylor, "Quirinius and the Census of Judaea," *American Journal of Philology* 54 (1933) 129; and R. E. Brown, *The Birth of the Messiah* (Garden City: Doubleday, 1977) 548–49.

3. Tacitus, *Annals* 6:41. The tribe involved (the Clitae) rebelled at the census concept in a manner parallel to the Judeans in A.D. 6.

4. H. Dessau, *Inscriptiones Latinae Selectae* (3d ed.; Berlin: Weidmann, 1962) 2683. Other provincial censuses are in Dessau 950, 1409, and 9011.

5. M. Hammond, *The Augustan Principate* (New York: Russell and Russell, 1968) 91.

Quirinius as governor of Syria and the census he administered in Judea dates to A.D. 6, a decade after the death of Herod the Great. The suggestion that Quirinius had a previous term as governor of Syria founders on the fact that the list of the relevant Syrian governors is not only apparently complete, but well peopled with personalities who are far more than names on a stone fragment somewhere.[6] Two of these governors play dramatic roles on the pages of Josephus in the final years of Herod the Great: C. Sentius Saturninus (9–6 B.C.) served as judge over Herod's sons Alexander and Aristobulus at Beirut (*Jewish War* 1:538–39, *Antiquities* 16:361ff.), and P. Quintilius Varus (6–4 B.C.), victim at the Teutoberger Forest massacre, judged Herod's son Antipater in Jerusalem (*Jewish War* 1:617–18, *Antiquities* 17:89ff.).[7]

Since Luke links Quirinius's name with a census famous enough to merit designation simply as "the census" without further description in Acts 5:37 (Gamaliel's controversial speech), it becomes difficult to dislodge Quirinius and the Luke 2 census from a dating of A.D. 6—so difficult, in fact, that Tertullian sought to cut the Gordian knot by simply stating that the census was taken under the governorship of Saturninus instead of Quirinius (*Against Marcion* 4:19).

Those seeking to preserve Lukan accuracy had best resort to alternate translations, such as, "This enrollment was *before* that made when Quirinius was governor of Syria," which is possible according to Greek syntax and the textual variants.[8] An alternative suggestion turns on the idea that since it took forty years to complete one of the censuses in Gaul, the registration process could have begun under Herod, but then been completed under Quirinius, who was sent to clean up the mess left by Herod's son, Archelaus (*Antiquities* 17:355). Quirinius, in any case, helps but little in dating the Nativity.

The Last Years of Herod the Great (Matt 2:1, Luke 1:5)

Both Matthew (2:1) and Luke (1:5) agree that Herod was on the throne at the time Jesus was born. Indeed, his death between a lunar eclipse (12/13 March 4 B.C.) and the spring Passover festival (April 11) has for many years pointed to the error in our present calendar, made

6. [The list is open in 12–10 B.C., however—J. Vardaman.]

7. *Antiquities* 16:361 speaks of "governors of Syria" in the plural—Saturninus and Volumnius are intended—even though the latter was procurator. Still, this lax reference may offer some fuel to those seeking an earlier term or similar governing role for Quirinius.

8. For further discussion, see Brown, *Birth of the Messiah*, 394ff., 414–15, 547ff.; and Hoehner, *Chronological Aspects*, 13ff.

by the sixth-century Scythian monk who fathered reckoning in years B.C. and A.D. Recently, however, several scholars have claimed that Dionysius Exiguus may not have committed such a gaffe after all, particularly W. E. Filmer, who argues that the lunar eclipse of 9 January 1 B.C. was the one Josephus had in mind (*Antiquities* 17:167). By adjusting the traditional dating of Herod's accession (when he was declared king by the Romans) from 40 to 39 B.C., or (when he actually conquered Jerusalem) from 37 to 36 B.C., and using accession-year reckoning, Filmer claims to satisfy the Josephan parameters for Herod's life.[9]

A major difficulty in this otherwise attractive thesis is the chronology of the Herodians after Herod. Josephus's accounts of the reigns of Archelaus, Antipas, and Philip all correlate perfectly with a 4 B.C. date for their father's death—and not with 1 B.C. Filmer resorts to coregencies by which the reigns of the first two sons overlapped Herod's by several years, and he emends the text in the case of Philip to adjust his reign appropriately, but T. D. Barnes has convincingly refuted this attempt to transpose Herod's death.[10] Resort to coregencies is a malady that should never have infected New Testament chronological research to the extent it has. Having for years displaced the Crucifixion by three years due to the almost universal adoption of a joint rule of Augustus and Tiberius, this "solution" has now affected Nativity chronology as well. To arguments that Herod's sons and successors would try to augment the length of their reigns in this fashion, I note that Josephus was under no necessity to let them get away with it, writing as he did in Rome, under no pressure from any Herodian prince. His time grid for the Herodians holds up well enough without tampering.

Recently, P. M. Bernegger has underlined Barnes's refutation of a post-4 B.C. date for Herod's death by further elucidating Josephan chronology and confirming 37 B.C. (the year of Antigonus's death) as the start of Herod's *de facto* kingship.[11] Josephus's precise statements in both *Jewish War* (1:665) and *Antiquities* (17:191) that Herod reigned thirty-four years from the death of Antigonus can, by inclusive reckoning—that is, counting fractional portions of the years at the beginning and end of Herod's reign as complete years—point only to 4 B.C. as the year of his death.

9. W. E. Filmer, "The Chronology of the Reign of Herod the Great," *JTS* 17 (1966) 283–98. A similar chronology has been proposed by E. L. Martin, *The Birth of Christ Recalculated* (2d ed.; Pasadena: Foundation for Biblical Research, 1980).

10. T. D. Barnes, "The Date of Herod's Death," *JTS* 19 (1968) 204–9.

11. P. M. Bernegger, "Affirmation of Herod's Death in 4 B.C.," *JTS* 34 (1983) 526–31.

Both Barnes and Bernegger, however, argue that the precise date of Herod's death need not be in March/April 4 B.C., according to the standard chronology, but may instead have occurred in December 5 B.C. The eclipse of the moon that preceded Herod's death (*Antiquities* 17:167) is usually dated 12/13 March 4 B.C., but a slightly larger eclipse of the moon was visible in Jerusalem on the night of 15/16 September 5 B.C. And since the *Megillat Ta'anit* speaks of Kislev 7 (December) as a Jewish festival, with a later commentator suggesting that this marked the date of Herod's death, an alternate reckoning would place Herod's death in December 5 B.C. Because so many events seem crowded into the time frame between March 12 and the following Passover of April 11, Barnes finds the December date "clearly preferable."[12]

On the contrary, the traditional dating of Herod's death in 4 B.C. seems preferable for several reasons. First, by inclusive reckoning on the Julian calendar, which Josephus regularly employs for the reign of Herod, 5 B.C. would mark only the thirty-third year since the death of Antigonus (not the thirty-fourth), and the thirty-sixth following his *de jure* kingship announced by the Romans (not the thirty-seventh, as Josephus specifies).

Next, too much time would have to be inserted between a December death for Herod in 5 B.C. and the Passover of 11 April 4 B.C. to accommodate the accounts in Josephus. In these, Herod's principal successor, Archelaus, is shown observing the customary seven days' mourning for his father, but after that, he is understandably eager to sail to Rome as soon as possible in order to gain Augustus's confirmation of Herod's will and, thus, ratification of his own kingship. He had no interest in prolonging any interim period (when his own kingship was in question) that would have violated the provisions of Herod's will, thereby endangering his own political fortunes vis-à-vis the emperor. Indeed, Archelaus even gave in to pressures from hostile demonstrations in Jerusalem "because of his intention of making his way to Rome as quickly as possible in order to learn Caesar's decision" (*Antiquities* 17:209; cf. *Jewish War* 2:8: "in haste to depart"). The Passover, however, intervened, and he could not make the trip until afterward. If the December option for Herod's death were true, affairs would have dragged on at least four months prior to the trip, which is patently improbable.

Finally, the earlier eclipse and death for Herod are extremely unlikely when considered against the background of Herod's own living

12. Barnes, "The Date of Herod's Death," 209.

habits during the last months of his life, when advancing illness demanded optimal comforts. Josephus attaches the lunar eclipse preceding Herod's death to the night when he had burned to death the two teachers and their students who were responsible for the assault on the golden eagle that Herod had placed over the great gate of the temple. Their trial had taken place at his theater in Jericho, where Herod was apparently living at the time in his winter palace. Yet he would hardly have been living here in early September, the time of the earlier eclipse, when the Jordan valley at Jericho, over a thousand feet below sea level, is excessively hot. But he would have been staying at his winter palace in early March, the time of the later eclipse.

Against this background, the notation of Kislev 7 in *Megillat Ta ʾanit* as marking the presumed date of Herod's death must be interpreted for what it undoubtedly is: the untrustworthy tradition of a late scholiast.[13] Certainly something as significant as Herod's death—*if* it were commemorated as a holiday—would have been so recorded in *Megillat Ta ʾanit* from the start.

This leaves, then, the traditional date of Herod's death in March/April 4 B.C. Against all recent objections that Herod's funeral was too elaborate to compress into the time frame between the eclipse and the Passover, I argue that if Herod did indeed die at the close of March, the Passover would have followed inexorably—no matter whose funeral was involved—and events would have progressed almost exactly as recorded by Josephus.[14]

The last events in Herod's life after the eclipse of March 12 are a brief excursion (of unspecified duration) to neighboring Callirrhoe to try its medicinal waters, a summoning of Jewish leaders to the hippodrome at Jericho, and the execution of his son Antipater. Herod himself died five days after the last episode, or approximately the end of March. Counting backward from the Passover of April 11, the following occur: demonstrations against Archelaus, a seven-day mourning period, and Herod's own funeral, again pointing to the end of March for Herod's death. However, if Josephus were reckoning according to the Jewish calendar, Herod's thirty-fourth year of reign would have begun on 1 Nisan 4 B.C., or March 29. Accordingly, we should not miss the mark excessively to estimate Herod's death about 1 April 4 B.C., particularly if Josephus (as seems probable) was using the Julian calendar.

---

13. See Josephus, *The Jewish War* (trans. H. St. J. Thackeray; Cambridge: Harvard University, 1927), 1:314-15 n. *a*. [Is it possible that Kislev 7 alludes to Herod's *birthday*, which Jews of that period could well have observed as though it were the day of a *funeral*? This mocking practice would be full of biting sarcasm!—J. Vardaman]

14. Contra Martin, *Birth of Christ Recalculated*, 29ff.

The Star and the Magi (Matthew 2)

Granting historical problems in the Matthean account, the Star of Bethlehem *could* serve to anchor Nativity chronology were we sure of the phenomenon behind it. But the star (alas!) must always shine only as secondary or tertiary evidence for purposes of Nativity chronology, since enough celestial events seem to have filled the skies over Judea between 12 and 1 B.C. to preclude any sure conclusion. In dealing with this episode, one must resist the tendency to regard Jesus as around two years old when the magi visited (based on a confusion of Matt 2:7 and 2:16—Herod asked the magi "what time the star appeared," not the age of Jesus). The astral event could well have preceded the birth of Jesus and been in the heavens some months before the magi made their trip. Herod might also have allowed himself an extra year leeway in the infant massacre.

Against this background, Johannes Kepler's venerable suggestion of the triple conjunction of Jupiter and Saturn in 7–6 B.C. remains the most attractive hypothesis for the Star of Bethlehem amid the plethora of other explanations, since 7 B.C. minus two years yields 5 B.C., the most likely date for the Nativity, as demonstrated below.[15] This rare conjunction also satisfies a common critical complaint about the star and the magi, best expressed by Raymond E. Brown in his authoritative *The Birth of the Messiah*:

> A star that rose in the East, appeared over Jerusalem, turned south to Bethlehem, and then came to rest over a house would have constituted a celestial phenomenon unparalleled in astronomical history; yet it received no notice in the records of the times.[16]

But surely this critique is too literalistic an interpretation of Matthew, who implies that only the magi saw something in the heavens unique enough to draw their interest. Herod and his court did not respond to them (so far as we know), "Yes, we've been wondering about that star ourselves." The triple conjunction would have required some astronomical sophistication—as well as astrological credulity—to induce a long trip westward, but if Jupiter ("the king's planet") nearly impinged on Saturn ("the defender of Palestine") three times, then, in the lore of the times, "a king is coming to Palestine," and the magi set out.

This exhausts the chronological clues within the Christmas gospels, thus providing a terminus ad quem for the Nativity, but what about the

15. For a survey of other explanations for the Star of Bethlehem, see my *First Christmas* (San Francisco: Harper and Row, 1971) 69–81.
16. Brown, *Birth of the Messiah*, 188.

terminus a quo? How far in advance of March 4 B.C. was Jesus born? The answer necessarily involves further time references in the New Testament concerning Jesus' age during his maturity.

The Adult Ministry

"In the Fifteenth Year of the Reign of Tiberius Caesar" (Luke 3:1)

No date in the entire Bible is given with more exactitude than Luke 3:1. Luke almost seems to grasp for our B.C.—A.D. dating system, but cannot find it. In its place, he substitutes the relational mode of defining years in terms of then-contemporary rulers, international and regional. Beginning with the Roman emperor, Tiberius, and his governor, Pontius Pilate, he goes on to list other local political and religious rulers—seven in all. Clearly, Luke is making a stronger chronological point here than in the Augustus decree (2:1) or the Quirinius census (2:2), and some scholars have deemed this the original beginning of Luke's gospel.[17]

Two problems, however, are associated with this verse in which Luke is at such pains to give a firm dating schema: (1) This passage determines the start of John the Baptist's ministry, not Jesus', so we must learn something of the duration of John's ministry prior to that of Jesus. (2) From what year ought Tiberius's reign be dated, in Luke's reckoning?

An active, but brief ministry, measured in months rather than years, seems postulated for John the Baptist in Matthew (chap. 3), Mark (chap. 1), and John (chap. 1). The overlap between John and Jesus is almost immediate: "The next day he saw Jesus. . . ." (John 1:29). Luke switches John's incarceration on a thematic—not chronological—pattern, although he indicates that Jesus had clearly been baptized by John by that time (3:18ff.) Accordingly, a previous ministry by John the Baptist of approximately six to nine months seems not unreasonable. Anything longer would have vitiated John's role as "forerunner" in favor of a developing following of his own. Most scholars, therefore, find this a proximate reference to the beginning of Jesus' own ministry.

The other problem, to define the "fifteenth year" of Tiberius, seeks an instinctive solution by noting that if Augustus (Tiberius's predecessor) died on 19 August A.D. 14, and the Roman Senate confirmed Tiberius as emperor on September 17, then his fifteenth regnal year would be A.D. 28 or 29, depending on whether the accession-year

---

17. So B. H. Streeter, *The Four Gospels* (London: Macmillan, 1930) 209ff.; H. J. Cadbury, *The Making of Luke-Acts* (London: SPCK, 1958) 204ff.; Brown, *Birth of the Messiah*, 239ff.; and others.

system was used.[18] The simple arithmetic pointing to A.D. 28/29—which I believe accurate and what Luke intended—would probably never have been challenged had not Luke supplied another chronological clue twenty-two verses later.

"About Thirty Years of Age" (Luke 3:23)

Once it is established that Herod died in 4 B.C., it is apparent that Jesus' birth prior to Herod's death would have made him at least 32 or 33 in A.D. 28–29, rather than 30, as Luke states (3:23). But there is no need to rush to Luke's assistance with the wrong sort of first-aid: positing a coregency between Augustus and Tiberius in the last two years of Augustus's life, thus enabling the fifteenth year to be defined as A.D. 26 in behalf of a now-thirty year old Jesus, has skewed research into biblical chronology.

This standard reconciliation between Luke 3:1 and 3:23 has attained almost canonical status, but such a resort is absolutely unnecessary in terms of the New Testament text, as well as opposed to Roman imperial usage. First, Luke 3:23 must be translated correctly. The traditional rendition, "And Jesus himself began to be about thirty years of age" (AV), implying that he was on the verge of attaining his thirtieth year, is not correct. Ἀρχόμενος refers rather to the beginning of his ministry, and most contemporary translations reflect this:

Jesus, when he began his ministry, was about thirty years of age (RSV).

When Jesus began his work he was about thirty years old (NEB).

When he started to teach, Jesus was about thirty years old (JB).

Next, does Luke intend an exact registration of thirty as Jesus' age at the start of his ministry? Not with the qualifier ὡσεὶ 'about' (literally, 'as if'), which, when used with numbers and measures, has precisely the same definition as in English. Within the context of Luke's own writings, ὡσεὶ is used for the feeding of "about 5000 men" (9:14), and no one would doubt that there could have been several dozens or hundreds more or less—this very use of the larger units (dozens, hundreds) forming a parallel to Luke's usage. Similarly, Luke refers to "about 120" Jerusalem believers (Acts 1:15), "about 3000" converts at Pentecost (Acts 2:41), "about [ὡς] three months" for the duration of

18. Jack Finegan, with meticulous care and admirable objectivity, has demonstrated how the fifteenth year of Tiberius could be defined in a variety of eastern Mediterranean calendars; see his *Handbook of Biblical Chronology* (Princeton: Princeton University, 1964) 259–73.

Mary's stay with Elizabeth prior to John the Baptist's birth (Luke 1:56), and "about a stone's throw" for Jesus' withdrawal from the disciples at Gethsemane (Luke 22:41). Not one of these references intends mathematical precision, but rather an approximation to the nearest integral unit or round number.

Apart from Luke, the other evangelists use ὡσεὶ and ὡς in precisely the same manner, as do nonbiblical authors of the time.[19] Xenophon writes of "about 300" victims at a battle late in the Peloponnesian War (*Hellenica* 1:2:9) and of "about 70" horsemen (*Hellenica* 2:4:25), while Josephus has David amassing "about 400" followers at the Cave of Adullam (*Antiquities* 6:247) and Judas Maccabaeus killing "about 800" Syrians in battle (*Antiquities* 12:292). In this context, Luke's "about thirty" could well serve for any actual age ranging from 26 to 34, before and after which (presumably) the middle 5 might intrude before attraction to the next adjacent round number, 20 or 40 in this case. If Jesus was born in late 5 B.C., his age in A.D. 28–29 would have been 32 (since there in no 0 year, dates move from 1 B.C. to A.D. 1). Obviously, an age of 32 or 33 easily falls within the flexible parameters of ὡσεὶ.

The coregency device also flies in the face of Roman custom of that day. Unquestionably, Tiberius had *proconsular imperium* over the provinces along with Augustus from A.D. 12 on, but no source—Roman or otherwise—claims Tiberius as full *princeps* or emperor before his succession in 14. Nor was Tiberius the sort to poach on Augustus's turf once he controlled the empire: no shred of evidence exists in any of his inscriptions or coinage to support such an overlap. Certainly Tiberius knew he could never implement such a claim since he was an unpopular emperor following no less than "the Father of the Fatherland."

In terms of historiography, the coregency also has no basis. The principal sources for this era—Tacitus, Suetonius, and Dio Cassius—all date Tiberius's reign to full calendar years after the death of Augustus, as do the epigraphy, coinage, and papyri.[20] And since Luke-Acts is addressed to a "most excellent [κράτιστε] Theophilus" (Luke 1:3), a form of address used elsewhere by Luke only for a Roman official (Acts

19. Compare Matt 14:21; John 4:6, 6:10; 19:14. Other references in Luke include an interval of "about an hóur" before the third challenge to Peter in Caiaphas's courtyard (Luke 22:59) and "about the ninth hour" for Cornelius's vision in Caesarea (Acts 10:3).

20. See Fotheringham, "Astronomy and Technical Chronology," 146ff. See especially his reference to Oscar Kästner, "De Aeris quae ab imperio Caesaris Octaviani constituto initium duxerint" (Inaugural diss., Leipzig, 1890), on double-dated coins from Antioch and Seleucia, which show Tiberius' regnal years in terms of the Actian era. All date to his succession in A.D. 14. Significantly, many scholars posit an Antiochene provenance for Luke-Acts.

23:26, 24:3), the gospel was probably written for gentile Greco-Roman consumption and would hardly have ignored normal Roman chronology. Finally, evidence given below will demonstrate that to date the Crucifixion in A.D. 33 (rather than in 30) would extend Jesus' ministry too far—if it had already begun in A.D. 26 on the basis of a coregency for the "fifteenth year."

"Forty-six Years This Temple Has Been Built" (John 2:20)

When Jerusalemites requested a sign from Jesus at the first Passover, he responded, "Destroy this temple, and in three days I will raise it up" (John 2:19). To which his opponents replied (in traditional translation), "It has taken forty-six years to build this temple, and will you raise it up in three days?" Calculating the start of Herod's Temple construction as 19 B.C. (from Josephus), Finegan posits A.D. 27/28 as the date of the statement *if* a continuing building operation is what the passage intends—or A.D. 29/30 if dating from the completion of the sanctuary, which was built in one year and five months according to Josephus (*Antiquities* 15:420–21).[21] The latter interpretation would seem indicated by the verb οἰκοδομήθη 'was built', an aorist passive denoting a completed building operation, not one still going on. If it actually took one year and five months to build the temple proper or sanctuary (ναός, used in both John 2:20 and Josephus), then A.D. 29/30 is probable, and the meaning of the Jews' response is: "Rebuild in three days something that has stood for forty-six years?!"[22]

"Not Yet Fifty Years Old" (John 8:57)

Jesus told a hostile crowd, "Your father Abraham rejoiced that he was to see my day; he saw it and was glad"; to which they responded derisively, "You are not yet fifty years old, and have you seen Abraham?" (John 8:57). This verse has extremely low utility for any chronology of the life of Jesus, and of the church fathers only Irenaeus, strangely, thought otherwise (*Against Heresies* 2:22:6). Irenaeus's claim for a much older Jesus would have been impressive had he reported it as a common tradition, perhaps via Polycarp and others, but he does not. Instead, his sole source is this very passage, and his purpose is theological rather than chronological. The context shows a crowd furious enough to stone Jesus inside the temple (John 8:59), and the meaning of this reference is "Abraham died centuries ago, but this

---

21. Finegan, *Biblical Chronology*, 276–80.
22. I have discussed this issue in detail in my "Sejanus, Pilate, and the Date of the Crucifixion," 4–5; see also Finegan, *Biblical Chronology*, 276–80.

TABLE 1.   *Chronology of the Life of Jesus*

Date	Event
Nov.–Dec. 5 B.C.	Nativity
Nov.–Dec. 1 B.C.	Jesus' fourth birthday } (Included to demonstrate
Nov.–Dec. A.D. 1	Jesus' fifth birthday } absence of the year "0")
Nov.–Dec. A.D. 28	Jesus' thirty-second birthday
A.D. 29	Fifteenth year of Tiberius (by Roman reckoning), extending from 1 January to 31 December A.D. 29 (Luke 3:1)
	Ministry of John the Baptist early in the year and extending throughout A.D. 29
	Baptism and start of public ministry of Jesus, probably in the fall, since the Jordan valley is extremely hot during the summer months; Jesus "about thirty" (Luke 3:23)
Nov.–Dec. A.D. 29	Jesus' thirty-third birthday
A.D. 30	First Passover, forty-six years after the priests finished building the temple edifice proper (John 2:20)
A.D. 31	Second Passover
A.D. 32	Third Passover
A.D. 33	Final Passover
Friday, 3 April A.D. 33	Crucifixion

deceiver isn't even one century old, or even half a century old!" The attraction of round numbers only reinforces the comments on Luke 3:23 above.

The Crucifixion

The net results of all the chronological references above are incorporated in Table 1.[23] Briefly summarized, with the mission of John the Baptist beginning in A.D. 28/29, and Jesus' first public Passover in 29 or 30, the Passover of Good Friday should have been at least two and probably three Passovers later, since three Passovers are specifically cited in the Fourth Gospel (2:13, 6:4, 11:55), while a fourth is implied.

23. Compare the similar tables in Finegan, *Biblical Chronology*, 270 and 301.

This would allow a range of dates from A.D. 31 to 33 for the Crucifixion. But which year is the most probable?

The Fourth Gospel (19:14) states that Jesus was crucified on "the day of Preparation for the Passover" when the Passover lamb was slain—defined in Exod 12:6 as Nisan 14. And since all the gospels report Jesus' Crucifixion on the day before the Sabbath (Saturday), it is only necessary to determine when Nisan 14 fell on a Friday in the years appropriate (specified above). J. K. Fotheringham and others have calculated this date and found that Nisan 14 fell on a Friday in both A.D. 30 and 33: 7 April A.D. 30 and 3 April A.D. 33.[24]

The evidence for the latter is overpowering. The former would demand resurrection of the moribund device of a coregency between Augustus and Tiberius to make room for three Passovers prior to the Crucifixion. There is also fresh evidence to support A.D. 33 from the context of Roman imperial politics. In another study, I have demonstrated the startling shift in imperial policy vis-à-vis the Jews that took place after 18 October A.D. 31, when L. Aelius Sejanus, Tiberius' anti-Semitic Prefect of the Praetorian Guard, was executed. Briefly stated, Pontius Pilate's aggressive, anti-Judaic conduct prior to A.D. 31 contrasts sharply with his defensive posture after that date, in accord with Tiberius's new directives to favor Jews throughout the Roman Empire. In this context, the prosecution's threat on Good Friday at the trial of Jesus—"If you release this man, you are not Caesar's friend; every one who makes himself a king sets himself against Caesar" (John 19:12)— would have made no sense whatever prior to A.D. 31 and Pilate would cheerfully have disregarded it. But it reflects perfectly the political climate after that date and the cowed reaction of the Roman governor.[25]

If the Nativity has its star, the Crucifixion has its mysterious darkness. Phlegon, a Greek from Caria writing a chronology soon after A.D. 137, reported that in the fourth year of the 202d Olympiad there was "the greatest eclipse of the sun" and that "it became night in the sixth hour of the day [i.e., noon] so that the stars even appeared in the heavens. There was a great earthquake in Bithynia, and many things were overturned in Nicaea." An eclipse, of course, was impossible at

---

24. Fotheringham, "Astronomy and Technical Chronology," 146ff.; and R. A. Parker and W. H. Dubberstein, *Babylonian Chronology: 626 B.C.–A.D. 75* (Providence: Brown University, 1956) 34–69.

25. The detailed arguments set forth in my "Sejanus, Pilate, and the Date of the Crucifixion" have not been refuted to date. See also my "The Episode of the Golden Roman Shields at Jerusalem," *HTR* 62 (1969) 109–21; and *Pontius Pilate* (Garden City: Doubleday, 1968).

that time, but how intriguing that Year 4 of the 202d Olympiad should be A.D. 33![26]

Finally, and most recently, C. J. Humphreys and W. G. Waddington, using refined astronomical calculations, have not only reaffirmed Fotheringham's conclusion that 7 April A.D. 30 and 3 April A.D. 33 are the only possible calendrical candidates for the first Good Friday, but they also strongly support the latter by citing a lunar eclipse that took place that evening, thereby corroborating the reference in Peter's speech to Pentecost about the "moon turning into blood" (Acts 2:20).[27]

On many bases, then, 3 April A.D. 33 makes a strong claim as the date of the Crucifixion.

Chronological Conclusions

The birth of Jesus is most widely dated between 7 and 4 B.C., but further refinement within this range now seems possible. The terminus ad quem, the first week of April 4 B.C., must certainly be advanced by several months at the very least. Too much occurred between the birth of Jesus and the death of Herod to crowd into the early weeks of 4 B.C., as seen in Table 2. The events listed here required an estimated minimum of fourteen weeks—and the sojourn in Egypt could have been considerably longer—thereby excluding 4 B.C., since Herod lived only thirteen or fourteen weeks in this year.

But what of the terminus a quo? How far back into 5 or 6 B.C., or even earlier, was the birth of Jesus? Certainly Herod's massacre of infants "two years old and under" (Matt 2:16) establishes 7 B.C. as the limit, even though this refers to the star rather than the birth of Jesus and is of little help chronologically.[28]

A cluster of evidence, however, urges a date for the birth of Jesus as late as possible, up to the forward limit. The qualifier ὡσεὶ for Jesus being "about thirty years of age" at the start of his ministry will stretch only so far, and a dating back to 6 or 7 B.C. would make him 34 or 35 at

26. My translation from the fragmentary thirteenth book of Phlegon, *Olympiades he Chronika*, in *Rerum naturalium scriptores graeci minores* (ed. O. Keller; Leipzig: Teubner, 1877), 1:101. An actual eclipse of the sun was impossible on Nisan 14 since the Passover occurred at the time of the full moon.

27. C. J. Humphreys and W. G. Waddington, "Dating the Crucifixion," *Nature* 306 (22 Dec. 1983) 743-46. See also their essay in this volume.

28. While the historicity of the infant massacre has been called into question, along with most of the Matthean Nativity account, arguments for its validity are impressive; see my "The Infant Massacre—History or Myth?" *Christianity Today* 20 (19 December 1975) 7-10; and R. T. France, "Herod and the Children of Bethlehem," *NovT* 21 (1979) 98-120.

TABLE 2.   *Events between Jesus' Birth and Herod's Death*

Event	Number of Weeks
Purification of Mary and Presentation of Jesus Lev 12:2–4 specifies that a woman is ritually unclean for 33 days after the circumcision of a male child and can come to the sanctuary only after 40 days have elapsed. Six weeks includes two days for travel to and from Jerusalem.	6
Visit of the Magi Included here are Herod's awaiting the return of the Magi and the slaughter of the infants in Bethlehem. (See n 28 for a discussion of the historicity of the massacre.)	1
Flight to Egypt and sojourn there Even if Jesus' family merely fled over the border to Gaza—which seems doubtful according to any existing traditions—a minimal duration of three or four weeks is required (not including the return to Judea).	3 or 4
Herod's final illness This is an arbitrary guess for the duration of Herod's incapacitating final illness, which Josephus describes in repulsive detail. Herod tried desperately to cure himself, primarily at Jericho and Callirrhoe (the hot springs at the northeastern end of the Dead Sea). The Magi could hardly have found him in Jerusalem at this time or, if this had been the time of one of his last visits to the Jerusalem palace, surely Matthew would have made reference to Herod's malady.	3
Total:	13 or 14 weeks

that point, and thus a candidate for the next round number, "about forty years of age." Moreover, the testimony of the church fathers—disappointingly conflicting in matters chronological, particularly as regards the Crucifixion date—achieves some unanimity in assigning the years 3 or 2 B.C. for the birth of Jesus by correspondence with the regnal years of Augustus and other Roman emperors.[29]

While 3/2 B.C. is, of course, too late for the Nativity and may well have been based on counting backward from the Lukan "about thirty years of age"—the fathers using the same sources as we do—other evidence also appears to juxtapose the events of the Nativity into a rather short time frame. Justin Martyr, for example, claims the Magi visited "as soon as the child was born" (*Dialogue with Trypho* 88). In any case, there is much forward pressure on the date of Nativity, which

29. Finegan, *Biblical Chronology*, 222–30.

brings December 5 B.C. into focus. (This is, of course, "embarrassing" because it seems so very "uncritical" to opt for a date like this, which, in terms of our present celebration on December 25, was determined in the fourth century!)

If, however, the year 5 B.C. is posited as the twelvemonth that best satisfies all the evidence, is any further refinement possible aside from the forward pressure above? Finegan has demonstrated some patristic evidence for a spring conception and winter birth of Jesus.[30] It is especially interesting to note that John Chrysostom's defense of the Western date for Christmas, December 25, seems to have turned the tide against the Eastern date, January 6 (*Homily on Philogonius*, Dec 20, A.D. 386). Chrysostom, basing his argument on the earlier claim of Hippolytus, cleverly reckons back to the announcement in the temple to Zechariah that he would father John the Baptist. Luke identifies Zechariah as a "priest of the division of Abijah" (1:5), and Chrysostom assumed that he was high priest at the time and the occasion involved was the Day of Atonement followed by the Feast of Tabernacles (Tishri 10–15 or September 20–25). The Annunciation to Mary took place six months later according to Luke 1:26, or around March 25, with Christmas of course nine months later.

This interesting calculation (only sketched in the paragraph above) is based on the premise that Zechariah was high priest, but there is no evidence for this or the claimed festivals involved. Alfred Edersheim worked instead from Luke's reference that Zechariah's priestly division, Abijah, might be datable in terms of service in the temple. A Mishna tradition, *b. Ta ͨ an.* 29a, states that at the time the temple was destroyed, the course of Jehoiarib was on duty, the first of the twenty-four priestly courses (1 Chr 24:7–18), of which Abijah's was the eighth. The destruction occurred on 9 or 10 Ab A.D. 70 (August 4 or 5); this date is confirmed by Josephus (*Jewish War* 6:220, 250, where *Lous* equals *Ab*). Counting the priestly courses backward to 6 B.C., Edersheim found the Abijah course on duty the week of October 2–9, quite close to Chrysostom's reckoning, although he rightly admits that "absolute reliance cannot be placed on such calculations."[31] (The course of Abijah would also have been on duty twenty-six weeks earlier.)

A preliminary computer study that I authorized finds February 10 and July 28 in the year 6 B.C. as the two dates on which the course of

30. Ibid. However, arguments as to when sheep would have been in the fields are indeterminate, since sheep in the Bethlehem area destined for temple sacrifice were continually in the fields.

31. A. Edersheim, *The Life and Times of Jesus the Messiah* (London: Longmans, Green, 1883; repr. Grand Rapids: Eerdmans, 1936), 2:705.

Abijah would have begun its week of duty in the temple, using the same bases for calculation as above.[32] If the temple episode were dated approximately August 1 and Elizabeth conceived "after these days" (Luke 1:24)—two weeks?—Jesus' conception would come six (apparently lunar) months later.[33] This would move the Annunciation to Mary from March to February, and the Nativity from December to November.

A recent study by Roger T. Beckwith, however, denies that the twenty-four priestly courses followed one another inexorably regardless of the year involved.[34] While a six-year cycle based on the solar year controlled these courses at Qumran, the orthodox lunar calendar at Jerusalem seems to have compelled a recommencing of the cycle each year, beginning with the course of Jehoiarib on the sabbath on or immediately preceding Tishri 1. But because leap-year months (Second Adar) had to be included so frequently in the Jerusalem lunar calendar, and the starting point for the twenty-four courses and their progress is still much debated, this device has only questionable utility in establishing the Nativity month.

A better solution may be to recall again the earliest patristic date for the first Christmas, that given by Clement of Alexandria in his *Stromateis* (written about A.D. 194). Not only is it the earliest, but it is also the most exactly specified date: "From the birth of Christ . . . to the death of Commodus are, in all, a hundred and ninety-four years, one month, thirteen days" (1:21:145). Since Commodus was murdered on 31 December 192, this fixes Clement's date for the Nativity as 18 November 3 B.C. While this is two years too late—an error forgiveable in the absence of published records in those days—what is impressive are the fixed points involved in producing this date, for which the *time of year* would be much more easily remembered by the Egyptian church than the exact tabulation of the years since the Nativity. Clement knew categorically the date of Commodus's death since he wrote just two years afterward, and the date itself was unforgettable since it was the last day of the year in the Julian calendar. When he calculated the Nativity on November 18, then—in specific relation to so fixed a terminus as the end of the year—he gives not only the earliest patristic reference to the Nativity, but probably the most accurate one in terms

32. Courtesy of E. W. Faulstich of Ruthven, Iowa.

33. At the time of the Annunciation of Mary, Elizabeth was in her sixth month (Luke 1:26); but Mary stayed with her about three months and still left before the baby was born (Luke 1:56), suggesting a pregnancy of ten lunar months (280 days). See the discussion in Brown, *Birth of the Messiah*, 264.

34. R. T. Beckwith, "St. Luke, the Date of Christmas, and the Priestly Courses at Qumran," *RevQ* 9 (1977) 73-96.

of month and day. It also corresponds perfectly with the parameters of the chronology of the life of Christ as detailed above.

Because December 25 barely escapes the improbable time limitation of 4 B.C. and because it is suspect as coincidental with what was then deemed to be the winter solstice, not to mention its late observance in the early church, the November date is clearly preferable. In any case, a date late in 5 B.C. for the Nativity seems an optimal conclusion on the basis of all surviving evidence in the New Testament and beyond. A resulting chronology for the life of Jesus appears in Table 1.

Calendars and the Crucifixion

Crucifixion in A.D. 36:
The Keystone for Dating the Birth of Jesus

Nikos Kokkinos

If the evidence were such that one theory of Nativity chronology could be established to the exclusion of all others, the whole question would have been settled long ago. The question of the date of Jesus' birth, however, remains unsettled and therefore it must be admitted that at least part of the evidence is not in its purest condition. Once the task of reconsidering the evidence is carried out, several different interpretations may legitimately be made. Whether, of course, the interpretation presented here is preferable to others will depend on whether it will make the best sense of the greatest number of details.

It seems of vital importance to emphasize the need of reexamining the date of the Crucifixion, since the extant sources are far more interested in how Jesus' life ended than how it began. Only in the light of a reassessed date for the Crucifixion can the date of Jesus' birth be approached under positive perspectives.

Crucifixion in 36 and Josephus

The Gospels place the death of John the Baptist during the time that Herodias was living with Antipas. According to Josephus, Antipas proposed marriage to Herodias and it was arranged that on his return from a journey to Rome, he would divorce his wife (the daughter of Aretas the king of the Nabateans) and marry her. It is possible to establish the date of this journey using the account of Josephus. During Antipas's absence, Aretas's daughter learned the full details of his arrangements with Herodias and on his return she fled to her father (*Antiquities* 18:110–12). Antipas had been married to her for a long time

Nikos Kokkinos is Dorothea Grey Senior Scholar at St. Hugh's College, Oxford University.

(*Antiquities* 18:109), perhaps some twenty years. It had been a diplomatic alliance—possibly contrived by Augustus himself, who seems to have favored intermarriages among his client kings (Suetonius, *Augustus* 48)—and throughout its existence there had been no trouble along that borderland of the Roman Empire. Yet, as soon as the alliance between the two kings was broken, Aretas exploited the pretext of a border dispute and proclaimed war on Antipas, the preparation of which was accelerated by Aretas knowing that the Romans were engaged in a struggle against Artabanus III, king of Parthia (Tacitus, *Annals* 6:31–37, 41–44; Dio Cassius 58:26:1–4). In the ensuing battle Antipas's whole army was destroyed and he was forced to appeal to Rome. Tiberius ordered Vitellius to declare war on Aretas, but Vitellius, on his way to carry out this order, was notified of the death of the emperor and so decided to abandon his mission (*Antiquities* 18:124).

Tiberius died in March A.D. 37 (Tacitus, *Annals* 6:50; Suetonius, *Tiberius* 73). Thus, as a logical consequence, the war of Aretas is dated to 36, the death of John the Baptist to 35, and the journey of Antipas to Rome and his subsequent marriage to Herodias to 33 or 34. Therefore, Josephus provides all the historical elements needed for dating the Crucifixion of Jesus. The Gospels are clear that the death of John preceded Jesus', and John's death in 35 places the Crucifixion in 36, the last possible year due to the ending of Pilate's prefecture.

It has been presumed by many that by the phrase "the beginning of enmity" (*Antiquities* 18:113) Josephus means the dismissal of Aretas's daughter.[1] However, Josephus really indicates that the two kings were in dispute over frontier issues, but Aretas was avoiding military action since Antipas was married to his daughter (cf. Zonaras, *Annals* 6:6). The frontier questions were the initial cause of the enmity: ὁ δὲ ἀρχὴν ἔχθρας ταύτην ποιησάμενος περί τε ὅρων ἐν γῇ τῇ Γαβαλίτιδι, '[Aretas] made this the start of a quarrel: a dispute about boundaries in the district of Gabalitis' (*Antiquities* 18:113). Once his daughter was dismissed, Aretas was no longer under any obligation to avoid war and hence he could lead his army against Antipas.[2] This view was expressed as early as 1866 by T. Keim: "The *initium dissidii* is immediately followed by action: Aretas at once breaks with Antipas, brings on the controversy about the boundary, collects, troops, and strikes the blow: *initium belli.*"[3]

---

1. See, for example, C. J. Cadoux, "A Tentative Synthetic Chronology of the Apostolic Age," *JBL* 56 (1937) 181.

2. Cf. A. Negev, "The Nabateans and the Provincia Arabia," *Politische Geschichte (Provinzen und Randvölker: Syrien, Palästina, Arabien)* (ed. H. Temporini and W. Haase; Aufstieg und Niedergang der römischen Welt: Principat 8; Berlin: de Gruyter, 1977) 568.

3. T. Keim, *The History of Jesus of Nazara* (trans. A. Ransom; London: Williams and Norgate, 1883), 6:232.

It has been further argued that it should not be obligatory for Aretas's revenge to follow hard on his daughter's return.[4] One could suppose he needed time to collect troops, yet it is evident that Aretas was one of the most powerful independent rulers of the East and he would not have needed a lengthy period for preparations. As K. Lake explained, "Political or strategical reason for a long delay on the part of Aretas cannot be found."[5] I would also suggest that on psychological grounds it would have been impossible for an outraged and insulted father, who had the power to act, to have waited longer than a year or two before taking active measures.

The declaration by the Jews that Antipas's defeat was a judgment of God for killing John the Baptist (*Antiquities* 18:119) lends final support for my chronology. To argue that the Jews felt God's revenge did not occur immediately after the misdeed is deceptive.[6] Circumstances in the recent rather than the distant past would be more likely to make the Jews attribute divine punishments.

For example, God's punishment for the murder of Onias the rainmaker arrived immediately, as a vehement windstorm destroyed the crops of the whole country (*Antiquities* 14:25–28). It also did not take long for Agrippa I to die as God's avengement after he had killed James the son of Zebedee (Acts 12:2, 23). Again, it was soon after the execution of Mariamme I, ordered by Herod the Great in the presence of his close friends, that a pestilential disease arose that destroyed many of Herod's friends, afflicting him later as well. This too was seen as a direct expression of God's anger at the treatment of Mariamme (*Antiquities* 15:243). Josephus explicitly states at one point that the people suspected misfortunes emanated from the wrath of God, especially when such misfortunes occurred at a time appropriate to the event.[7] His statement concerns the attempt Herod made upon the tomb of David, soon after which the state of affairs in his household became worse, making the Jews attribute it to a divine punishment (*Antiquities* 16:188). Thus, the war won by Aretas in 36, which made the Jews instantly denounce Antipas for killing John the Baptist, should leave no doubt that the death of John took place in 35, immediately preceding this calamity.

4. E. M. Smallwood, *The Jews under Roman Rule: From Pompey to Diocletian* (Leiden: Brill, 1976) 185, suggests ten years between her return and Aretas's war; A. W. Zumpt, *Das Geburtsjahr Christi* (Leipzig: B. G. Teubner, 1869), 261 suggest twenty years.

5. K. Lake, "The Date of Herod's Marriage with Herodias and the Chronology of the Gospels," *Expositor*, 8th ser., 4 (1912) 469.

6. H. W. Hoehner, *Herod Antipas* (Cambridge: Cambridge University, 1972) 126.

7. See *Antiquities* 18:255, 308–9 and *Jewish War* 7:451–53 for further examples in Josephus of immediate divine punishment for misdeeds.

The hypothesis that Josephus may have introduced the death of John as a "flashback," or in other words without regard to chronological order, can no longer stand in view of the historical implications examined above or in light of a grammatical scrutiny of the passage.[8] Although Josephus from time to time does present such flashbacks in his narrative, John's death is not one of them. The present tense is used in both passages (κτείνει in *Antiquities* 18:117, κτίννυται in 18:119), and clearly indicates this is a current action, thus following a smooth chronological order.[9]

What is significant for the dating of John's death in 35 is that the Slavonic version of Josephus combines additional evidence, verifying this understanding of the Greek.[10] The Slavonic text, which, although containing the anachronistic tendency of introducing John the Baptist at the time of Archelaus, has John dying after Philip the Tetrarch's demise in 33/34. (This anachronistic tendency does not make the Slavonic version chronologically unreliable; for example, Luke's writings contain anachronistic tendencies such as the placing of Theudas [Acts 5:36; cf. *Antiquities* 20:97], but this does not make the whole text of Luke unsuitable source for dating purposes.)

In addition, the Slavonic version has Herodias as the wife of Philip the Tetrarch previous to her marriage to Antipas, thus dating her last marriage to 34.[11] This would harmonize with the Gospels, which timidly call Herodias's former husband, Philip.[12] Herodias's marriage to Philip the Tetrarch ties in accurately with the expedition of Antipas to Rome in 33/34 which was apparently connected with the death of Philip and Antipas's succession to his possessions. Perhaps Antipas undertook this

---

8. H. St. J. Thackeray, *Josephus: The Man and the Historian* (New York: Jewish Institute of Religion, 1929) 131, and Hoehner, *Herod Antipas*, 128, posit a "flashback" as the solution to this problem.

9. The English translation in the Loeb Classical Library edition is wrong. Here, as with other important passages, uncritical use of the Loeb translations has been partly responsible for the creation of paradoxes.

10. See R. Eisler, *The Messiah Jesus and John the Baptist* (London: Methuen, 1931) 229.

11. J. M. Creed, "The Slavonic Version of Josephus's History of the Jewish War," *HTR* 25 (1932) 307.

12. Herodias's former husband is called Philip in Mark 6:17 and Matt 14:3, with strong textual support in Luke 3:19 (manuscripts A, C, K, W, Ψ 33, 565, 1424, and others; and the Peshitta, Harclean, Sahidic (a few manuscripts) and Bohairic versions); cf. Luke 3:1 and Origen, *Commentary on Matthew* 10:21. This Philip is the only Philip who existed; the so-called "Herod-Philip" is an imaginary person created to resolve this apparent contradiction. See my article "Which Salome Did Aristobulus Marry?" *PEQ* 118 (1986) 33–50, for a detailed analysis of the problem of Herodias's marriages.

journey at the urging of Herodias, as he did on a later occasion in 38/39 (*Antiquities* 18:240–46).

Crucifixion in 36 and Luke

It has been said, unjustifiably, that the theory placing the Crucifixion in 36 makes havoc of the Gospels' chronology. In reality, all other theories make havoc of the Gospels' chronology, let alone of the chronology in Josephus.

Emil Schürer, disturbed by the implications of the late dating of the Crucifixion, stated that this falters on Luke's statement (3:1), for even if Luke was mistaken he would have hardly erred by as much as five years.[13] However, Luke does not suggest that the commencement of Jesus' ministry occurred in the fifteenth year of Tiberius, but that this was when John began to preach: Ἐν ἔτει δὲ πεντεκαιδεκάτῳ τῆς ἡγεμονίας Τιβερίου . . . ἐγένετο ῥῆμα θεοῦ ἐπὶ Ἰωάννην, 'In the fifteenth year of the reign of Tiberius . . . the word of God came to John.'

The Fourth Gospel may appear to indicate that Jesus' ministry commenced almost immediately after the Baptist began to preach, but one has to keep in mind that that same gospel places the cleansing of the temple episode almost at the outset of his public life, instead of at the end of it. The Synoptics are united in maintaining that the bulk of Jesus' mission came during the closing stages of the Baptist's preaching (Matt 4:12, 17; Mark 1:14; Luke 3:20, 4:16; cf. Acts 13:25). Luke is not even clear whether Jesus was really baptized by John,[14] and the ministry of Jesus began in the synagogue of his home town according to Acts 10:37.

However, although one could assert that Jesus was baptized by John, perhaps in the early part of John's career (despite the fact that "all of the people were baptized before Jesus," Luke 3:21), there is no

---

13. E. Schürer, *A History of the Jewish People in the Age of Jesus Christ* (trans. J. Macpherson; Edinburgh: Clark, 1890), 2:31. The decision of the revisers of the new edition (ed. G. Vermes and F. Millar; Edinburgh: Clark, 1973) of Schürer's work to omit his original discussion (2:30–32) on the date of the Crucifixion is wholly inadmissible. They simply refer the reader (1:350 n. 32) to Hoehner's work (*Herod Antipas*, 307–12), which, although fairly up to date on this aspect, can hardly justify the omission. Schürer, disturbed by the theory of the late Crucifixion (A.D. 35) proposed in his time by T. Keim, complained that Keim had "completely turned [chronology] upside down" (2:30). It seems to me, however, that Schürer demurred, not because of contrary evidence, but because Keim's thesis was too new and unprecedented. Schürer uneasily declared that he would continue to date the Crucifixion to A.D. 30 (2:32).

14. See J. Van Goudoever, *Biblical Calendars* (Leiden: Brill, 1961) 268.

support for the idea that Jesus' ministry commenced in the fifteenth year of Tiberius. Evidently, it could not have begun in any of the immediately following years, for Jesus himself spoke of the duration of John's work that occurred before Jesus began public life: Ἀπὸ δὲ τῶν ἡμερῶν Ἰωάννου τοῦ Βαπτιστοῦ ἕως ἄρτι ἡ βασιλεία τῶν οὐρανῶν βιάζεται, 'From the days of John the Baptist until now, the kingdom of heaven has been forcefully advancing' (Matt 11:12; cf. Luke 16:16).[15] Between the baptism and the commencement of the ministry of Jesus, a substantial interval is surely essential; and a five-year interval, in connection with Josephus's chronological arrangement of John's death, must be seriously taken into account.

In conclusion, whereas the theory of the late Crucifixion was once said to be in collapse before Luke 3:1, it now appears reasonable to say that at this point it is far from collapsing. To the contrary, this is the only chronological framework that may canonically verify that Jesus was active when a sabbatical year overlapped with a Roman census year; all other theories fail to do this.[16] The year 33/34 was sabbatical, an echo of which might be discerned in Jesus' reading of Isa 61:1, 2 in the synagogue (Luke 4:17-20), in the incident of the plucking of grain by Jesus and his disciples on the Sabbath (Luke 6:1-5), and perhaps in the miracle of feeding the 5,000 (Luke 9:10-17). The following year 34/35 was a Roman census year and taxes were collected in 35/36— a most probable reason for the hostility toward the tax-collector Zacchaeus (Luke 19:1-10), the timeliness of the question put to Jesus in Jerusalem, "Shall we pay tribute to Caesar?" (Luke 20:21-25), and the unfairness of the system as reflected in Jesus' words (Luke 8:18, 19:26).

The sabbatical cycle was decisively established by B. Zuckermann as early as 1857, and sporadic attempts to disrupt his definition of these years by moving the cycle forward one year have not succeeded.[17] The evidence for certain years is strong enough to require no change, and the two main objections that have so far been advanced against Zuckermann cannot be justified.

The first objection is that Simon Bar Giora attacked Idumaea in the winter of 68/69 and his army ravaged the land "like a host of locusts,"

15. Cf. C. King, "The Outlines of New Testament Chronology," *CQR* 278 (1945) 134.

16. See. H. J. Schonfield, *The Pentecost Revolution* (London: Macdonald and Jane's, 1974), 54; and my *The Enigma of Jesus the Galilean* (Athens: Chryssi Tomi, 1980) 64-65 [Greek].

17. B. Zuckermann, *Über Sabbatjahrcyclus und Jobelperiode* (Jahresbericht des jüdisch-theologischen Seminars "Fränckelscher Stiftung"; Breslau: W. G. Korn, 1857).

consuming all that grew in the country (*Jewish War* 4:535), which would mean that the earth had been sown that year. However, the sabbatical laws affected only the land of Palestine and had no application in Edom or in any other region annexed to Palestine.[18] The second objection concerns the Jewish demonstration before Petronius in 40, which Josephus dates to the seedtime in early autumn (*Antiquities* 18:272, *Jewish War* 2:200), meaning again that the earth had been sown that year. However, E. M. Smallwood, from the evidence in Philo (*Embassy to Gaius* 249), showed that the demonstration actually took place during harvest-time in the early summer of 40, therefore posing no problem for the sabbatical year in 40/41.[19] On the contrary, it is my belief that the evidence for the commencement of a sabbatical year in Tishri 40 accurately explains the anxiety of Petronius to urge the Jews to return to their fields for the harvest earlier the same year, which would have been vital in view of the forthcoming sabbatical year.

A recent attack on Zuckermann's cycle by B. Z. Wacholder was likewise unsuccessful. The evidence that Wacholder produced agrees no better with his proposition than with Zuckermann's; in fact, Wacholder is in error when he dates a Hebrew tombstone discovered in 1924 by John Philby to A.D. 434/435.[20] The inscription is dated to the 364th year of the Hurban era, which it calls the first year of Shemitah, or in other words a postsabbatical year. The Hurban era commenced in A.D. 70/71— which is year 1 of the era not year 0 as Wacholder would have it— hence, year 364 is the equivalent of A.D. 433/434, and since this was a postsabbatical year the inscription testifies that the previous year was sabbatical. This is in disagreement with Wacholder, but in total agreement with Zuckermann's cycle.

The provincial Roman census cycle has been established by the discovery of the Egyptian papyri, which document censuses in 20/21 (*P.Oxy.* 2:254), 34/35 (*P.Oxy.* 2:256), and 48/49 (*P.Oxy.* 2:255).[21] H. J. Cadbury holds that after the census of 6/7 in Judea there is no trace of a census in 20/21, 34/35, 48/49, or 62/63[22]; however, it seems clear that

18. S. Zeitlin, "Megillat Taanit as a Source for Jewish Chronology and History in the Hellenistic and Roman Periods," *JQR* 9 (1918) 101. Cf. m. Šeb. 6:1.

19. Smallwood, *Philonis Alexandrini: Legatio ad Gaium* (Leiden: Brill, 1961) 283.

20. B. Z. Wacholder, "The Calendar of Sabbatical Cycles during the Second Temple and the Early Rabbinic Period," *HUCA* 44 (1973) 182.

21. For the census in 34/35 see also S. Eitrem, "Drei neue griechische Papyri," *Philologus* 71 (1912) 24–25 no. 1.

22. H. J. Cadbury, "Acts of the Apostles," *The Beginnings of Christianity* (ed. F. J. Foakes Jackson and K. Lake; London: Macmillan, 1933), 4:62 n. 4.

there is enough indirect evidence for these censuses. After all, regularity of censuses in Egypt—a necessity for the exaction of a capitation tax— would imply the regularity of censuses in Judea, Syria, and the other Eastern provinces. Despite the fortuitous nature of this evidence,[23] such regularity can be demonstrated directly in Gaul (Livy, *Periochae* 134, 138; Tacitus, *Annals* 1:31, 33, 14:46; Dio Cassius 59:22; and Frontinus, *Strategemata* 1:1:8). That Syria and Judea must have followed the same Egyptian fourteen-year cycle in the first century A.D. is made clear by the statements of Ulpian (*De Censibus 2, Digesta* 50:15:3) that men in Syria were liable to this tax from the age of fourteen.[24] The indirect evidence for this cycle is easily traced:

1. Census year 6/7 (collecting year 7/8). When Luke (2:2) refers to the census of Quirinius (during which Judas the Galilaean was active; Acts 5:37, *Antiquities* 18:4), he refers to it as ἀπογραφὴ πρώτη 'first census', which undoubtedly means that others regularly followed.

2. Census year 20/21 (collecting year 21/22). Tacitus (*Annals* 2:42) relates that in 17 a Jewish delegation, along with a delegation from Syria, made the long journey to Rome to protest against the excessive taxes that were being levied by the Roman governors and to ask for a diminution of the tribute. Apparently, this was a most appropriate time in view of the forthcoming census year in 20/21. Germanicus in 18/19 was sent to effect the needed reforms in the East and many tributes were diminished (Tacitus, *Annals* 2:56).

3. Census year 34/35 (collecting year 35/36). At Passover 36 Jesus was asked whether people should pay the Roman tribute, the κῆνσος 'census, census tax' (Matt 22:17, Mark 12:14). Jesus asked to be shown τὸ νόμισμα τοῦ κήνσου 'the coin used for paying the census tax'.[25] The Palmyra Tariff inscription shows that the census tax had to be paid in Roman currency, and Jesus was accordingly presented with a Roman silver denarius (δηνάριον; Matt 22:19, Mark 12:15). Other indirect evidence for a census in 34/35 is the

---

23. Cf. P. A. Brunt, "The Revenues of Rome," *JRS* 71 (1981) 164.

24. B. P. Grenfell and A. S. Hunt, *The Oxyrhynchus Papyri* (London: Egypt Exploration Fund, 1899), 2:207–8.

25. κῆνσος is also found in *BGU* 917:6 (*Aegyptische Urkunden aus den Königlichen Museen zu Berlin: Griechische Urkunden*, vol. 3 [Berlin: Weidmann, 1903]) and *P.Amh.* 83:2 (*The Amherst Papyri*, vol. 1 [ed. B. P. Grenfell and A. S. Hunt; London: Frowde, 1901]); cf. F. W. Hasluck, "Inscriptions from Bizye," *Annual of the British School at Athens* 12 (1905) 177–78 no. 2. The Palmyra Tariff inscription is published as text no. 629 in *Orientis graeci inscriptiones selectae* (ed. W. Dittenberger; Leipzig: Hirzel, 1903–5).

refusal of the Cietae (in Cilicia) to pay their census tax in 36 (Tacitus, *Annals* 6:41), and the reduction of certain Judean taxes even further when Vitellius finally visited Jerusalem after the deposition of Pilate (*Antiquities* 18:90).

4. Census year 48/49 (collecting year 49/50). Josephus confirms, without giving a full account, that Simon and James were crucified in 49 (*Antiquities* 20:102). They were the sons of Judas the Galilean, who had resisted the payment of the taxes at the time of the first census (see no. 1 above). It is reasonable to assume that Simon and James followed in the footsteps of their father, resisting the payment of the census to the Romans. Apparently, at the same time (48/49), the Cietae of Cilicia again refused to pay the census tax, with the result of the complete destruction of their fortress by the governor Q. Veranius.[26]

5. Census year 62/63 (collecting year 63/64). A census fell on the year during which the completion of the work undertaken by Agrippa II on the temple left a great number of people jobless (*Antiquities* 20:219). Many people then put pressure on the king to provide them with work, for otherwise they could not pay the Roman taxes (*Antiquities* 20:220). The presence of tax collectors in the following year is evident (*Jewish War* 2:287), and when the deadline had well passed and the payment of the tribute was in arrears, Florus decided to extract the amount from the temple's treasury (*Jewish War* 2:293)—the first step toward the Jewish Revolt. Agrippa, hastening his return from a trip to Egypt, urged the people to pay the tax and he succeeded temporarily in sending members of the council to collect some of the dues (*Jewish War* 2:403-5). However, the trouble soon spread again and Agrippa's expulsion from Jerusalem left Florus in Caesarea to deal with the uncollected taxes (*Jewish War* 2:406-7). It is significant that Josephus's narrative continues with the introduction of the man responsible for the trouble: Menahem the grandson of Judas the Galilaean (*Jewish War* 2:433).

To return at this point to the sabbatical cycle, it is also possible to calculate that 33/34 was the sixty-ninth sabbatical year after that of 444/443 B.C., when the decree of Artaxerxes was given to Nehemiah

26. A. E. Gordon, "Q. Veranius, Consul A.D. 49," *University of California Publications in Classical Archaeology* 2/5 (1952) 231-351; idem, *Album of Dated Latin Inscriptions* (Berkeley: University of California, 1958), 1:109 no. 109; *L'Année Épigraphique* 1953: no. 251; E. M. Smallwood, *Documents Illustrating the Principates of Gaius, Claudius, and Nero* (Cambridge: Cambridge University, 1967) 68 no. 231c.

(Neh 2:1–8).[27] This would present an attractive hypothesis for Daniel's prophecy (9:24–27) for the sixty-ninth sabbatical could have marked the commencement of the official ministry of Israel's Messiah. Jesus, at the appropriate time (cf. Gal 4:4), announced to the people on 1 Tishri 33: Πεπλήρωται ὁ καιρός, 'The time has come' (Mark 1:15). On 10 Tishri 33 he proclaimed, Πνεῦμα κυρίου ἐπ' ἐμέ, οὗ εἵνεκεν ἔχρισέν με . . . κηρύξαι ἐνιαυτὸν κυρίου δεκτόν, 'The Spirit of the Lord is on me; therefore he has anointed me to preach . . . to proclaim the year of the Lord's favor' (Luke 4:18–19, cf. Isa 61:2; according to Lev 25:18 the sabbatical year was followed by the jubilee year). And 15 Tishri 33 is the possible date of Pilate's episode with the shields at the Feast of Tabernacles (Philo, *Embassy to Gaius* 299–305). When Jesus later was asked for the signal of his coming he replied that the signal was "the abomination of desolation," in other words, Pilate's act (Matt 24:15–6), and thus the commencement of the Messianic age was at hand (Dan 9:27).

Hoehner admits that the incident of the shields could have taken place at any time between 32 and 36; although he would have preferred a later date[28] he settles for 32 since he places the Crucifixion in 33. Yet Pilate set up the shields in honor of Tiberius, who was celebrating his seventy-fifth birthday in 33.[29] This was an exceptional year because of the coincidence of the *dicennium* of Drusus's death with the semicentenary of Augustus's *saeculum*, the games in honor of the emperor, the Olympic Games, and the Games of Caesarea. It was then, on the emperor's birthday, that Pilate dedicated a *tiberieum* in Caesarea.[30] Pilate appears to have attempted to ingratiate himself with Tiberius by such dedications, especially after the fall of Sejanus in 31.[31] According to Daniel's prophecy, the Messiah would have been cut off some time after this; perhaps in the middle of the seventieth week,[32] or within a

27. Cf. Hoehner, *Chronological Aspects of the Life of Christ* (Grand Rapids: Zondervan, 1977) 128.

28. Hoehner, *Herod Antipas*, 180.

29. W. F. Snyder, "Public Anniversaries in the Roman Empire: The Epigraphical Evidence for Their Observance during the First Three Centuries," *Yale Classical Studies* 7 (1940) 235. See also M. Grant, *Roman Anniversary Issues: An Exploratory Study of the Numismatic and Medallic Commemoration of Anniversary Years* 49 B.C.–A.D. 375 (Cambridge: Cambridge University, 1950) 10, for Roman elasticity in celebrating anniversaries.

30. Cf. E. Weber, "Zur Inschrift des Pontius Pilatus," *Bonner Jahrbücher* 171 (1971) 194–200. See also Smallwood, *The Jews under Roman Rule*, 167; and J.-P. Lémonon, *Pilate et le gouvernement de la Judée: Textes et monuments* (Paris: Gabalda, 1981) 31–32.

31. Cf. H. Volkmann, "Die Pilatusinschrift von Caesarea Maritima," *Gymnasium* 75 (1968) 133; and L. I. Levine, *Roman Caesarea: An Archaeological-Topographical Study* (Jerusalem: Institute of Archaeology, Hebrew University, 1975) 21.

32. J. B. Payne, *The Imminent Appearing of Christ* (Grand Rapids: Eerdmans, 1962) 148.

gap prior to the beginning of the seventieth week.[33] Either way, the year 36 for the Crucifixion meets the evidence positively.

In *Egesippus*, the Latin version of Josephus's works, the Crucifixion of Jesus follows the uprising of the Samaritan prophet,[34] but in the Greek version of *Antiquities* the Crucifixion preceded this uprising (18:63–64; cf. 85–87). That the two events occurred close together in the year 36 may explain *Egesippus's* confused chronological arrangement. Additionally, the Crucifixion in *Antiquities* immediately follows the episode of Pilate's aqueduct (18:63–64; cf. 60–62), but is represented in the *Jewish War* as prior to the time of Agrippa I's journey to Rome in 36 (2:175–77; cf. 178).

Furthermore, the *Chronicon Hieronymis* and the Byzantine *Chronicon Paschale* have Pilate reporting the case to Tiberius, when the consuls in Rome were Gallus and Nonianus (A.D. 35).[35] Finally, the medieval Jewish chronicle *Sepher ha-Yuhasin* of Avraham ben Samuel Zacuto, names the thirty-fifth year before the destruction of Jerusalem (A.D. 36) as the year of Jesus' Crucifixion.[36] (See Table 1.)

Crucifixion in 36 and Paul

Although one must not base the chronology of the Gospels on the chronology of the Apostolic Age, it is necessary for the sake of clarity to take the latter into consideration.

It has been asserted that Paul's statement in Gal 2:1 creates an impasse to a Crucifixion date of 36. The reading "fourteen years later" does create a difficulty, but not as formidable as it first appears.[37] This is a superficial difficulty because it also affects the proposed Crucifixion dates of 33, 30, and even 27. Therefore, one may question whether this reading of Gal 2:1 is correct.

Peter escaped from prison and permanently left Jerusalem after a Passover before the death of Agrippa I (Acts 12:17–23). This Passover must be that of 44 at the latest. On Paul's "second" visit to Jerusalem, fourteen years after his "first," he was appointed, among others, by Peter to begin a mission to the nations (Gal 2:9). Hence, his second visit

---

33. R. H. Gundry, *The Church and the Tribulation* (Grand Rapids: Zondervan, 1973) 190.

34. Eisler, *The Messiah Jesus and John the Baptist*, 293.

35. *Die Chronik des Hieronymus: Hieronymi Chronicon* (ed. R. Helm; 2 vols.; Leipzig: J. C. Hinrich, 1913–26; repr. Berlin: Akademie, 1956); and *Chronicon Paschale* (ed. L. A. Dindorf; 2 vols.; Bonn: E. Weber, 1832).

36. *Yuhasin ha-shalem* (ed. H. E. Filipowski; Frankfurt: M. A. Wahrmann, 1924).

37. Cf. R. Jewett, *Dating Paul's Life* (London: SCM, 1979) 52; and C. J. Hemer, "Observations on Pauline Chronology," *Pauline Studies: Essays Presented to F. F. Bruce* (ed. D. A. Hagner and M. J. Harris; Grand Rapids: Eerdmans, 1980) 12.

TABLE 1. *The Age of Jesus in Relation to Sabbatical Years and Roman Census Years, as well as the Reign of Tiberius and the Governorships of Gratus and Pilate*

Sabbatical and Census Years	Age of Jesus	Sabbatical and Census Years	Age of Jesus	Roman Rulers
	12 B.C	1	A.D. 14	26	Tiberius 1
	11	2	15	27	Tiberius 2, Gratus 1
Sabbatical year 63 { 10	3	16	28	Tiberius 3, Gratus 2
9	4	17	29	Tiberius 4, Gratus 3
8	5	18	30	Tiberius 5, Gratus 4
7	6	Sabbatical year 67 Roman census year 2 { 19	31	Tiberius 6, Gratus 5
6	7	20	32	Tiberius 7, Gratus 6
5	8	21	33	Tiberius 8, Gratus 7
4	9	22	34	Tiberius 9, Gratus 8
Sabbatical year 64 { 3	10	23	35	Tiberius 10, Gratus 9
2	11	24	36	Tiberius 11, Gratus 10
1 B.C	12	25	37	Tiberius 12, Gratus 11
A.D. 1	13	Sabbatical year 68 { 26	38	Tiberius 13, Pilate 1
2	14	27	39	Tiberius 14, Pilate 2
3	15	28	40	Tiberius 15, Pilate 3
4	16	29	41	Tiberius 16, Pilate 4
Sabbatical year 65 Roman census year 1 { 5	17	30	42	Tiberius 17, Pilate 5
6	18	31	43	Tiberius 18, Pilate 6
7	19	32	44	Tiberius 19, Pilate 7
8	20	Sabbatical year 69 Roman census year 3 { 33	45	Tiberius 20, Pilate 8
9	21	34	46	Tiberius 21, Pilate 9
10	22	35	47	Tiberius 22, Pilate 10
11	23	36	48	
Sabbatical year 66 { 12	24			
13	25			

should apparently be dated at the latest to 44, while Peter was still in Jerusalem. Under this order Paul's first visit would have taken place in 30 (Gal 1:18), and his conversion three years before that, in 27 (Gal 1:17). However, by following this process, we are tied to a Crucifixion before 26, which is incompatible not only with Luke 3:1, but also with Josephus and the numismatic evidence. For example, Josephus brings Pilate to Judea in 26/27.[38]

38. P. L. Hedley, "Pilate's Arrival in Judaea," *JTS* 35 (1934) 57; E. M. Smallwood, "The Date of the Dismissal of Pontius Pilate from Judaea," *JJS* 5 (1954) 12; and my, "A Retouched New Date on a Coin of Valerius Gratus," *Liber Annuus* 36 (1986) 241–46.

It therefore seems compulsory to adopt the variant reading of τεσσάρων found in the twelfth-century manuscript 1241ˢ (Sinai, Gr. 260), instead of δεκατεσσάρων. Otherwise there has to be a blank space and Paul's history has to stand still for fourteen years—although it moves rapidly before and after these years. Also, not only do none of Paul's letters come out of this period, but Acts has little to say of any activity of Paul during this time.[39] My conclusion on this point is in agreement with past research. For example, K. G. Wieseler wrote: "Aus chronologischer Verlegenheit haben nicht wenige Gelehrte (Cappellus, Grotius, Semmler, Heinrichs, Bertholdt, Künül, Lüchler, Wurn, Ulrich, Böttger, früher auch Schott) für *decatessáron, tessáron* schreiben wollen, allein gegen alle Handschriften. . . ."[40]

Thus, by adopting the τεσσάρων solution, the first two visits of Paul are made to occur in the years 40 and 44, the conversion three years before that in 37 and the Crucifixion in 36.

As M. Lindner has shown, it was Caligula who transferred Damascus to Nabataean control.[41] Thus, the negotiations with Aretas could not have been completed before the summer of 37. Paul's presence in Damascus must have occurred approximately at this time, or not later than 39/40 when Aretas died.[42] Additionally, the persecution in the course of which Stephen was stoned and Paul converted must have taken place after the deposition of Pilate and before his successor was securely invested.[43] By dating the Crucifixion in 36 the event is no longer in isolation, but in the context of conditions that have an important bearing on what took place.[44] (See Tables 2 and 3.)

Crucifixion in 36 and Astronomy

Astronomical analysis of the year 36 lends support to the theory of the late Crucifixion. It is widely accepted that Jesus was crucified on a

39. Cf. J. Knox, "Fourteen Years Later: A Note on the Pauline Chronology," *JR* 16 (1936) 342.

40. K. G. Wieseler, *Commentar über den Brief Pauli an die Galater* (Göttingen: Dietrich, 1859) 91.

41. M. Lindner, *Petra und das Königreich der Nabatäer: Lebensraum, Geschichte und Kultur eines arabischen Volkes der Antike* (2d ed.; Munich: Delp, 1974) 130–31.

42. Y. Meshorer, *Nabataean Coins* (Jerusalem: Institute of Archaeology, Hebrew University, 1975) 47.

43. F. Hitzig, *Geschichte des Volks Israel* (Leipzig: S. Hirzel, 1869) 578; D. J. O'Herlihy, "The Year of the Crucifixion," *CBQ* 8 (1946) 303; and J. Finegan, *The Archaeology of the New Testament: The Mediterranean World of the Early Christian Apostles* (Boulder, CO: Westview, 1981) 12.

44. Cf. my *Enigma of Jesus the Galilean*, 256.

TABLE 2.   *Chronological Synthesis of Events During the Ministry and Crucifixion of Jesus*

33	August	Death of Philip the Tetrarch
	September	Commencement of the ministry of Jesus in Galilee on Tishri 1 (Rosh Hashanah) at the beginning of the sabbatical year 33/34 (Daniel's sixty-ninth year)
	October	Incident of the votive shields by Pilate at the Feast of Tabernacles (Daniel's abomination of desolation and the commencement of the Messianic era)
		Journey of Antipas to Rome for the succession to Philip's possessions
34	March	Return of Antipas and the flight of his wife to Petra
		First Passover of Jesus' ministry (in Jerusalem); the question of his and the Temple's age
	April	Marriage of Antipas and Herodias and its subsequent denunciation by John the Baptist
	May	Imprisonment of John the Baptist
	June	Proclamation of the third Roman census year 34/35 in Judea (censuses also in Egypt and Cilicia)
	July	Appointment of Agrippa I in Tiberias at the request of his sister Herodias to Antipas
	September	Commencement of the Jubilee Year 34/35
	October	Visit of Agrippa I to Syria with Flaccus
35	March	Execution of John the Baptist
	April	Second Passover of Jesus' ministry (in Galilee)
		Massacre of the Galileans in Jerusalem by Pilate
	June	Beginning of the census tax collection (35/36)
	July	Breaking of the friendship of Agrippa I and Flaccus, and the former's departure from Syria
		Arrival of Agrippa I at Ptolemais, the incident with the soldiers of Capito, and his departure to Alexandria
	August	Death of Flaccus in Syria
	October	Uprising of the Jews against Pilate for the aqueduct in Jerusalem
	November	Vitellius in Syria to replace Flaccus
		Struggle of Rome with the Parthians (lasts into A.D. 36)
		Negotiations begun by Antipas for the peace treaty between Rome and Parthia

TABLE 2, *continued*

36	March	Arrival of Agrippa I in Rome
		Third Passover of Jesus' ministry (in Jerusalem); the question of the payment of the census tax, the trial by Antipas, and the Crucifixion by the order of Pilate
	April	Refusal of the Cietae in Cilicia to pay the census tax
	May	Execution of Tigranes IV in Rome
	July	Defeat of Antipas by Aretas of Petra, his denunciation by the Jews, and his appeal to Tiberius
	September	Imprisonment of Agrippa I by Tiberius in Rome
	October	Revolt in Samaria and the attack by Pilate at the Feast of Tabernacles
		Great fire in Rome
	December	Dismissal of Pilate by Marcellus after the order of Vitellius
		First visit of Vitellius to Jerusalem on Kislev 25 at the feast of Hanukkah
		Replacement of Caiaphas by Vitellius and appointment of Jonathan to the high priesthood
37	January	Disturbances at Jerusalem; persecution of the followers of Jesus and the death of Stephen
	March	Death of Tiberius
		Arrival of Pilate at Rome
	April	Second visit of Vitellius to Jerusalem at the time of the Passover, replacement of Jonathan, and the abandonment of his mission against Aretas of Petra
	May	Transfer of Damascus's rule to Aretas by Caligula
	June	Conversion of Paul on the road to Damascus

Friday and on Nisan 14. Astronomical chronology, although it leads to no certain result, establishes the probability that Nisan 14 fell on Friday in the years 27, 30, and 33. The year 36 was formerly discounted *a priori*,[45] but recently has been mentioned as a possible astronomical nomination.[46] Computations by the Physics Department at the University of Athens confirm the date Friday, 30 March A.D. 36, as Nisan 14,

45. For example, J. Jeremias, *The Eucharistic Words of Jesus* (London: SCM, 1966) 38.
46. See Hoehner, *Chronological Aspects of the Life of Christ*, 100.

TABLE 3.   *Chronological Reconstruction of the First Part of Paul's Christian Life*

36	Crucifixion of Jesus
36/37	Persecution of the followers of Jesus (Gal 1:13, Acts 8:1)
37	Conversion of Paul (Gal 1:12, 16; Acts 9:3–9, 22:6–11)
38/39	Paul in Arabia on a mission (Gal 1:17; not recorded in Acts)
40	First visit of Paul to Jerusalem (on a sabbatical year) and his stay with Peter for fifteen days (Gal 1:18; Acts 9:26–29, 22:17–21)
41	Paul in Syria and Cilicia (Gal 1:21, Acts 9:30)
42/43	Barnabas and Paul in Antioch for one year; the naming of the "Christians" (Acts 11:25–26)
44	Second visit of Paul to Jerusalem with Barnabas and Titus and discussion of the circumcision question while Peter was still in the city; this is the visit after "four" *not* "fourteen" years (Gal 2:1–9, Acts 15:1–35)
44/45	Flight of Peter from Jerusalem, introduction of John Mark, and Agrippa I's death in Caesarea (Acts 12:1–23)
45	Peter in Antioch and the confrontation with Paul (Gal 2:11–21; not recorded in Acts)
45/46	Paul in Galatia on a mission (Gal 1:6–11; not recorded in Acts)
46/47	Writing of Paul's letter to the Galatians by his own hand: the earliest extant Christian document
47	Third visit of Paul to Jerusalem: the "famine visit" (on a sabbatical year) during the time of a universal famine under Claudius (Gal 2:10?; Acts 11:27–30, 12:24–25)
48	Council of Antioch (Acts 13:1–3)
48–49	First official apostolic journey of Paul with Barnabas and part way with John Mark (Acts 13:4–14:28)
49–52	Second official apostolic journey of Paul with Silas after the departure of Barnabas with John Mark to Cyprus (Acts 15:36–18:19)
52	Fourth visit of Paul to Jerusalem on his return from Corinth (Acts 18:20–22)

but with the caution that such computations can be no more than probable.[47]

Of the possible years mentioned above, 27 is the least likely astronomically. In fact, in this year Nisan 14 seems to have fallen on

47. Personal communication from P. Pappas, 7 June 1982.

Thursday.[48] At all events, the early year of 27 is biblically inconceivable and inevitably must be left out.

The year 30 has also been questioned since a recent computerized study seems to indicate that Nisan 14 occurred on Thursday.[49] Also, this year is biblically improbable for it compresses the time of John's and Jesus' ministries. To fit the duration of their ministries, the proponents of this theory employ Tiberius's "joint rule" sophism, which is "distasteful, unlikely, and forced."[50] Additionally, a further objection exists that has never really been obviated: April 7 was a *dies nefastus*, an unlucky day to the Romans, a day in which certain judicial actions were avoided.[51]

The year 33 is also vulnerable, for Nisan 14 may have fallen on a Thursday (April 2 in the Julian calendar). With good atmospheric visibility, to say nothing of "transparency," at the time of the new moon (the sighting of which determined Nisan's first day), the new moon may have been observed after sunset on Thursday, March 19 (or perhaps, better, after sunrise on Friday, March 20—depending on the beginning of the Hebrew day and the official reckoning that part of a day equals a whole day), thus making Friday, March 20, the first day of Nisan. Of course false allegations or even approximate calculations made to the authorities could have started Nisan earlier, but obviously this could have affected any other year as well. Unlike the other years proposed, however, a major problem for 33 is the increasing probability that it was a leap year, since it was presabbatical (the sabbatical year was from Tishri 33 to Elul 34).[52] If this were the case, then another month, VeAdar, was intercalated between Adar and Nisan (see *y.Sanh.* 18d; cf. Julius Africanus as recorded in Eusebius, *Demonstration of the Gospel* 7:2:54) and therefore Nisan 14 fell on Saturday.[53] Further, historically, the year 33 can by no means stand against the chronological

---

48. J. K. Fotheringham, "The Evidence of Astronomy and Technical Chronology for the Date of the Crucifixion," *JTS* 35 (1934) 158.

49. H. H. Goldstine, *New and Full Moons: 1001 B.C. to A.D. 1651* (Philadelphia: American Philosophical Society, 1973) 86.

50. P. L. Maier, "Sejanus, Pilate, and the Date of the Crucifixion," *CH* 37 (1968) 8. Cf. M. M. Sage, "Tacitus and the Accession of Tiberius," *Ancient Society* 13/14 (1982) 293–321.

51. Cf. U. Holzmeister, "Neuere Arbeiten über das Datum der Kreuzigung Christi," *Bib* 13 (1932) 99.

52. Cf. P. Scheff, *Das Todesjahr des Königs Herodes und das Todesjahr Jesu Christi* (Munich: E. Stahl, 1882) 49–50.

53. Cf. T. Nicklin, *Gospel Gleanings* (London: Longmans, 1950) 152.

elements of the Baptist's story.[54] Josephus makes shipwreck of the 33 hypothesis.

Since the original presentation of this paper at the Nativity Conference, C. J. Humphreys and W. G. Waddington have published another article concerning the date of the Crucifixion.[55] However, they do not acknowledge that 33 was a presabbatical year and hence likely a leap year; thus their calculations do not take into account the intercalation of VeAdar. Besides, 33 cannot be reconciled with the chronology of Josephus (especially the death of John the Baptist) or the New Testament (for example, John's three Passovers). Also, this hypothesis does not deal adequately with the age of Jesus at his death or with the date of his birth. There is, further, a theological problem concerning the lunar eclipse they propose.

Although this is not the place for a detailed reply, a clarification has to be made regarding Humphreys and Waddington's presentation that 14 Nisan 36 fell on Saturday, March 31. Their assumption, I presume, implies the following:

1. The new moon was not observed during the night of Friday, March 16 (presumably the beginning of Saturday in the Hebrew calendar), but it was seen twenty-four hours later on the night of Saturday, March 17 (the beginning of Sunday). Therefore, Sunday, March 18, became the first day of the new month, that is, Nisan 1.
2. The previous month Adar had one extra day—the new moon had not been observed on Adar 29—and therefore a thirtieth day was added to this month.
3. The Passover of Nisan 14, which ought to have fallen on the first full moon after the spring equinox, was not celebrated accordingly in 36, for Nisan 14 fell on the following day of the full moon; of course, the full moon occurred on Friday, March 30.

Concerning (1), even accepting the arithmetic values of Humphreys and Waddington—that the astronomical new moon occurred on March 16, Jerusalem time 17:50, plus the fact that the new moon could not have been seen after sunset—it is still not impossible that the new moon was detected after sunrise of the following day (in the Julian calendar), some twelve hours later. There are several variables that may have affected the beginning of Nisan: atmospheric visibility, extreme

54. See my "Which Salome Did Aristobulus Marry?"
55. C. J. Humphreys and W. G. Waddington, "Dating the Crucifixion," *Nature* 306 (22 Dec. 1983) 743–46.

transparency (a real phenomenon), approximate calculations by the authorities, the varying official beginning of the day (for example, the day began at sunrise in Egypt and Qumran), and even false or inaccurate sightings of the new moon (examples of this are known from Hebrew history). Thus the official beginning of Nisan may well have been on Saturday, March 17.

It is commonly held that the new day in Israel started at sunset of the previous day, but this is by no means certain. Even if the public reckoned its day this way, the priests and authorities may have followed a different system. In fact, Pliny (*Natural History* 2:79:188) says that the official day began at midnight. Jack Finegan has pointed out that the best that can be said is that day began before sunrise.[56]

Finally, the argument of the so-called "crescent invisibility" may also be put forward as an explanation, according to which a month could occasionally have been started prematurely.[57]

Concerning (2) above, no Hebrew month had less than twenty-nine or more than thirty days, and there had never been more than eight or less than four months of thirty days in one year (cf. *m. ʿArak.* 2:2). It is not possible at present to say which months in a specific year had thirty days. However, according to the Babylonian Talmud (*b. Roš Haš.* 19b–21a)—and contrary to Humphreys and Waddington—it may not have been permissible to add a day to Adar.

Concerning (3) above, I note that it was a requirement for the Passover feast to be celebrated at the first full moon after the spring equinox, that is, on Nisan 14 (see Anatolius, as recorded in Eusebius, *Ecclesiastical History* 7:32:16–19). In 36 the first full moon after the spring equinox fell on Friday, March 30. Hans Achelis was one of the first to calculate the Crucifixion on the basis of the full moon falling on a Friday; he determined that this only happened in 30, 33, and 36.[58] (The unpublished *Mishmarot* from Qumran Cave 4 also testify that the Qumran community calculated full moons.) Achelis, concluding that the Crucifixion occurred in 30, rejected 33 and 36 as not satisfying the evidence. Unfortunately, as was later discovered, Achelis had made a miscalculation: the full moon of 30 did not fall on a Friday. And equally unfortunately, Achelis had rejected 36 since he held that Pilate had left

---

56. Finegan, *Handbook of Biblical Chronology* (Princeton: Princeton University, 1964) 9–10, no. 13.

57. Cf. L. W. Casperson, "The Lunar Dates of Thutmose III," *JNES* 45 (1986) 139–50.

58. "Ein Versuch, den Karfreitag zu datieren," *Nachrichten von der Königlichen Gesellschaft der Wissenschaften zu Göttingen* (Phil.-hist. Klasse) 1902: 707–17.

Judea in 35, but recent studies have established that Pilate was in Judea in 36.[59]

Finally, the connection between the Crucifixion and a lunar eclipse is not as new as Humphreys and Waddington make it appear. J. K. Fotheringham before them proposed the same link and he also mentions similar investigations, including those by C. Schoch and others, even as early as Sethus Calvisius (1556–1615).[60] Fotheringham calculated that this partial eclipse—if it were visible at all in Jerusalem—would not have lasted more than nineteen minutes, and it gave no "blood moon" and no upheaval. He evidently knew that a lunar eclipse at the Crucifixion could not be connected with Peter's eschatological speech at Pentecost (the eschatological nature of his speech is seen when it is compared to Rev 6:12). It is of interest that Revelation 6 reports a darkened sun and a blood moon as the result of an earthquake; therefore, should one look at this case in an unorthodox fashion—that is, the only return of Jesus was at his resurrection—one may be able to identify this earthquake with the one in Matt 27:54, which is given as the explanation for the darkening of the sun and the tearing of the temple's curtain (borrowed from Mark 15:33, 38). Some manuscripts of Luke 23:45 replace the earthquake explanation with an eclipse of the sun, possibly because it was felt that an earthquake could not explain a "darkening of the sun." But, of course, a solar eclipse cannot occur at the time of a full moon; therefore this variant reading is in error.

One form of tectonic activity that may give an account for the red moon, the dark sun, and the tearing of the curtain is a volcanic eruption (compare the effects of the eruption of Krakatoa and other volcanoes). Perhaps, then, such a natural catastrophe has to be sought in the year 36. Quite apart from the fact that an eclipse is out of context in the present argument, a total eclipse would have given the most dramatic effect of a blood moon, as Humphreys and Waddington claim. It is significant that not one but two such eclipses took place in 36 at Jerusalem: the first before Crucifixion at Passover (January 31) and the second after Pentecost (July 26). Further, as will be noted later, meteor showers are on record as having fallen on March 15 and July 17 of that year.

59. Smallwood, *The Jews under Roman Rule*, 160–74; idem, "The Date of the Dismissal of Pontius Pilate"; Schürer, *History of the Jewish People* (rev. ed.), 1:383; M. Stern, "The Province of Judaea," *The Jewish People in the First Century* (ed. S. Safrai and M. Stern; Assen: Van Gorcum/Philadelphia: Fortress, 1974) 320.

60. Fotheringham, "The Evidence of Astronomy and Technical Chronology for the Date of the Crucifixion," *JTS* 35 (1934) 158.

In conclusion, as the result of eliminating years 27, 30, and 33, we are left with the year 36 (with its full moon on Nisan 14, Friday, March 30) for the date of Jesus' Crucifixion. This is the only year that, with the highest degree of probability, takes full account of all the evidence: biblical, historical, calendrical, and astronomical. However, it must be stressed again at this point that the coordination of the Hebrew calendar and astronomical data is ambiguous. No positive result can be achieved, and astronomy alone cannot arrive at the date of the Crucifixion. Astronomy may be used tentatively as supporting evidence only after the historical and archaeological arguments have been advanced.

John and the Age of Jesus

The belief that the Fourth Gospel contains primitive and reliable historical tradition has been reinforced by numerous studies in recent years. The work of C. H. Dodd began a new phase in accepting that, regardless of the degree of the cross-fertilization between the traditions, John is not dependent upon the Synoptic Gospels for his material and therefore does not have to be dated after them.[61] Certainly Dodd himself ascribed the gospel to an Ephesian elder writing between 90 and 100, but he combined this view with the conviction that the tradition behind it goes back a great deal further.[62]

The Fourth Gospel is the only one that presents three Passovers in Jesus' ministry (2:13, 6:4, 11:55). Furthermore, its last pericope (21:25) gives special attention to the length of Jesus' ministry. Consequently, it is not coincidental that John discloses the age of Jesus as being "not yet fifty" (8:57). Even more so, is John's striking revelation (2:20) of the precise age of Jesus, providing that reader perceives the statement as an allegorical pun: the Jews speak of the temple while Jesus speaks of his body. At his first Passover in Jerusalem (in A.D. 34) Jesus was forty-six years old and obviously not yet fifty; the temple was the same age. Often in the New Testament Jesus is equated with the temple.[63]

Some have put forward the suggestion that the conversation in John 2:20 has reference to the First Temple of Solomon or to the

61. See F. L. Cribbs, "A Reassessment of the Date and the Destination of the Gospel of John," *JBL* 90 (1970) 38; O. Cullmann, *The Johannine Circle* (London: SCM, 1976) 97; and J. A. T. Robinson, *Redating the New Testament* (London: SCM, 1976) 284.

62. C. H. Dodd, *Historical Tradition in the Fourth Gospel* (Cambridge: Cambridge University, 1963) 120.

63. Cf. Matt 12:6, Eph 2:21, Rev 21:22. Jesus is also referred to as a stone in Matt 21:42, Mark 12:10, Luke 20:17, Acts 4:11, Rom 9:32-33, and 1 Pet 2:4-8 (cf. Matt 7:24, Luke 6:48, 1 Cor 10:4, and Eph 2:20).

Second Temple of Zerubbabel.[64] This proposal is irreconcilable with the evidence. First, according to the Old Testament Solomon's Temple was built in seven years (1 Kgs 6:37–38) and Zerubbabel's in five years (compare Zech 1:1, 4:9 with Ezra 6:15). Second, there is no extrabiblical evidence that either of these temples was built in forty-six years, despite the claims of *Acta Pilati* 5:1 (for the Temple of Solomon) and George Syncellus (*Chronicle* 234b, for Zerubbabel). Origen (*Commentary on John* 10:38) bitterly opposed both of these groundless contentions. Third, the word οὗτος clearly refers to the structure standing at that time, that is, the Herodian Temple.

Others have paraphrased John's passage, regarding it as indicative of the year in which the conversation took place: the forty-six years should be reckoned from the commencement of the work undertaken by Herod on the temple.[65] This suggestion is likewise incompatible with the evidence. First, the Greek text has οἰκοδομήθη not οἰκοδομεῖται, a tense that would be appropriate for something begun in the past and continuing at the time of the narration. Second, counting forty-six years from 19 B.C. (the commencement of Herod's work) gives the year A.D. 27 as the date of Jesus' first Passover.[66] But this would date the Crucifixion in 29, a year that has been excluded on astronomical grounds, among others. Third, the reconstruction undertaken by Herod finished after eight years with a great celebration for its completion (*Antiquities* 15:420–21). Fourth, had any kind of work continued after Herod's (unlikely in view of *Antiquities* 15:391), it would not have been terminated at the time of Jesus (any future work could have been done only under Agrippa II; see *Antiquities* 20:219).

A better suggestion is that the forty-six years should be reckoned subsequent to the completion of the work of Herod, for in this way Jesus' conversation would be transposed to a later date, nearing the period in which Jesus was active.[67] However, because such a venture would require a transposition of eight years (the length of Herod's work), advocates of this theory ingeniously distinguished between the Greek words ἱερόν and ναός. They proposed that since the ναός was

---

64. E. A. Abbott, "John 2:20," *Classical Review* 8 (1894) 89.

65. T. D. Woolsey, "The Year of Christ's Birth," *BSac* 27 (1870) 325.

66. Finegan has proven that the work by Herod on the temple was begun in 19 B.C. (see *Handbook of Biblical Chronology*, 279). If one accepts T. Corbishley's earlier suggestion of 23/22 B.C. as the starting date, the completion of the work would have been in A.D. 23/24—much too early to date Jesus' first Passover (see "The Chronology of the Reign of Herod the Great," *JTS* 36 [1935] 26).

67. E. Power, "John 2:20 and the Date of the Crucifixion," *Bib* 9 (1928) 268.

completed by the priests in one year and six months (*Antiquities* 15:421), the forty-six years should be reckoned from that event. Yet, counting from 17 B.C. (when the ναός was finished)[68] yields a date of A.D. 29 for the first Passover of Jesus. (This would result in the Crucifixion being dated to 31, which has been totally excluded by the astronomical data.) But it is not possible to make such a sharp distinction between the two Greek words, which in many cases in early Christian literature are interchanged (cf. 1 *Clement* 41:2; Ignatius, *Letter to the Magnesians* 7; and *Gospel of Peter* 7:26). Even in the Gospels the two words are often uncertain (cf. Matt 12:5, 27:5; Mark 12:35; Luke 21:5; John 8:20). Their meaning has remained interchangeable through the years. Modern Greek contradicts the Greek of Josephus: presently ἱερόν is used for the Most Holy Place situated inside the ναός 'temple'. Additionally, Josephus's text contains a third related, but distinct, word (νεώς), whose meaning is best ignored as it adds further to the confusion (*Antiquities* 15:380, 401).

In reality, the completion of all the work undertaken in the temple area must have been particularly memorable in light of the great festival that Herod organized after the eight-year building period (*Antiquities* 15:420). It is from this event that one should count the forty-six year period (if this is to be calculated literally at all). It seems highly unlikely that the priests would have held extensive celebrations before Herod had completed his part; after all, it was Herod's idea to rebuild the temple, a plan that in the beginning the priests had opposed (*Antiquities* 15:389).[69] The amazing part of this argument is that the completion occurred in 12 B.C., and adding forty-six years gives a date of A.D. 34—exactly the year that I have already established as the first Passover of Jesus.

From all this I conclude that John's statement (2:20) is a characteristic pun conveying the real age of Jesus. C. H. Kraeling wrote, "It is quite as possible that Jesus was between 40 and 50 when he died, as that he was between 30 and 40. The only question is which is more probable, and the answer to this question depends upon the validity of the arguments advanced in support of the two alternatives."[70] I disagree with Kraeling only in that there is no comparison as to the validity of the two alternative arguments. The advanced age of Jesus is evident from the following:

68. Finegan, *Handbook of Biblical Chronology*, 280.
69. Cf. G. Wissowa, *Religion und Kultus der Römer* (2d ed.; Handbuch der klassichen Altertumswissenschaft 5/4; Munich: Beck, 1912) 472–73.
70. C. H. Kraeling, "Olmstead's Chronology of the Life of Jesus," *ATR* 24 (1942) 337.

1. The passages of John (2:20, 8:57, 21:25) and the absolute necessity of accepting the truthfulness of at least 8:57 in view of the apologetic temper of the redactor of the Fourth Gospel, who would have excised it had it not been taken as correct.
2. A general assumption about the necessary age for one who might claim authority.
3. The observation of the collectors of the temple tax (Matt 17:24), who thought Jesus was over the requisite age to pay the tax (which was apparently the age of fifty; *Antiquities* 3:196).
4. The fact that Jesus died so quickly upon the cross (John 19:33; cf. Mark 15:44).
5. The disagreement of the data supplied by the synoptic infancy narratives, but their general agreement that Jesus was born under Herod the Great (Matt 2:1; Luke 1:5, 26); that is, he was well over thirty years old at the time of his ministry, in any system of chronology.
6. The verification of Irenaeus (*Against Heresies* 2:12:5) who claimed to have corroborative testimony to the effect that Jesus was about fifty years of age when he preached. Irenaeus had been a listener to Polycarp (*Against Heresies* 3:3:4), who had "intercourse with John [the Presbyter] and with the others who had seen the Lord" (Irenaeus, *Letter to Florinus*, in Eusebius, *Ecclesiastical History* 5:20:4–8). Irenaeus has preserved the most valuable oral tradition, which interlocks with the text of John's Gospel,[71] and Rev 1:14 where Jesus is visualized with white hair.[72]

A. T. Olmstead argued strenuously for the Crucifixion in 30, yet had to admit: "These who know their Near East will be difficult to convince that a man of thirty could have been accepted as a teacher of authority. . . . But if Jesus was not far from fifty, then the story of his ministry gains in plausibility, and for the first time we can understand how he came to be accepted as an authoritative Rabbi."[73] The view that Jesus was precisely in his forty-sixth year was held by several early writers, according to Augustine (*De Doctrina Christiana* 2:28). Unfortunately these writings are not extant, nevertheless, this idea is found in the pseudo-Cyprianic tract *De Montibus Sina et Sion*.[74]

71. Cf. G. Ogg, "The Age of Jesus When He Taught," *NTS* 5 (1959) 296.
72. Cf. A. Cabaniss, "The Year of Jesus' Birth," *Studies in English* 11 (1971) 86.
73. A. T. Olmstead, "The Chronology of Jesus' Life," *ATR* 24 (1942) 26; cf. King, "The Outlines of New Testament Chronology," 146.
74. See *Cypriani Opera Spuria* (ed. W. A. Hartel; Corpus Script. Eccles. Lat. 3/3; Vienna: C. Geroldi, 1871) 104–19.

T. Corbishley has written, "On any tolerable system of dating our Lord will be several years over thirty when he begins his ministry."[75] If, inevitably, it is accepted that Jesus was well over thirty—since Herod the Great died in 4 B.C.[76]—then Luke's statement in 3:23 should have nothing to do with chronology. The figure might have been taken from 2 Sam 5:4, for it is appropriate that the Son of David should inaugurate his activities at David's age.[77] Or, one has to consider the possibility that Luke might have originally written "forty" instead of "thirty"; that Luke wrote a higher number has been strongly argued in the past by T. Lewin and J. Van Bebber.[78] What is surprising in this approach is that, if Jesus was forty in the fifteenth year of Tiberius (28/29),[79] he must have been forty-six in the year 34, which also agrees with my dating of Jesus' conversation about his body in the temple. Whichever way we gain no less unique a light on the question of the birth of Jesus: he was born in 12 B.C. under Herod the Great, in the heyday of the king's reign (cf. Matt 2:1). (See Tables 1 and 2.)

Matthew and the Datum of the Star

There are three data that the nativity narratives provide for determining the year of Jesus' birth: the reign of Herod the Great, the enrollment ordered by Augustus, and the governorship of Quirinius in Syria. The first one is found in Matthew and all three in Luke. At the present state of historical knowledge, a scientific reconciliation of these data cannot be achieved.[80] Luke seems to contradict Matthew as well as himself. For example, an enrollment ordered by Augustus while Quirinius was governor of Syria, in the time of Herod the Great, cannot be solidly proved. However, it must be allowed that it can neither be solidly disproved.

It is my belief that Luke was presented with a tradition, from a strong source, that placed the birth of Jesus at the time of a taxation

75. Corbishley, "The Date of Our Lord's Birth," *Scripture* 1 (1946) 80.

76. J. Van Bruggen, "The Year of the Death of Herod the Great," *Miscellanea Neotestamentica* (ed. T. Baarda, A. F. J. Klijn, and W. C. Van Unnik; Leiden: Brill, 1978), 2:1–15; and P. M. Bernegger, "Affirmation of Herod's Death in 4 B.C.," *JTS* 34 (1983) 526–31.

77. Cf. J. D. M. Derrett, "Further Light on the Narratives of the Nativity," *NovT* 17 (1975) 84.

78. T. Lewin, *An Essay on the Chronology of the New Testament* (Oxford: J. H. Parker, 1854) 11; idem, *Fasti Sacri; or, A Key to the Chronology of the New Testament* (London: Longmans, Green, 1865) xv; J. Van Bebber, *Zur Chronologie des Lebens Jesu* (Münster im Westphalia, 1898) 147.

79. Cf. R. W. Husband, "The Year of the Crucifixion," *PAPS* 46 (1915) 26.

80. Cf. R. E. Brown, *The Birth of the Messiah* (Garden City: Doubleday, 1977) 555.

assessment in Herod the Great's Judea. Luke searched unsuccessfully in history for this taxation, and, unable to reject this tradition, he finally associated it with the well-known census of Quirinius. Unfortunately, the census he chose to link it to can today be decisively dated long after the death of Herod. I am assuming, therefore, that in his effort to fix the date of the Herodian taxation assessment, Luke erroneously identified it with the first Roman census of Judea undertaken by Quirinius. As to whether such a Herodian assessment is historically possible, one has to rely on two statements of Josephus that relate that Herod remitted taxes after a presupposed enrollment.[81] Nevertheless, since a new attempt to reconcile Luke with Matthew has been made by Jerry Vardaman (partly published in this volume), my exposition at this point can be reserved until Vardaman's complete thesis is published, because, now he also has concluded that Jesus was born in 12 B.C.[82]

Another datum, but of secondary importance, is provided by Matthew as a supplement to the three main points above: the star of the Magi. The conclusion that 12 B.C. is the date of Jesus' birth requires reexamination of the astronomical evidence surrounding this year.

It has been proposed that the star in Matthew is a midrash on the text of Num 24:17, that is, an elaboration to give fulfillment to the Old Testament prophecy: "a star shall come forth out of Jacob." But such a thought is founded on the presumption of the historical incredibility of Matthew's narrative.[83] Therefore, investigation of the star may render it subservient to the purpose of chronological inquiry. After all, Matthew might have elaborated a piece of historical information that chronologically connected the birth of Jesus with the appearance of a heavenly body, using it to give fulfillment to the prophecy.

The question that arises is whether Matthew's account allows us to conceive of an actual star.[84] Upon a closer examination of his text, one cannot help being struck by the pragmatic nature of the star. The whole description obliges the reader to assume a physical object explicable by scientific law, and it is difficult to regard it as merely a figment of a fertile imagination. The purport of ἐν τῇ ἀνατολῇ 'in the east' (2:2) presupposes an ordinary heavenly body, προῆγεν 'went ahead' (2:9) implies motion and direction in the sky, and ἐστάθη 'stopped' (2:9)

81. Cf. A. Schalit, *König Herodes: Der Mann und sein Werk* (Berlin: de Gruyter, 1969) 274. The statements from *Antiquities* are found in 15:365 and 16:64. It is perhaps necessary to also take into account *Antiquities* 15:300–303 and 17:25.
82. Cf. Finegan, *The Archaeology of the New Testament: The Mediterranean World*, 236 n. 13, for Vardaman's earlier view of 11/10 B.C.
83. Cf. Brown, *The Birth of the Messiah*, 195.
84. Cf. Derrett, "Further Light on the Narratives of the Nativity," 102.

conveys a change of speed and position. There seems to be only one type of object that can be identified with confidence in respect to the star's description: a comet. The following facts support this conclusion.

1. The huge size. Comets sometimes extend 90° or more on the vault of heaven; for example, the comet of 1861 had a tail 118° in length.[85] It should be noted that Matthew refers to a single star, not to a group of stars.[86]

2. The strange appearance. Comets always capture the imagination, especially spectacular ones like the comet of 1744, which had six tails.[87] The appearance of the star in Matthew, first in the east and then for a second time when the Magi were on their way from Jerusalem to Bethlehem, is in accord only with the theory of a comet.

3. The quick motion. Comets move fast in their journey through the inner solar system: they move across the sky with a speed of about 10° per day, moving from one constellation to the next every three or four days.[88] Hence, comets are distinguishable simply by their movement. John Chrysostom (*Homily* 6) rightly questioned if the star could have been a star, since stars do not move and cannot show the way! He concluded, subjectively, that it was an invisible force or an angel who directed the Magi. A similar view is encountered later in the visions of St. Maria de Agreda. ("The Holy Town," 1655).

4. The prolonged manifestation. Comets remain visible for days, weeks, and months, and often reach a maximum brilliance considerably brighter than Jupiter. They appear twice: once as they

85. C. Flammarion, *Astronomie populaire* (Paris: E. Flammarion, 1922) 646.

86. A. J. Sachs and C. B. F. Walker, in their article "Kepler's View of the Star of Bethlehem and the Babylonian Almanac for 7/6 B.C.," *Iraq* 46 (1984) 43–55, put the record straight concerning the theory that the star was a conjunction of planets. According to their research this theory was not originated by Johannes Kepler—but by a misunderstanding of his texts—and it has been followed by almost all astronomers since Christian Ludwig Ideler. Sachs and Walker also point out that the Babylonian Almanac for 7/6 B.C. does not refer to any conjunction of Jupiter and Saturn, merely to the movements of these planets. (Additionally, Kepler's view of the star being a nova cannot add to our understanding of the date of Jesus' birth.) Sachs and Walker also point out that, according to B. Tuckerman's calculations (*Planetary, Lunar, and Solar Positions* 601 B.C. to A.D. 1 [Philadelphia: American Philosophical Society, 1962]), the two planets did not approach sufficiently close to each other in 7 B.C. to give the appearance of a single star. Above all, Sachs and Walker give, for the first time, the complete collated and translated text of the almanac.

87. Flammarion, *Astronomie populaire*, 623.

88. D. Hughes, *The Star of Bethlehem Mystery* (London: Dent, 1979) 145.

approach the sun and again after perihelion. Their brightness can
be seen occasionally even during the day. Maximus the Confessor
remarked on the star in Matthew that: καί ἐν ἡμέρα φαινόμενος, 'it
could be seen during the day' (*Philocalia* 2:92). Comets can be seen
near the disc of the sun, like those of 1843 and 1882.[89]

5. The ability to stop overhead. The description, the star "stood over"
(that is, in astronomical parlance, "it reached its zenith" directly
above the observer), could only reasonably apply to a comet. It was
regarded in this manner as early as the time of Origen (*Against
Celsus* 1:58) and probably even earlier in the time of Ignatius (*Letter
to the Ephesians* 19:2). One only has to compare Matt 2:9, ἐστάθη
ἐπάνω οὗ ἦν τὸ παιδίον, 'it stopped over the place where the child
was', with similar terminology in Dio Cassius 54:29:8, ὑπέρ αὐτοῦ
τοῦ ἄστεως αἰωρηθείς 'hung over the city' (describing the comet of
12 B.C., which stood over Rome at the time of Marcus Agrippa's
death), and Josephus (*Jewish War* 6:289), ὑπὲρ τὴν πόλιν ἄστρον
ἔστη 'a star stood over the city' (describing the comet in A.D. 66
that stood over Jerusalem).

The Greeks and the Romans observed and described 135 comets
before the coming of Christianity.[90] The last two comets before our era
appeared in 17 B.C. and 12 B.C.[91] Other presumed comets have been
suggested for 4 B.C. (later shown to be a fireball) and 5 B.C. (probably a
nova).[92] Chinese records about the 12 B.C. comet reveal that this is the
comet later named after Edmund Halley.[93]

Halley's Comet, one of the brightest comets known, has always
been an object of great fascination and wonder to humankind. It returns

89. For the 1843 comet see Flammarion, *Astronomie populaire*, 639; for the comet of
1882 see S. M. Plakidēs, *The Star of Bethlehem* (Athens: Hestia, 1952) 14 [Greek].
90. K. S. Chasapes, *The Star of Bethlehem* (Athens: A. Karabia, 1970) 79 [Greek].
91. On these two comets see, respectively, W. Keller, *The Bible as History* (London:
Hodder and Stoughton, 1956) 329; and E. Burrows, *The Oracles of Jacob and Balaam*
(London: Burns Oates and Washbourne, 1938) 100.
92. C. St. J. H. Daniel, who followed J. Pingré (*Cometographie* [Paris: Imprimerie
Royale, 1783], 1:281), suggested that the object in the sky in 4 B.C. was a comet (see his
"The Star of Bethlehem," *Planetarium* 1 [1967] 40). However, R. K. Marshall has proven
that it was really a fireball (*The Star of Bethlehem* [2d ed.; Chapel Hill, NC: Morehead
Planetarium, University of North Carolina, 1956] 15). On the nova of 5 B.C., see D. H.
Clark, J. H. Parkinson, and F. R. Stephenson, "An Astronomical Re-Appraisal of the Star
of Bethlehem: A Nova in 5 B.C.," *Quarterly Journal of the Royal Astronomical Society* 18
(1977) 443.
93. See H. P. Yoke, "Ancient and Medieval Observations of Comets and Novae in
Chinese Sources," *Vistas in Astronomy* 5 (1962) 147 no. 61, for citation of Pan Ku's first-
century A.D. work, *Chhien Han Shu*.

approximately every seventy-six years, most recently in 1985–1986.[94] It appeared in the autumn of 12 B.C., twenty-six solar passages previously. The 12 B.C. apparition has been calculated as 0 magnitude, an extremely impressive sight that will unfortunately remain unrepeated since its brightness is decreasing with time—about 2.5 units of magnitude every millennium—and by 1910 it had already decreased to 4.6 magnitude.[95] One of the first modern scholars to associate Halley's Comet with the star of Jesus in 12 B.C. was A. Stenzel.[96] However, as early as 1301 the painter of Florence, Giotto di Bondone, incorporated this comet in a fresco at Padua that showed the Magi adoring the infant Jesus.

The comet interpretation of the nativity star faces fewer difficulties than any other interpretation.[97] In fact there is only a single objection: that comets were usually thought to herald a catastrophe rather than the birth of a salvific figure. However, according to the astrological faith of the ancient world, extraordinary events—especially the birth and death of distinguished people—were indicated by heavenly bodies, particularly comets.[98] A comet was also connected with the birth of Mithridates VI Eupator of Pontus in 134 B.C. (Justinus, *History* 37:2). This comet was regarded, like the comet of Jesus in Matthew, as a mere symbolical legend,[99] but J. K. Fotheringham proved with the assistance of the Chinese records that it was historical![100] The Jews anticipated a celestial phenomenon—probably a comet—with the birth of the Messiah (Num 24:17; *Testament of Levi* 18:2–3; *Testament of Judah* 24:1). When Abraham was born a comet was seen coming from the east, traversing the heavens (*Ma ʿaseh Avraham Avinu; The Book of Jasher* 8:2; *Chronicles of Jerahmeel* 34). Also when John the Baptist was born, at least according to the Mandaean belief, a comet (Halley's?) flew over Judea (*Sidra d̲-Yahya* 18). Thus, the appearance of comets in antiquity might have been occasionally regarded as signs from heaven of impending calamity and divine displeasure, but that they were also regarded as predicting major

94. See D. K. Yeomans, "Comet Halley: The Orbital Motion," *Astronomical Journal* 82 (1977) 435–40.

95. Hughes, *The Star of Bethlehem Mystery*, 144.

96. A. Stenzel, *Jesus Christus und sein Stern* (Hamburg: Verlag der Astronomischen Korrespondenz, 1913) 73.

97. See my *Enigma of Jesus the Galilean*, 72–75.

98. For ancient deaths and births heralded by comets see Cicero, *De Divinatione* 1:23:47; Lucan 1:529; Virgil, *Aeneid* 2:694; Pliny, *Natural History* 2:6:28; Seneca, *Naturales quaestiones* 1:1; Suetonius, *Julius Caesar* 88; Servius, *Ad. Virgil Eclogues* 9:47; and *Historia Augusta*, §12 on Alexander Severus.

99. T. Reinach, *Mithridate Eupator: Roi de Pont* (Paris: Didot, 1890) 51 n. 2.

100. Fotheringham, "The New Star of Hipparchus and the Date of the Birth and Accession of Mithridates," *Monthly Notes of the Royal Astronomical Society* 89 (1919) 162.

political changes can scarcely be doubted. The death of Marcus Agrippa (Augustus's deputy in the east), thought to have been predicted by the comet of 12 B.C., was followed by the birth of Jesus in the same year.

The year 12 B.C. not only presents Halley's Comet, but also two other major celestial phenomena. First, a most unusual triple conjunction in the constellation of Capricorn on January 22 when Mars, Saturn, and Venus came within a circle of diameter 0.8°.[101] Second, great meteor showers on May 23.[102] It is noteworthy that after 12 B.C. and within Jesus' lifetime meteor showers only occurred twice (15 March 36 and 17 July 36)—at the very time of Jesus' Crucifixion according to my theory presented here.

J. E. Bruns submitted the ingenious proposition that the Magi, among numerous foreign guests and envoys, visited Herod on the occasion of the festival for the completion of Caesarea (*Antiquities* 16:140).[103] However, in such a case one would expect the Magi to have visited Herod in Caesarea, rather than in Jerusalem. Additionally, it can be forcibly argued that the completion of Caesarea occurred late in 13 B.C.,[104] before Herod set sail for Rome to meet Augustus, (*Antiquities* 16:90), and not after his return late in 12 B.C.[105] It is my belief that it was the temple in Jerusalem that was finished on Herod's return from Rome (*Antiquities* 16:132) in the early autumn of 12 B.C., after eight years of work (*Antiquities* 15:420). If I may judge from the astronomical calculation of Halley's Comet, the Magi should have reached Herod by mid-September 12 B.C. Significantly, Quirinius was consul in Rome for at least part of this year (cf. Luke 2:2). (See Table 1.)

Summary and Conclusion

According to Josephus, John the Baptist died in 35 and according to the Gospels the death of John preceded that of Jesus. The death of John in 35, therefore, places the Crucifixion of Jesus in 36.

The statement of Luke 3:1 refers to the commencement of John's preaching, *not* to the commencement of Jesus' ministry. Jesus began his public life only at the closing stage of John's career, and John (according to Josephus) was not arrested before 34. The sabbatical year 33/34 and

101. R. B. Sinnott, "Thoughts on the Star of Bethlehem," *Sky and Telescope* 36 (1968) 384–85.

102. S. Imoto and I. Hasegawa, "Historical Records of Meteor Showers in China, Korea, and Japan," *Smithsonian Contributions to Astrophysics* 2 (1958) 137.

103. J. E. Bruns, "The Magi Episode in Matthew 2," *CBQ* 23 (1961) 54.

104. M. Avi-Yonah, "The Foundation of Tiberias," *IEJ* 1 (1951) 169.

105. Corbishley, "The Chronology of the Reign of Herod the Great," 29.

the Roman census year 34/35 are indicative of the time in which Jesus was active.

The statement of Paul in Gal 2:1 does not present an insurmountable problem to all systems of Jesus chronology, including the Crucifixion in 36 A.D. A feasible solution exists by reading "four" instead of "fourteen" years.

Although calculations are only probable, astronomy can confirm 36 as the most likely year for the Crucifixion of Jesus.

John records three Passovers in the duration of Jesus' life; consequently the first was in 34, the second in 35, and the third in 36. Both Matthew and Luke place the birth of Jesus at the time of Herod the Great, in other words, prior to 4 B.C.; henceforth it is inevitable that Jesus was *over forty years old*. John's Gospel indeed reveals that Jesus was *forty-six* at the time of his first Passover in 34, and that he was *not yet fifty* at the time of the Feast of Tabernacles (after the second Passover) in 35. It follows that Jesus was born in 12 B.C.

Luke's "about thirty years old" was meant to symbolize the age of king David and it need not be used for dating purposes. Alternatively, it is possible that "forty" was initially written, since Luke 3:23 remains in contradiction with the other chronological data that this gospel provides for the determination of Jesus' birth.

The datum of the star included in Matthew may now be accurately explained: in 12 B.C. Halley's Comet passed the earth. It is likely therefore that the Magi visited Herod in Jerusalem at the time of the celebrations for the completion of the temple in the early autumn of that year.

Astronomy and the Date of the Crucifixion

Colin J. Humphreys and W. G. Waddington

As Jack Finegan has pointed out,[1] the date of the Crucifixion is the key date in the chronology of the life of Jesus, since it is directly relevant to the date and nature of the Last Supper, and to the length of his ministry; it is also indirectly relevant to his date of birth. The only certainty is that Jesus' death occurred during the ten years that Pontius Pilate was procurator of Judea (A.D. 26–36). There are advocates for nearly every year in this period.[2] In addition to the unknown year, the day of the execution of Jesus is also uncertain since there appears to be a difference of one day between the date given by the Gospel of John and that indicated by the Synoptics.

Previous attempts to date the Crucifixion have used a process of elimination, showing that every year other than the one chosen (usually A.D. 30 or 33) is incompatible with the available evidence.[3] In this essay we consider the first positive dating of the Crucifixion, using lunar eclipse evidence.[4] We also reassess the "elimination method" using a new technique for reconstructing the first-century-A.D. Jewish Calendar, which should be more reliable than previous versions.

1. Biblical Evidence

There are three main pieces of biblical evidence for dating the Crucifixion:

Colin J. Humphreys is Henry Bell Wortley Professor of Materials Engineering at University of Liverpool. W. G. Waddington is Research Assistant in the Department of Astrophysics at Oxford University.

1. J. Finegan, *Handbook of Biblical Chronology* (Princeton: Princeton University, 1964) 285–301.

2. See, for example, H. W. Hoehner, *Chronological Aspects of the Life of Christ* (Grand Rapids: Zondervan, 1977) 95–97.

3. Finegan, *Handbook of Biblical Chronology*, 300–301.

4. See our previous article, "Dating the Crucifixion," *Nature* 306 (22 Dec. 1983) 743–46.

1. Jesus was crucified when Pontius Pilate was procurator of Judea during A.D. 26–36 (all four Gospels; also Tacitus, *Annals* 15:44).
2. All four Gospels agree that Jesus died a few hours before the commencement of the Jewish Sabbath, that is, he died before nightfall on a Friday. In addition, the earliest writings that explicitly state the date of the Crucifixion all have it as a Friday.[5]
3. All four Gospels agree to within about a day (see below) that the Crucifixion was at the time of Passover.

In the official festival calendar of Judea, as used by the priests of the temple, Passover time was specified precisely.[6] The slaughtering of the lambs for Passover occurred between 3 P.M. and 5 P.M. on the fourteenth day of the Jewish month Nisan. The Passover meal commenced at sunset that evening, that is, at the start of Nisan 15 (the Jewish day running from evening to evening; Lev 23:5, Num 28:16). There is, however, an apparent discrepancy of one day in the Gospel accounts of the Crucifixion, which has been the subject of considerable debate. In John's Gospel, it is stated that Jesus' trial and execution was the day before Passover (John 18:28, 19:31). Hence John places the Crucifixion on Nisan 14. The correct interpretation of the Synoptics is less clear and we consider briefly three of the many possible interpretations that have been proposed.[7]

a. A straightforward reading of the Synoptics would seem to indicate that the Last Supper was a Passover meal, eaten in the evening at the start of Nisan 15, with the Crucifixion occurring later that Jewish day (that is, still on Nisan 15; e.g., Mark 14:12). This disagrees with John's date of Nisan 14.[8]
b. Many scholars propose that the Last Supper described by the Synoptics was not a strict Passover meal. It is suggested that Jesus, knowing of his imminent arrest, held a Passover-like meal on the evening before Passover (see Luke 22:15). Supporters of this interpretation note that the Synoptics make no mention of a Passover lamb being slain and roasted for the Last Supper. This interpreta-

---

5. For a discussion of the three days and three nights of Matt 12:40, and the arguments against a Wednesday or Thursday Crucifixion, see Hoehner, *Chronological Aspects*, 65–71.

6. B. Reicke, *The New Testament Era* (London: Black, 1968) 178–79.

7. For a review, see I. H. Marshall, *Last Supper and Lord's Supper* (London: Paternoster, 1980), chap. 3.

8. J. Jeremias, *The Eucharistic Words of Jesus* (London: SCM, 1966) 15–20.

tion is in broad agreement with the Johannine account in which the farewell meal is explicitly stated to have occurred before the feast of Passover (John 13:1). The timing also agrees, so that on this theory all four Gospels would give Nisan 14 as the Crucifixion date. A number of variations on this basic interpretation exist.[9]

c. A. Jaubert has proposed that the Last Supper reported by the Synoptics was a strict Passover Meal, but held at Passover time as calculated according to the "sectarian" calendar of the Qumran community and others.[10] According to this theory the Last Supper was held on Tuesday evening, that is, at the start of the Jewish Wednesday (the sectarian calendar Passover day; recorded by the Synoptics), the Crucifixion was on Friday (all four Gospels), and the official Passover was on Saturday (recorded by John). According to this theory all four Gospels again give Nisan 14 (official calendar) as the Crucifixion date.[11]

Some scholars thus believe that all four Gospels place the Crucifixion on Friday, Nisan 14, while others believe that according to the Synoptics it occurred on Friday, Nisan 15. At this stage for the sake of discussion we assume that both dates may be possible. The problem that then has to be solved is determining in which of the years A.D. 26–36 the fourteenth and fifteenth Nisan fell on a Friday. As is well known, various authors have attempted to use astronomy to provide a solution to this problem.[12] This is not entirely straightforward however, since, although astronomical calculations can accurately specify the times of new and full moons, we do not know with what skill the Jews of the first century could detect the first faintly glowing lunar crescent following conjunction with the sun (the new moon itself being invisible, of course).

9. Reicke, *New Testament Era*, 180–84; F. F. Bruce, *New Testament History* (London: Thomas Nelson, 1969) 183.

10. A. Jaubert, *La Date de la Cène* (Paris: Gabalda, 1957); see also Finegan, *Handbook of Biblical Chronology*, 44–49.

11. For a discussion of calendars in use in the first century A.D. see, for example, E. Schürer, *The History of the Jewish People in the Age of Jesus Christ* (rev. ed. by G. Vermes and F. Millar; Edinburgh: Clark, 1973), vol. 1: appendix 3.

12. Finegan, *Handbook of Biblical Chronology*, 291–98; Hoehner, *Chronological Aspects*, chap. 5; E. W. Maunder, "On the Smallest Visible Phase of the Moon," *Journal of the British Astronomical Association* 21 (1911) 355; J. K. Fotheringham, "The Evidence of Astronomy and Technical Chronology for the Date of the Crucifixion," *JTS* 35 (1934) 146–62; H. H. Goldstine, *New and Full Moons, 1001 B.C. to A.D. 1651* (Philadelphia: American Philosophical Society, 1973).

2. Reconstructing the First Century A.D. Jewish Calendar

The Jewish calendar is a lunar calendar, which, in the first century A.D., was determined by observing the new lunar crescent. Each Jewish month began with the evening when the new crescent was for the first time visible, shortly after sunset. Hence the Jewish day began in the evening, and the first day of each month was the day of first visibility. Consecutive reappearances of the new crescent from its period of invisibility (when it is lost in the glare of the sun) are separated by twenty-nine or thirty days, hence each lunar month is either twenty-nine or thirty days long. The main problem in reconstructing the Jewish calendar is to determine which months were twenty-nine days long and which thirty days.

In our previous paper we considered the problem of first crescent visibility from first principles by comparing the apparent visual contrast between the crescent moon and the surrounding twilight sky with the contrast threshold of the eye (which itself depends on the sky brightness and size of object). This enabled us to compute (1) the lunar crescent visibility as a function of time after sunset for the beginning of each lunar month in the period of interest, and (2) the dates of Nisan 14 for the period A.D. 26–36.

Although in the first century A.D. the beginning of the Jewish lunar month (in the official calendar) was fixed rigorously by astronomical observation, there remain two uncertain calendrical factors: intercalary (or leap) months and the possibility of a cloudy sky rendering the moon invisible. In the case of adverse weather conditions, preventing the observation of the "new light," the new month commenced on the thirty-first day of the old one, since the maximum length of any month was thirty days. Hence, although the visibility calculation cannot unambiguously determine that the moon *was* observed, it does tell when, even under perfect atmospheric conditions, the moon could *not* be seen and can thus be used to determine the earliest possible start to each lunar month. (It may be worth adding that the meteorology of a desert region, such as around Jerusalem, gives a high proportion of cloudless nights.)[13] In addition, since in our previous paper we considered the possibilities of both Nisan 14 and 15 falling on a Friday, we implicitly allowed for the possibility of the start of a month being delayed for a day due to the presence of clouds.

Twelve lunar months total approximately eleven days less than a solar year. For agricultural and religious festival reasons the Jews kept

13. N. V. Vidal and U. Feldman, "Meteorological Conditions near the Wise Observatory, Israel," *Quarterly Journal of the Royal Astronomical Society* 15 (1974) 462.

TABLE 1. *Calendrically Possible Dates for the Crucifixion*

Jewish Day	Source*	Date (Julian Calendar)
Nisan 14	John's Gospel and Synoptics (b, c)	Friday, 11 April A.D. 27†
		Friday, 7 April A.D. 30
		Friday, 3 April A.D. 33
Nisan 15	Synoptics (a)	Friday, 11 April A.D. 27†
		Friday, 23 April A.D. 34‡

* Synoptics (a, b, c) refers to the three possible interpretations mentioned on pp. 166–67.
† There is some uncertainty, depending on the atmospheric conditions, as to whether this day was on Nisan 14 or 15. We include all possibilities for completeness.
‡ Only in the case of a leap month being inserted because of exceptionally severe weather (see text).

lunar months at approximately the same place in the solar year by the intercalation of a thirteenth month when necessary. Different methods of intercalation were used at different periods of Jewish history, but in the first century A.D. intercalation was regulated annually by proclamation of the Sanhedrin according to certain criteria.[14] The most important of these was that Passover must fall after the vernal equinox. If it was noticed (for example, from the position of sunrise or sunset relative to the "Gates of Heaven" arcs of the Horizon)[15] toward the end of a Jewish year that Passover would fall before the equinox, the intercalation of an extra month before Nisan was decreed. However, a leap month could also be decreed if the crops had been delayed by unusually bad weather (since the first fruits of barley had to be ripe for presentation on Nisan 16) or if the lambs were too young. Unfortunately we possess no historical reports as to the proclamation of leap-months in the years A.D. 26–36. It is therefore possible that in some years Nisan was one month later on account of unusually severe weather. Our calculations show that in the period A.D. 26–36, if Nisan was one month later, Nisan 14 would not fall on a Friday in any year and Nisan 15 would only fall on a Friday in A.D. 34 (April 23).

3. *Possible Dates for the Crucifixion*

Table 1 lists the possible dates of a Friday Crucifixion, on Nisan 14 or 15, and including 23 April A.D. 34. These dates are the only ones that

14. Finegan, *Handbook of Biblical Chronology*, 42–44; Schürer, *History of the Jewish People*, 1:589–95; Jeremias, *Eucharistic Words*, 37; Fotheringham, "The Evidence of Astronomy," 156–57; G. Ogg *The Chronology of the Public Ministry of Jesus* (Cambridge: Cambridge University, 1940) 263.
15. O. Neugebauer, "Notes on Ethiopic Astronomy," *Or* 33 (1964) 50.

are astronomically and calendrically possible for the Crucifixion. Table 1 is identical to the possible dates given by Finegan (based on the calculations of J. K. Fotheringham),[16] except that our more accurate calculations show that Friday, 11 April A.D. 27, could have fallen on either Nisan 14 or 15, depending upon the atmospheric conditions pertaining at the start of that month.

The year A.D. 27 is almost certainly too early for the Crucifixion. Luke 3:1-2 carefully states that John the Baptist commenced his ministry in the fifteenth year of Tiberius Caesar (Jesus was baptized by John subsequently). Depending on whether Hellenistic (Roman) civil or the Jewish ecclesiastical reckoning is used, the fifteenth year (=340 Seleucid Era) is autumn A.D. 28-29 or spring A.D. 29-30.[17] In addition most scholars believe that Pilate had been procurator for some time before the Crucifixion (see Luke 13:1, 23:12). These two points render the possibility of an A.D. 27 Crucifixion unlikely.

The year A.D. 34 is almost certainly too late for the Crucifixion since it would conflict with the probable date of Paul's conversion. We can quite confidently date the later events in Paul's life. Working back from these, and using time intervals given by Paul himself (for example, three years and 14 years, see Gal 1:18, 2:1) leads many scholars to infer that Paul's conversion was in A.D. 34.[18] In addition, A.D. 34 is only a possibility for the Crucifixion date if the weather was exceptionally severe. There is no positive evidence in favor of A.D. 34 and we therefore rule it out. (The only eminent supporter of 23 April A.D. 34 that we have come across was Sir Isaac Newton, and his main reason seems to have been that April 23 is St. George's Day!)

Having effectively eliminated A.D. 27 and A.D. 34 as possible years for the Crucifixion, we note from table 1 that the Crucifixion must have occurred on Nisan 14 and that the previously listed interpretation (a) of the Last Supper cannot be correct. It is perhaps also worth noting that science has been used here to distinguish between different theological interpretations of the nature of the Last Supper, and has shown on calendrical grounds that the Last Supper cannot have been a Passover meal held at the official Passover meal time. In addition, we have shown that the Crucifixion occurred on Nisan 14, not Nisan 15. Thus Jesus died at the same time as the Passover lambs were slain. This is consistent with many Pauline statements, for example, "Christ our

16. Finegan, *Handbook of Biblical Chronology*, 295.

17. O. Edwards, "Herodian Chronology," *PEQ* 114 (1982) 29; idem, *The Time of Christ* (Edinburgh: Floris, 1986) 102, 196.

18. R. Jewett, *A Chronology of Paul's Life* (Philadelphia: Fortress, 1979) 30; Edwards, *The Time of Christ*, 174.

Passover is sacrificed" (1 Cor 5:7). In addition, Paul refers to Christ as the first fruits of those who rise from the dead (1 Cor 15:20), a clear analogy with the offering of the first fruits of barley in the temple, which occurred on Nisan 16. It is unlikely that Paul would have used this symbolism if it were inconsistent with the chronology. Thus, in describing Christ symbolically as the Passover lamb and as the first fruits, the Pauline chronology of the Crucifixion events (recorded in one of the earliest New Testament documents, 1 Corinthians, about A.D. 55)[19] is identical to that of John. Both are consistent with the synoptic chronology, provided the Last Supper was not a Passover meal held at the official time. In addition, the apocryphal "Gospel of Peter" states explicitly that Jesus' death was on the eve of Passover, that is, on Nisan 14,[20] and a Jewish source, the Babylonian Talmud, records that "on the eve of Passover they hanged Yeshu," earlier referred to as "Yeshu the Nazarene" (*b. Sanh.* 43a; "Jesus" is the Graeco-Roman equivalent of the Semitic "Yeshu"). Thus there is a striking unanimity from all sources that the Crucifixion was on Nisan 14 and consequently the only two plausible years for the Crucifixion are A.D. 30 and A.D. 33.

The earliest possible date for the commencement of the ministry of Jesus is autumn A.D. 28,[21] and John's Gospel records three different Passovers occurring during his ministry (including the one at the Crucifixion). Hence, if this evidence is accepted, A.D. 30 cannot be the Crucifixion year, leaving A.D. 33 as the only possibility, which year is also consistent with the "temple reference." At the first Passover of Jesus' ministry, John 2:20 records that the Jews said to Jesus "It has taken forty-six years to build this temple." Assuming this refers to the inner temple, the forty-six years leads to the first Passover of Jesus' ministry being in the spring of A.D. 30 or 31, depending upon how much preparation time was involved before building commenced.[22] In addition, an A.D. 33 Crucifixion is consistent with the known political situation in Judea.[23] It has puzzled some theologians that at the trials of Jesus, the Gospels depict Pilate as weak and subject to the pressure of the Jews, whereas Josephus, and also Luke 13:1, depict him as ruthless and anti-Semitic. Pilate was appointed procurator of Judea in A.D. 26 by Sejanus,

---

19. Jewett, *Chronology of Paul's Life*, 104; J. A. T. Robinson, *Redating the New Testament* (London: SCM, 1976) 54–55.

20. M. R. James, *The Apocryphal New Testament* (Oxford: Clarendon, 1953) 91.

21. Edwards, *The Time of Christ*, 104.

22. Hoehner (*Chronological Aspects*, 43) gives A.D. 30; Edwards (*The Time of Christ*, 128) gives A.D. 31, assuming eighteen months building preparation time. For an A.D. 33 Crucifixion these interpretations support a three-year and a two-year ministry, respectively.

23. Hoehner, *Chronological Aspects*, 108–9; Reicke, *New Testament Era*, 236.

a noted anti-Semite. Tiberius executed Sejanus for sedition in October A.D. 31, and subsequently ordered all governors not to mistreat the Jews. Hence the portrayal of Pilate in the Gospels is consistent with the Crucifixion occurring after October A.D. 31, that is, in A.D. 33. If the only Passovers of Jesus' ministry were the three explicitly mentioned in John's Gospel, an A.D. 33 Crucifixion implies a ministry of about two and one-half years. Many scholars believe that John omitted mention of a further Passover, which would imply a ministry of three and one-half years.

This date, 3 April A.D. 33, is supported by many scholars.[24] However, not all scholars accept that A.D. 33 is preferable to A.D. 30, and the date 7 April A.D. 30 is also strongly supported.[25] Without further evidence it does not seem possible to decide conclusively between these two dates, although we consider 3 April A.D. 33 to be the more probable for the reasons given above. In addition a few scholars support dates other than A.D. 30 or A.D. 33 (for example, A.D. 36 has been revived recently), although these do not seem calendrically possible. In order to differentiate between these two calendrically possible dates we now consider the new evidence presented in our previous paper, which, if accepted, provides the first positive dating of the Crucifixion.

4. *The Moon turned to Blood*

The new evidence concerns the meaning and significance of the moon being "turned to blood," referred to in the Bible and elsewhere. In Acts 2:14–21 it is recorded that on the day of Pentecost the apostles were accused by a crowd of being drunk. Peter stood up and said, "No, this is what was spoken by the prophet Joel: In the last days, God says, 'I will pour out my spirit on all people . . . I will show wonders in the heavens above . . . The sun will be turned to darkness and the moon to blood before that great and glorious day of the Lord shall come. And everyone who calls on the name of the Lord shall be saved.'"

Commentators are divided upon whether Peter was claiming that all the prophecy quoted from Joel had recently been fulfilled[26] or whether the words refer to the future. We will investigate the former interpretation further, and demonstrate that "the moon turned to blood" probably refers to a lunar eclipse, and show that this interpretation is self-consistent and enables the Crucifixion to be dated precisely.

24. Hoehner, *Chronological Aspects*, 145; Reicke, *New Testament Era*, 183-84; Ogg, *Chronology of the Public Ministry*, 277.

25. Finegan, *Handbook of Biblical Chronology*, 300-301; Bruce, *New Testament History*, 192 n. 2; Robinson, *Redating the New Testament*, 37.

26. W. Neil, *The Acts of the Apostles* (Grand Rapids: Eerdmans, 1973), in loc.

Peter prefaces his quotation from Joel with the words, "Let me explain this to you . . . this is what was spoken by the prophet Joel." Peter therefore appears to be arguing that recent events had fulfilled the prophecy he was about to quote. If this interpretation is correct "the last days" (v 17) began with Christ's first advent (for similar usage see 1 Pet 1:20, Heb 1:1-2) and the outpouring of the spirit (vv 17-18) commenced at Pentecost; "that great and glorious day" (v 20) refers to the resurrection, since which time "everyone who calls on the name of the Lord will be saved" (v 21). "The sun will be turned to darkness" (v 20) refers back to the three hours of darkness that occurred only seven weeks previously, at the Crucifixion (Matt 27:45), and would be understood as such by Peter's audience. As is well known, the mechanism by which the sun was darkened may have been a khamsin dust storm.[27] In addition, a Messianic section of the Sibylline Oracles, probably written before A.D. 160, states, "And straightway dust is carried from heaven to earth, and all the brightness of the sun fails at midday from the heavens."[28] (This would seem to indicate an early tradition that the darkness at noon was due to a dust storm.) Since the darkened sun occurred at the Crucifixion, it is reasonable to suppose that the moon turned to blood that same evening, "before that great and glorious day"—the resurrection. This interpretation of Acts 2:20 is supported by the New Testament scholar, F. F. Bruce, who states in his commentary on the Acts, "Peter's hearers may have associated the phenomena described in vv. 19 f. with those which attended the preternatural darkness on Good Friday."[29]

There is some other evidence that on the evening of the day of the Crucifixion the moon appeared like blood. The so-called "Report of Pilate," a New Testament apocryphal fragment states, "Jesus was delivered to him by Herod, Archelaus, Philip, Annas, Caiphas, and all the people. At his Crucifixion the sun was darkened; the stars appeared and in all the world people lighted lamps from the sixth hour till evening; the moon appeared like blood."[30]

Much of the New Testament Apocrypha consists of highly theatrical literature, which cannot be used as primary historical evidence. Tertullian records that Pilate wrote a report of all the events surrounding the Crucifixion and sent this to the Emperor Tiberias (*Apologeticus* 5 and 21). The manuscript fragments that we possess of the "Report of

27. G. R. Driver, "Two Problems in the New Testament," *JTS* 16 (1965) 334-35.

28. Sibylline Oracles 3:800-802 in R. H. Charles (ed.), *The Apocrypha and Pseudepigrapha of the Old Testament* (Oxford: Clarendon, 1913), 2:392.

29. Bruce, *The Acts of the Apostles* (Grand Rapids: Eerdmans, 1952), in loc.

30. James, *Apocryphal New Testament*, 154.

Pilate" are all of later date, but may be partly based on this very early
lost document.[31] If this is the case, the report may provide independent
evidence that the moon appeared like blood following the Crucifixion.
On the other hand, the report may have used Acts as a source and not
be independent from it. If this is the case, however, the event described
by Peter is clearly stated in the report to have occurred at the Crucifixion. A third possibility is that the so-called report is a late Christian
"forgery." If this is correct, there must have been a tradition that at the
Crucifixion the moon appeared like blood: to what extent this document
is an invention is unimportant in this context, it is the terminology
employed that is, however, significant.

Further evidence is provided by Cyril of Alexandria, the orthodox
Patriarch of Alexandria in A.D. 412. After stating that there was darkness at the Crucifixion he adds, "Something unusual occurred about the
circular rotation of the moon so that it even seemed to be turned into
blood," and notes that the prophets foretold such signs.[32] It is concluded
that the "Report of Pilate" and the words of Cyril may be used as
secondary supporting evidence that the moon appeared like blood on
the evening of the Crucifixion.

5. A Lunar Eclipse following the Crucifixion

The moon turning to blood is a graphic description of a lunar
eclipse. The reason an eclipsed moon appears bloodred is well known
and the effect has been well documented. Even though during an eclipse
the moon is geometrically in the earth's shadow, some sunlight still
reaches it by the refraction of light passing through the earth's atmosphere. The light reaching the moon is red since scattering by air
molecules and very small particles along its long path through the
atmosphere preferentially removes the blue end of the spectrum.

The phrase "moon turned to blood" has been used by writers and
historians to describe lunar eclipses for many centuries, and the expression dates back to at least 300 B.C. Descriptions of some well-
documented ancient eclipses have been compiled by F. K. Ginzel and
matched with his calculated eclipse dates.[33] We quote three examples:

31. Ibid., 153. See F. Scheideweiler, "The Gospel of Nicodemus, Acts of Pilate and
Christ's Descent into Hell," *New Testament Apocrypha* (ed. E. Hennecke and W. Schneemelcher; Philadelphia: Westminster, 1963), 1:444–49.

32. P. E. Pusey, *Sancti patris nostri Cyrilli . . . in XII Prophetas* (Oxford: Clarendon,
1868), 1:341–42, on Joel 2:30–31; cited in Driver, "Two Problems in the New Testament,"
333.

33. F. K. Ginzel, *Spezieller Kanon der Sonnen- und Mondfinsternisse* (Berlin: Mayer und
Müller, 1899).

1. The lunar eclipse of 20 September 331 B.C. occurred two days after Alexander crossed the Tigris and the moon was described by Quintus Curtius (*History of Alexander* 4:10:2) as "suffused with the colour of blood."

2. The lunar eclipse of 31 August A.D. 304, which (probably) occurred at the martyrdom of Bishop Felix, was described in *Acta Sanctorum* as "when he was about to be martyred the moon was turned to blood."

3. The lunar eclipse of 2 March A.D. 462 was described in the *Hydatius Lemicus Chronicon* thus: "On March 2 with the crowing of cocks after the setting of the sun the full moon was turned to blood."

In the medieval European annals compiled by G. H. Pertz there are so many lunar eclipses described by "the moon turned to blood" that the phrase appears to be used as a standard description.[34] F. R. Stephenson considers that the prophecy of Joel clearly alludes to a lunar eclipse.[35]

There is therefore strong evidence that when Peter, the "Report of Pilate," and Cyril of Alexandria refer to the moon turning to blood on the evening of the Crucifixion, they were describing a lunar eclipse. It is surprising that this deduction does not appear to have been made before, although F. F. Bruce almost reaches this conclusion. He states, with reference to Peter's Pentecost speech, "It was little more than seven weeks since the people in Jerusalem had indeed seen the sun turned into darkness, during the early afternoon of the day of our Lord's Crucifixion. And on the same afternoon the paschal full moon may well have appeared blood-red in the sky in consequence of that preternatural gloom."[36] Presumably Bruce and other commentators have not been aware that a bloodred moon is a well-documented description of a lunar eclipse.

6. *Lunar Eclipses visible from Jerusalem A.D. 26–36*

We have determined the eclipses relevant to our work by the use of J. Meeus and H. Mucke's *Canon of Lunar Eclipses*, the most comprehensive data available, as corrected by F. R. Stephenson and L. V. Morrison, who used ancient Babylonian eclipse records to refine the

34. G. H. Pertz (ed.), *Monumenta germaniae historica . . . scriptorum* (Hanover: Hahn, 1826–1934; repr. New York: Kraus, 1963), vols. 16–19.

35. F. R. Stephenson, "The Date of the Book of Joel," *VT* 19 (1969) 224.

36. Bruce, *Commentary on the Book of the Acts* (NICNT; Grand Rapids: Eerdmans, 1981), in loc.

calculations to take into account more accurately the long-term changes in the earth's rate of rotation.[37] These calculations agree very well with records of Babylonian and Chinese eclipse observations (the probable error in an eclipse time 2000 years ago is typically five minutes). In the period A.D. 26–36 the computations show that there was one, and only one, lunar eclipse at Passover time visible from Jerusalem, namely that of Friday, 3 April A.D. 33. This date appears to be the most probable date for the Crucifixion deduced independently using other data. The interpretation of Peter's words in terms of a lunar eclipse is therefore not only astronomically and calendrically possible, but it also allows us with reasonable certainty to specify Friday, 3 April A.D. 33, as being the date of the Crucifixion. The random probability of a lunar eclipse occurring at moonrise on a particular date is, of course, small (see below).

It is interesting to note that there have been a few references to this eclipse in the past, for example, J. R. Hind calculated that there was a lunar eclipse on 3 April A.D. 33, however his calculations showed that this eclipse was not visible from Jerusalem, and presumably it was therefore considered irrelevant to the date of the Crucifixion.[38] It is only recently, especially following the work of F. R. Stephenson,[39] that we have been able accurately to take into account the effects of long-term changes in the earth's rate of rotation. We can now state with confidence that this lunar eclipse would have been visible from Jerusalem: that is its importance.

7. *The Lunar Eclipse on Friday, 3 April A.D. 33*

Calculations show that the eclipse on 3 April A.D. 33 was visible from Jerusalem at moonrise. (All times quoted below are local Jerusalem times as measured by a sundial.) The start of the eclipse was invisible from Jerusalem, being below the horizon. The moon rose above the Jerusalem horizon at about 6:20 P.M. (the start of the Jewish Sabbath and also the start of Passover day in A.D. 33), with about 20% of its disc in the umbra of the earth's shadow and the remainder in the penumbra

---

37. J. Meeus and H. Mucke, *Canon of Lunar Eclipses: −2002 to +2526* (Vienna: Astronomy Buro, 1983); F. R. Stephenson and L. V. Morrison, "Long-term Changes in the Rotation of the Earth: 700 B.C. to A.D. 1980," *Philosophical Transactions of the Royal Society of London* A313 (1984) 47; idem, "History of the Earth's Rotations since 700 B.C.," in P. Brosche and J. Sundermann (eds.), *Tidal Friction and the Earth's Rotation* (Berlin/New York: Springer Verlag, 1982), 2:29–50.

38. J. R. Hind, "Historical Eclipses," *Nature* 6 (1872) 251.

39. Stephenson and Morrison, "Long-term Changes in the Rotation of the Earth"; Stephenson, "Historical Eclipses," *Scientific American* 247.4 (1982) 154–63 [American edition pp. 171–73].

(that is, about 31% in the shadow as perceived by the eye).[40] The true umbral eclipse finished some 25 minutes later at 6:45 P.M. (and the perceived eclipse ended at 6:55 P.M.).

Although at moonrise only 20% of the total area of the moon's disc was in the true umbral shadow, this "bite" was positioned close to the top (that is, leading edge) of the moon. Figure 1 shows the appearance of the moon at, and shortly after, moonrise on 3 April A.D. 33. As the true umbral shadow (in which the sun is geometrically entirely hidden) was near the top of the moon, about two-thirds of the visible area of the rising moon would initially have been seen as fully eclipsed (see bottom of Figure 1), while the remainder would have been in the penumbral shadow.

There is great variability in exact coloration from eclipse to eclipse owing to atmospheric conditions. As explained previously, the umbral shadow is normally bloodred. However, this color is most noticeable during total lunar eclipses. For partial eclipses, particularly with the moon at high altitude against a starry background, there is a large contrast between the obscured and unobscured part of the moon, so that the moon often appears almost white with a very dark "bite" removed. However for some partial eclipses the red color of the umbral shadow is clearly visible. For example, D. Davis has recently depicted in color an eclipse sequence as seen by the human eye with the moon low in the sky; the coloration of the umbra in the partial eclipse phase is almost as vivid as when the eclipse is total.[41]

For the case of the eclipse of 3 April A.D. 33 the moon was just above the horizon and was seen against a relatively bright sky background (the sun having just set). The most probable color of the rising moon would be red in the umbral shadow (shaded in fig. 1) and yellow-orange elsewhere. At moonrise the initially small yellow-orange region would indicate that the moon had risen, but with most of its visible area "turned to blood." If in fact a massive dust storm was responsible for darkening the sun, and this storm subsided at about 3 P.M. (the darkness is recorded in the Gospels to have lasted from noon to 3 P.M.), any dust still suspended in the atmosphere would tend to modify the above colors. The nature of such a modification would depend upon the size distribution of the particles.

The majority of lunar eclipses pass unnoticed, occurring when people are asleep or indoors. This eclipse however would probably have been seen by most of the population of Israel, since the Jews on

40. Stephenson and Morrison, "History of the Earth's Rotation," 45.

41. D. Davis's illustration accompanying D. di Cicco, "More about July's Lunar Eclipse," *Sky and Telescope* 64 (1982) 391.

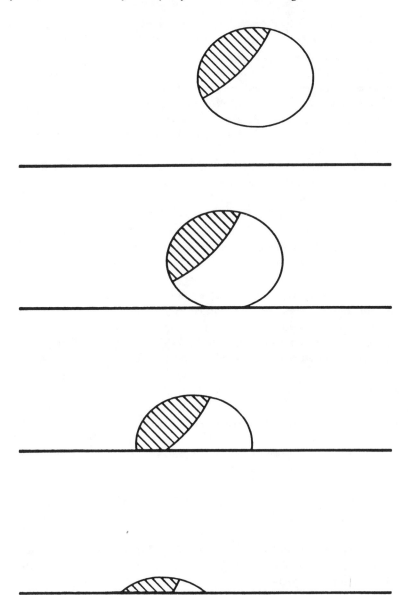

Fig. 1. *Moonrise on Friday,* 3 *April* A.D. 33, *as seen from Jerusalem.* The effects of atmospheric refraction have been included and give rise to the distorted shape of the moon. The time interval between successive diagrams is one minute. The most probable colors of the moon were red (shaded area) and yellow-orange (unshaded area).

Passover Day would be looking for both sunset and moonrise in order to commence their Passover meal. Instead of seeing the expected full Paschal moon rising, they would have initially seen a moon with a red "bite" removed (fig. 1). The effect would be dramatic. The moon would appear to grow to full in the next half hour. The crowd on the day of Pentecost would undoubtedly understand Peter's words about the moon turning to blood as referring to this eclipse that they had seen.

8. *The Apparent Mention of a Solar Eclipse in Some Texts of Luke's Gospel*

Whereas Mark 15:33 records the three hours of darkness accompanying the Crucifixion without comment—as if there were nothing particularly untoward about its occurrence—Luke 23:45 apparently appends, by way of explanation, a specific reference to a solar eclipse. As is well known, such an event is a scientific impossibility at Passover (full moon) time, and we give two possible explanations below.

In addition to the earliest known Lucan papyrus (ca. A.D. 200), all the major manuscripts of Luke's Gospel (Sinaiticus, Vaticanus, Ephraemi [C], and L) contain what appears to be the standard technical description of a solar eclipse (τοῦ ἡλίου ἐκλιπόντος); other Lucan manuscripts dating from before A.D. 900, however, lack any trace of these three words. Moreover, recent computer-based textual analysis of these primary manuscripts shows that the early papyrus p 75 is closely related to Vaticanus and often also to Sinaiticus, as well as to L and perhaps also to C.[42] It would thus appear that the specific reference to a solar eclipse was established uniquely in one family of the Lucan text by about A.D. 200 and is absent from all other families of related manuscripts. Furthermore, since the three words in question occur at the end of an otherwise complete sentence, and apparently refer to a scientific impossibility, we consider them to be an intrusion in p 75 and its related manuscripts, rather than being an intrinsic part of the original Lucan text that was later replaced by a more general phrase (ἐσκοτίσθη ὁ ἥλιος) in the other manuscript families.

Now, the context in which the solar eclipse phrase is presented in the isolated Lucan manuscript family is one of explanation: consequently, the phrase itself does not make sense unless it was intended by its author to refer to the darkness previously mentioned by Mark. Since the occurrence of a solar eclipse at Passover time has long been known to be astronomically impossible, but that of a lunar eclipse may well occur, it is possible that this particular passage is a direct result of confusion arising from a widespread tradition of *an* eclipse at the

---

42. As communicated personally to us by J. G. Griffith.

Crucifixion.[43] In this respect it is, perhaps, significant that, in attempting to identify the cause of the Crucifixion darkness as a solar eclipse, Julius Africanus (*Chronicon* 50) erroneously attributed to Phlegon the statement that the eclipse noted by him occurred at full moon; this particular eclipse (Phlegon's eclipse) was subsequently identified by Kepler as that of 24 November A.D. 29, in spite of the A.D. 32–33 date given by Phlegon.

The lunar eclipse of 3 April A.D. 33 may thus explain the curious reference to a Crucifixion solar eclipse in some manuscripts of the Luke text, which may be an intrusion inserted by a scribe knowing the oral tradition of a Crucifixion eclipse without appreciating that it was in fact a *lunar* eclipse.

An alternative explanation is that the Greek word ἐκλιπόντος in Luke is better translated "failed" than "eclipsed." Support for this interpretation comes from the Sibylline Oracles quoted earlier, where the same verb is translated "failed" in R. H. Charles's *Apocrypha and Pseudepigrapha of the Old Testament*, and clearly the darkening mechanism in the Oracles is a dust storm not an eclipse.[44] On this interpretation, Luke's apparent mention of a solar eclipse was not meant to be interpreted literally.

9. Some Implications of the Crucifixion Lunar Eclipse

In ancient times eclipses (total or partial) were regarded as a supernatural sign, often associated with the wrath of a god. For example, the first-century Jewish historian Flavius Josephus records that a lunar eclipse occurred on the same night as Herod the Great burnt alive Matthius and some other Jews for sedition (*Antiquities* 17:167).[45] A lunar eclipse on the same night as the Crucifixion would similarly have been interpreted by many as a supernatural sign associated with the wrath of God. This eclipse may well have been an important factor producing the overnight change of mind of the Jews and Pilate toward the body of Jesus, leading to the placing of the guard on the tomb, although previously Joseph of Arimathaea had apparently had no difficulty in obtaining the body for burial.

43. Fotheringham, "The Evidence of Astronomy," 160–61.

44. Charles, *Apocrypha and Pseudepigrapha of the Old Testament*, 2:392.

45. Ginzel (*Spezieller Kanon*, 127) takes this to be the partial eclipse of 13 March 4 B.C. Hind ("Historical Eclipses," 252) prefers the total lunar eclipse of 10 January 1 B.C. This latter identification is strongly supported by E. L. Martin, *The Birth of Christ Recalculated* (Pasadena: Foundation for Biblical Research, 1978), chap. 2. The possible astronomical relevance of these two dates is discussed by R. W. Sinnott, "Computing the Star of Bethlehem," *Sky and Telescope* 72 (1986) 632–35.

We have already noted the symbolism of Christ as the Passover lamb and the first fruits. The lunar eclipse may provide further symbolism in that it provides a striking parallel between the Crucifixion and the original Passover. The last plague before the Passover was three days of darkness, "darkness that can be felt" (Exod 12:13), which again could have been a massive dust storm. The Passover lamb was slain toward the end of Nisan 14. This was followed by blood being smeared on the door frames: "the blood will be a sign for you" (Exod 12:13). At the Crucifixion there was three hours of darkness, then the Lamb of God died toward the end of Nisan 14. This was followed by the moon "turning to blood," which could have been regarded as "a sign for you."

Finally, at first sight it might be thought curious that a Crucifixion lunar eclipse is not mentioned in the Gospel. However, although at the time of the Crucifixion this eclipse would have seemed of great significance and indeed Peter apparently referred to it about seven weeks later, in retrospect this lunar eclipse would have seemed insignificant to the Gospel writers compared with the Crucifixion and resurrection. The Gospel writers were not primarily interested in providing clues for chronologists.

10. Conclusions

Establishing the precise date of any ancient event is well known to be extremely difficult. It is probably not an exaggeration to state that only when ancient chronology is based upon calculable astronomical phenomena can we have certainty and precision. In this article, astronomy has been applied in two different ways to date the Crucifixion. First, in reconstructing the first-century-A.D. Jewish calendar and, second, in determining that there was a lunar eclipse visible from Jerusalem at moonrise on the evening of one of the only two days considered to be calendrically possible for the Crucifixion: Friday, 3 April A.D. 33. If this date was indeed the date of the Crucifixion we would expect some textual reference to this lunar eclipse. This article presents three such textual references: the Acts of the Apostles, the "Report of Pilate," and the writings of Cyril of Alexandria. There are therefore strong convergent arguments pointing to 3 April A.D. 33 as being the date of the Crucifixion.[46]

46. D. E. H. Whiteley, "Was John Written by a Sadducee?" *Religion* (*Vorkonstantinisches Christentum: Leben und Umwelt Jesu; Neues Testament* [*Kanonische Schriften und Apokryphon*], Forts.) (ed. W. Haase; Aufstieg und Niedergang der römischen Welt: Principat 25; Berlin: de Gruyter, 1985), 3:2504–5, has accepted our conclusions.

Cautionary Notes on the Use of Calendars and Astronomy to Determine the Chronology of the Passion

Roger T. Beckwith

The simplicity, clarity, and convenience of having a single system of chronology for world history is something that is tacitly confessed by the general and long-standing acceptance of such a system, though its benefits are more often taken for granted than explicitly recognized. It is true that, from one point of view, the introduction of our present Christian system of chronology by Dionysius Exiguus in the sixth century A.D. and its subsequent adoption worldwide was only a natural sequel to the conversion of the Roman Empire. Nevertheless, the system has served the human race well, and so much so that even those who do not acknowledge the central place of Jesus Christ in world history remain glad to use it (sometimes under an adapted nomenclature) for ordinary purposes. Even the discovery that Dionysius placed the transition between B.C. and A.D. a few years too late has simply been accepted as a fact, without any serious attempt being made to supersede or even modify his system.

The very different situation that obtained at the beginning of the Christian era is outlined with masterly lucidity in the opening chapters of Professor Finegan's *Handbook of Biblical Chronology*. A variety of eras then served as reference points for chronology. Among others, there were the Greek Olympiads (four-year periods, dating from an early celebration of the Olympic Games in what we call 776 B.C.); the era of the foundation of the city of Rome (which the learned Roman historian Varro had placed in the year 753 B.C.); the Seleucid era (dating from the victory of Seleucus I, the founder of the Greek dynasty in Syria, at the Battle of Gaza, 312 B.C.); and the era of the creation of the world (which

Roger T. Beckwith is Warden of Latimer House, Oxford.

the rabbinical chronicle *Seder ʿOlam Rabbah* fixed at about 3759 B.C.). Often, however, years were identified from the accession of a particular ruler or official, and it is in this way that the beginning of the ministry of John the Baptist is dated in Luke 3:1. In any case, a modern student needs to determine how the years are being counted, that is, at what season does the new year begin? And does the numbering start from the year in which the great event occurred or the ruler took office, or from the first complete year after it? And then again, one needs to investigate how the year itself is being reckoned, and what calendar is being used. Is it a lunar calendar of 354 days, or a solar calendar of something approaching 365 days? And is it an exact calendar, fixed by careful astronomical calculation, or an approximate calendar, intended for practical utility rather than scientific precision? Only when all these considerations have been taken into account can one begin to transpose the chronological information given by ancient writings into terms of our own chronology, and one must not be surprised if the conclusions that are reached are at best probable rather than certain, especially when one is trying to fix the month or the day of a particular occurrence, as well as the year.

The development of a scientifically exact calendar occurred in different nations at different periods, according to the rate at which the study of astronomy advanced there, and gained acceptance for its findings. In the lands of the Bible, Babylon and Egypt were the countries where astronomy was earliest studied, but Greece had caught up by the fifth century B.C., when the Greek astronomer Meton devised or adopted the nineteen-year cycle (afterwards refined by Callippus and Hipparchus) for reconciling the lunar year to the solar; though in practice Greece continued to use a less accurate eight-year cycle. Since twelve lunar months amount to only about 354⅓ days, the lunar calendar has to be adjusted periodically to the solar year of about 365¼ days, by the addition of a thirteenth month, so as to keep it in line with the seasons. Originally this was done irregularly, whenever it was seen to be necessary from the lateness of the seasons, but the nineteen-year cycle (adopted also by the Babylonians in the fifth or fourth century B.C.) made it possible to add the thirteenth month at fixed intervals, and to settle in advance the leap years in which it needed to be added.

Babylon and Greece both used a lunar calendar, adjusted in the way described, and lunar calendars also existed in Egypt. In Egypt, however, an important solar (or stellar) calendar also existed, governed by the heliacal rising of the Dog Star (i.e., its rising in proximity to the sun). Since Egypt is a flat country with a true horizon, the heliacal rising of the brightest of the stars was easily seen, and from very early times Egyptian astronomers noted that this happened about every 365 days. The 365-day calendar based on this fact was not, of course, absolutely exact, and in 238 B.C. one of the Greek kings of Egypt, Ptolemy Euergetes I, issued his Decree of Canopus, proposing the addition of a day to every fourth year so as to rectify the discrepancy. This reform was not actually adopted, however, until between 30 and 26 B.C., by which time a solar calendar based on similar principles had also been introduced at Rome. This was the famous Julian calendar, introduced by Julius Caesar in 46 B.C. under the guidance of the Egyptian astronomer Sosigenes, and it was sufficiently accurate to retain its place, without amendment, down to the sixteenth century A.D.[1]

It so happens that the chronological records of Babylon, Egypt, and Greece are remarkably full. Hence, with the aid of their relatively accurate calendars, the transposition of their statements into terms of the familiar Roman calendar and Christian system of chronology is fairly straightforward. Additional checks are provided when the records mention astronomical phenomena, since it is possible for modern astronomers to calculate with a high degree of accuracy the dates when such phenomena must have occurred. Roman chronological records are also full, and after the introduction of the accurate Julian calendar the chronology of Roman history can be established with considerable exactness.[2]

The Jewish Calendar: Scientific or Practical?

Since this was the situation in Babylon, Egypt, Greece, and Rome by the beginning of the Christian era, it is not unnatural to assume that the situation was the same in Palestine. After all, Palestine was now within the Roman Empire, and it had previously been under the authority of the Greek rulers of Syria and the Greek rulers of Egypt, and at a more remote period it had been part of the empire of Babylon. From their exile in Babylon, indeed, the Jews had brought back the Babylonian names for the months, which are found in the latest books of the Old Testament and subsequent Jewish literature. Is it not likely that, from

1. On the Babylonian, Egyptian, Greek, and Roman calendars, see for example O. E. Neugebauer, *The Exact Sciences in Antiquity* (2d ed.; Providence, RI: Brown University, 1957); R. A. Parker, *The Calendars of Ancient Egypt* (Studies in Ancient Oriental Civilization 26; Chicago: University of Chicago, 1950); the article "Calendar" in *Encyclopaedia Britannica* (15th ed.; 1974); and the articles "Calendar" and "Horae" in *Encyclopaedia of Religion and Ethics*.

2. On all this, see P. R. S. Moorey, *Excavation in Palestine* (Guildford: Lutterworth, 1981), chap. 5, "Establishing Time Scales."

one or other of these sources, they had also acquired a sufficient knowledge of astronomy to regulate their calendar and consequently their chronology with precision?

This inviting presumption is actually made by many writers on New Testament chronology, and it has the great convenience that it enables one to exploit fully the limited chronological data that the New Testament provides. The tables of new moons, new years, and leap years in antiquity that have been compiled by Parker and Dubberstein for Babylon and that have been calculated by Ginzel for Israel can then be applied to the events recorded in the New Testament without further ado.[3] All that is necessary is to allow for the fact that the new moon was visible in Jerusalem thirty-seven minutes before it was visible in Babylon, so that on occasion the Jewish month would have begun a day earlier.[4]

In reality, however, such a procedure involves a great fallacy. As noted earlier, from the fifth or fourth century B.C. onward the Baby- lonians employed the nineteen-year cycle for reconciling the lunar year with the solar. Aided by this, they were able to make an accurate calculation of new moons, new years, and leap years, and to fix them accordingly. These data serve as the basis of Parker and Dubberstein's tables. Nowadays the Jews also use, for religious purposes, the nineteen- year cycle, and by working backward from modern times Ginzel was able to calculate on the principles of this cycle how the Jewish new moons, new years, and leap years would have fallen in antiquity. What needs to be realized, however, is that Ginzel's tables are largely theoreti- cal. To treat them as historical is to ignore the clear evidence that the Jews did not use such a cycle until several centuries after the beginning of the Christian era.

Our evidence is partly Jewish and partly Christian. The Jewish evidence is mainly found in the rabbinical literature, of which the earliest substantial parts to be written down were the Mishna, the Tosepta, the Halakic Midrashim (such as Mekilta), and the quotations called baraitas, cited from earlier compilations at many places in the two Talmuds. This part of the rabbinical literature dates from about A.D. 200–300, though, as it is a record of oral tradition, it speaks for an earlier period and sometimes reaches back to the first century A.D. and

---

3. R. A. Parker and W. H. Dubberstein, *Babylonian Chronology 626 B.C.–A.D. 75* (revised edition; Brown University Studies 19; Providence, RI: Brown University, 1956); F. K. Ginzel, *Handbuch der mathematischen und technischen Chronologie* (Leipzig: Hinrichs, 1906–14).

4. Parker and Dubberstein, *Babylonian Chronology*, 25.

even before that. From these sources we learn that the Jewish months, years, and festivals were fixed not by calculation in advance but by continuous observation. The beginning of each month was announced when the new moon was sighted in Palestine. In months containing festivals, once the witnesses had given their reports and the announcement had been made, messengers were sent out to inform the Jews of the Dispersion (m. Roš Haš. 1–2). The addition of a thirteenth month to the year depended likewise upon observation; here, upon observing whether signs of spring had appeared or not. If they had not, the thirteenth month was added, and once again messengers were sent out to the Jews of the Dispersion to inform them of the fact (t. Sanh. 2:2–7, 12; Mekilta, Pisha 2; Baraitas in b. Sanh. 11a–13b).

The Christian evidence to the same effect relates to the fixing of Easter. When Christians first began to observe Easter, they evidently fixed it by working from the Jewish reckoning of the Passover, on Nisan 14. About A.D. 190 there was a sharp controversy among Christians, the Quartodeciman controversy, on the question whether to observe Easter on the Sunday after Nisan 14 or on Nisan 14 itself. Both parties to the controversy based their reckoning on the date when the Jews were observing the Passover, which they had first to inquire or discover from the Jews. This gave rise to the mocking taunt from the Jewish side that Christians could not fix Easter without their help. In response, third-century Christians began to calculate the date of Easter astronomically: first Hippolytus of Rome, adapting the old Greek eight-year cycle, and then Anatolius of Alexandria, using the more accurate nineteen-year cycle. The influential churches of Rome and Alexandria were among the first to adopt the new method. This, however, gave rise to the second Christian Easter controversy, which was settled in principle at the great council of Nicaea in A.D. 325: whether to fix Easter by astronomical calculation or to continue holding it on the Sunday after the Jewish Passover. The decision was in favor of the new method, though the old one lingered on for a time in the East.[5] Now, if the Jews had already been calculating the Passover by the nineteen-year cycle, this second Easter controversy could hardly have arisen, and certainly

5. The evidence about these two controversies and the distinction between them is set out in my article "The Origin of the Festivals Easter and Whitsun," Studia Liturgica 13 (1979) 1–20. The contention of August Strobel, in his learned and comprehensive book Ursprung und Geschichte des frühchristlichen Osterkalenders (TU 121; Berlin: Akademie-Verlag, 1977), that the Roman eighty-four-year cycle (though much later attested, much more elaborate, and much more accurate than Hippolytus's doubled eight-year cycle) is in fact older, cannot be regarded as plausible—still less his claim that it goes back to the first beginnings of Christianity and was taken over from the Jews.

not in the form in which it did, since both parties would in principle have agreed with each other.

It seems, in fact, that the Jews did not begin to calculate the date of the Passover astronomically, or to employ the nineteen-year cycle for this purpose, until between the fourth and the seventh centuries A.D.[6] If this appears surprising, one should recall the stubborn and commendable independence of the Jews in religious matters, which naturally made them slow to adopt either the conclusions or the methods of pagan or Christian scientists.

Of course, the most responsible writers on New Testament chronology are well aware that in the first century the Jewish year was governed by observation and not by calculation. Nevertheless, they often seem unconscious of the degree of irregularity that the old Jewish method of observation could introduce. This affects the dating of the most important of all first-century events, the death and resurrection of Jesus. George Ogg, author of two standard works in this general field, *The Chronology of the Public Ministry of Jesus* (1940) and *The Chronology of the Life of Paul* (1968), writes in his article on "Chronology of the New Testament" (contributed to *The Illustrated Bible Dictionary*):

> Of attempts to determine the year of the crucifixion the most fruitful is that made with the help of astronomy. According to all four Gospels, the crucifixion took place on a Friday; but whereas in the Synoptics that Friday is 15 Nisan, in John it is 14 Nisan. The problem then that has to be solved with the help of astronomy is that of determining in which of the years 26-36 the 14th and 15th Nisan fell on a Friday. But since in NT times the Jewish month was lunar and the time of its commencement was determined by observation of the new moon, this problem is basically that of determining when the new moon became visible. Studying this problem, [J. K.] Fotheringham and [K.] Schoch have each arrived at a formula by applying which they find that 15 Nisan was a Friday only in 27 and 14 Nisan a Friday only in 30 and 33. Since as the year of the crucifixion 27 is out of the question, the choice lies between 30 (7 April) and 33 (3 April).[7]

As will be noted, Ogg considers that astronomical and calendrical considerations (1) narrow down the possible years for the Crucifixion to two, A.D. 30 and A.D. 33, (2) fix the only date in each of those two years

---

6. See B. Z. Wacholder and D. B. Weisberg, "Visibility of the New Moon in Cuneiform and Rabbinic Sources," *HUCA* 42 (1971) 227-42. In earlier centuries, the rabbis did apparently keep some record of new moons, but from this they could draw only limited conclusions.

7. *The Illustrated Bible Dictionary* (ed. N. Hillyer et al.; Wheaton: Tyndale, 1980), 1:278-79.

when it could have occurred, April 7 or April 3 respectively, and (3) exclude the synoptic chronology of the passion in favor of the so-called Johannine chronology. Using more refined criteria for determining the time when the new moon became visible at Jerusalem, C. J. Humphreys and W. G. Waddington have recently reached the same three conclusions.[8] While grateful for all further light astronomy can provide, it is the contention of the present essay that, once the irregularities possible under the Jewish calendar have been appreciated, it will be seen that none of these three conclusions is legitimate.

Even that profound scholar of Judaism, Joachim Jeremias, who in his book *The Eucharistic Words of Jesus* has so thoroughly demonstrated to most people's minds that the Last Supper was an actual Passover meal and has so fully answered the customary objections to this conclusion, creates unnecessary difficulties for his own case by his presentation of the astronomical evidence. He speaks of the uncertainty about which years had twelve months and which thirteen, with leap years falling every two to three years on average, but says that the uncertainty is greatly reduced by "the rule that the passover must fall after the spring equinox."[9] He concludes that the only possible year for the passion in which there is much likelihood that Nisan 14 can have been a Thursday, in accordance with the synoptic chronology, is A.D. 31, and only then provided it included a thirteenth month, and the sighting of the new moon was delayed that year for a day by poor visibility.

The Passover and the Equinox

The alleged rule that the Passover must always fall after the spring equinox is so much taken for granted in discussions of the astronomical evidence that it calls for special attention. No doubt it is true that the Passover *usually* fell at or after the spring equinox (not necessarily after it), but was this an invariable rule? The proof that Jeremias offers is the fragment of Anatolius quoted by Eusebius in his *Ecclesiastical History* 7:32:13-19. Anatolius was the third-century church father from Alexandria who taught Christians to use the nineteen-year cycle for calculating Easter. He was one of those responsible for introducing the present Christian rule that Easter must never fall before the spring equinox. In his fragment he says that those who place "the first month [Nisan]" before it, "and determine the fourteenth day of the Pascha

---

8. "Dating the Crucifixion," *Nature* 306 (22 Dec. 1983) 743-46.
9. (London: SCM, 1966) 37. Jeremias's presentation of the astronomical evidence covers pp. 36-41.

accordingly, are guilty of no small or ordinary mistake." It is not clear whether he is here criticizing Jews or Christians or both, but he claims that the rule was known to "the Jews of old, even before Christ," and names Philo, Josephus, Musaeus, the two Agathobuli, and Aristobulus in proof of his assertion, laying particular emphasis on the last named. The writings of the Agathobuli and (pseudo-)Musaeus are lost to us, but it is likely that all of these authors, with the partial exception of Josephus, were Hellenistic Jews, and we know that Philo and Aristobulus were Alexandrian Jews. Josephus merely says that the sun is in the sign of Aries at the Passover (*Ant.* 3:248), which implies that the equinox is past, though he does not insist on the point. Philo more definitely says that Nisan commences with the spring equinox (*Questions and Answers on Exodus* 1:1), which may reflect the fact that Alexandria was a center of Greek learning, and Philo an ardent student of it. But the only one of these writers who is known to have insisted on the point, treating it as an invariable rule, is the other Alexandrian, Aristobulus. Aristobulus lived at Alexandria in the mid-second century B.C., at the same place and time as one of the greatest of Greek astronomers, Hipparchus, who perfected the nineteen-year cycle. The writings of Aristobulus, like those of Philo later, aimed to recommend Judaism by showing that it conformed to the highest standards of Greek wisdom. In his contemporary situation at Alexandria, it would have been natural for him to maintain that the Jewish year was truly scientific, in that it took as its invariable starting point the spring equinox.

In Palestine, however, the situation was quite different. Astronomy was not studied there, and the year was regulated not by calculation but by observation. It seems clear that the decision to add a thirteenth month to the old year was often taken without any attention to the equinox at all. In Mekilta (Pisha 2) the only factor considered is whether the first-ripe grain has appeared or not, basing this criterion on the old name for Nisan, "Abib" (ʾabîb 'the first-ripe ear'), Abib being the month in which the Passover is commanded to be held (Deut 16:1). If the first-ripe grain appears early, one must not lop off the twelfth month, we are told, but if it is still being awaited, one must add on a thirteenth month.

Nor is the equinox mentioned in two extant letters written to Jews of the Dispersion by Rabban Gamaliel II (first century A.D.) and Rabban Simeon ben Gamaliel II (second century A.D.) announcing that the thirteenth month has been added. The earlier of these letters reads, "May your peace be great for ever! We beg to inform you that the turtledoves are still tender and the lambs too thin and that the first-ripe grain has not yet appeared. It seems advisable to me and my colleagues to add thirty days to this year." Apart from the reference to the patriarch's 'colleagues', the other letter is virtually identical, and an oral saying by the patriarch who sent it is also on record: "He used to say: 'In that the turtledoves are still tender and the spring-lambs too thin, it is advisable in my opinion to add thirty days to this year.'"[10] The formula used in each of these places is probably an old one, since by the time of these two patriarchs the temple had been destroyed, and even though Passover lambs were still being killed (nonsacrificially), turtledoves were no longer being offered for the purification of the unclean.

Nevertheless, it may have been in the time of the later of these two patriarchs, Simeon ben Gamaliel II (mid-second century A.D.), that the Palestinian Jews first started to pay attention to the equinox. Simeon himself had the unusual reputation of having been trained in Greek learning, and many of his reported sayings reflect scientific knowledge.[11] In a passage recording that people rejoiced when the premature state of the grain was one of the reasons for adding the thirteenth month, the comment is made, "Rabban Simeon ben Gamaliel says, 'Also if it be the lateness of the *tekuphah*'" (*t. Sanh.* 2:2, and Bar. in *b. Sanh.* 11b).[12] Certainly the first known rabbis to discuss the equinox—Rabbi Judah ben Ilai, Rabbi Jose, and Rabbi Simeon ben Yohai—were contemporaries of Rabban Simeon in the mid-second century A.D. These rabbis believed that they could count the number of days before the equinox would arrive, and they discussed how many days distant the equinox must be (whether sixteen or twenty) if the new year were to be delayed (*t. Sanh.* 2:7, and *b. Sanh.* 12b–13b). Presumably, this knowledge of the equinox had been acquired from non-Jewish sources, but how accurately it had been acquired is open to question, since it is well known that inexact dates for the equinoxes and the solstices had wide currency in the early Christian centuries. As late as the fifth century A.D. the church of Rome, at the very heart of the Empire, was maintaining in opposition to the church of Alexandria that the spring equinox

---

10. For the two letters and the saying, see *t. Sanh.* 2:5–6 and *b. Sanh.* 11a–b. The lambs would, of course, be needed for the Passover itself; the turtledoves would be needed to purify the unclean before they partook of the Passover (cf. Lev 12:8; 14:22, 30; 15:14, 29; Num 6:10); while the first-ripe grain would be needed for the offering of the Sheaf during Passover week.

11. See J. Z. Lauterbach, "Simeon (ben Gamaliel II)," *The Jewish Encyclopedia* (ed. I. Singer; New York: Funk and Wagnalls, 1905), 11:347–48.

12. As the new grain was not to be eaten until after the Sheaf was offered, the Israelites would be sorry if the offering of the Sheaf were delayed on any grounds other than the premature state of the crop. The *tekuphah* is the new season or quarter, beginning with one of the equinoxes or solstices.

fell on March 18 and not March 21.[13] Yet even after the rabbis started paying attention to the equinox they refused to acknowledge the fact that it would fall after the Passover as an adequate reason in itself for adding the thirteenth month—there had to be an additional reason. The formula used was, "A year may be intercalated on three grounds: on account of the premature state of the corn-crops; or that of the fruit-trees; or the lateness of the *tekuphah*. On the basis of any two of these they may intercalate, but not one only" (*t. Sanh.* 2:2, and Bar. in *b. Sanh.* 11b).

But since the decision whether to add the thirteenth month was often made without any attention being paid to the equinox, and since when attention was paid to it it was not allowed to be the sole determining factor, it is inevitable that, at times when spring weather came early, the new year must often have been announced without waiting for the approach of the equinox. That this actually happened is proved by a Christian work produced in Syria in the latter half of the fourth century, the so-called Apostolic Canons. Syria was one of the three regions in the East where, at the time of the Council of Nicaea (A.D. 325), Easter was still being observed on the Sunday after the Jewish Passover instead of being calculated astronomically.[14] Syria was, of course, a country adjacent to Palestine, and it was heavily populated by Jews, so it was easy for Christians there to discover the date each year when the Passover would fall. The old custom was consequently still persisting sufficiently strongly when the Apostolic Canons were written to call forth the following denunciation: "If any bishop, presbyter, or deacon shall celebrate the holy day of the Pascha before the spring equinox, with the Jews, let him be deposed" (Canon 7).[15] It is clear from the language here used that the Jews of that time held the Passover before the spring equinox often enough for this to have come to be regarded as a characteristic Jewish practice.

But if the Passover quite frequently fell before the spring equinox, this at once opens new possibilities for the dates of Christ's death and resurrection. It means in particular that, working from the figures for the appearance of the new moon provided by Humphreys and Waddington and confining our attention to the most plausible period for the passion (A.D. 30–36), there is an additional year (A.D. 36) when Nisan 14

13. See C. J. Hefele, *A History of the Christian Councils* (Edinburgh: T. & T. Clark, 1894–96), 1:328–29.

14. Beckwith, "The Origin of the Festivals," 12. The other two regions were Cilicia and Mesopotamia.

15. *Pascha* in Greek can mean either the Passover or Easter, and here it embraces both.

may have been a Friday, and there are two years when Nisan 14 may have been a Thursday, in accordance with the synoptic chronology, and not a Friday.[16] In A.D. 33, although the fourteenth day of the lunar month immediately after the equinox would have been Friday, April 3, the fourteenth day of the lunar month immediately before the equinox would have been Thursday, March 5.[17] Again, in A.D. 30, although the fourteenth day of the lunar month immediately after the equinox would have been Friday, April 7, the fourteenth day of the lunar month immediately before the equinox would have been Wednesday, March 8, or, if the announcement of the new moon had been delayed a day by poor visibility, Thursday, March 9. March 5 or 9 (about a fortnight before the equinox) would be rather early for the Passover to fall, but since the climate of Palestine is not mechanically regular, and there is a great deal of variation in the time when the rainy season (with its agricultural activities) begins and ends, an early spring and therefore an early Passover is entirely possible.[18]

16. The main limiting factors for the date of the Crucifixion are the procuratorship of Pontius Pilate (A.D. 26–36), the commencement of John the Baptist's ministry in the fifteenth year of Tiberius (probably A.D. 28–29), the subsequent three Passovers of Jesus' ministry mentioned by John, and the fourteen or more years mentioned in Gal 1:18 and 2:1 between Paul's conversion (after Jesus' resurrection) and the Jerusalem council in A.D. 48–50. (Recent studies that have supported the historical value of the Fourth Gospel should warn us to take its three Passovers seriously.)

17. When it became customary to prohibit a thirteenth month within either a sabbatical year or the year following, as being years of scarcity because of the suspension of agriculture, a thirteenth month was added, by way of compensation in advance, to the year preceding (*t. Sanh.* 2:9, and Bar. in *b. Sanh.* 12a). As A.D. 33–34 was probably a sabbatical year (the sabbatical year began six months after the festal year, and so spanned parts of two calendar years), this would mean that a thirteenth month would have been added in A.D. 32–33, with the result that Passover in A.D. 33 would have been unlikely to fall before the equinox. However, as the latter of the two passages cited says, the family of Rabban Gamaliel (which held the patriarchate for most of the first two centuries A.D.) only prohibited intercalation in the sabbatical year itself, not the year following. This is confirmed by the evidence that the year of the destruction of Jerusalem, A.D. 69–70, which was the year after a sabbatical year, contained a thirteenth month. See my article "St. Luke, the Date of Christmas, and the Priestly Courses at Qumran," *RevQ* 9 (1977) 73–94.

18. See D. Baly, *The Geography of the Bible* (London: Lutterworth, 1959) 47–52 on the climate of Palestine. Another factor that would sometimes have caused an early Passover was the prohibition against adding a thirteenth month in a year of famine (*t. Sanh.* 2:9, and Bar. in *b. Sanh.* 11b–12a). This was to allow the Sheaf to be offered and the new crop to be released for use as soon as possible. However, there is no record of a year of famine in the period that concerns us. See J. Jeremias, *Jerusalem in the Time of Jesus* (London: SCM, 1969) 140–44, for a survey of famines occurring in Palestine around the beginning of the Christian era.

The Passover and the Thirteenth Month

In the course of the nineteen-year cycle a thirteenth month is added to the year seven times. Thus, to rectify the discrepancy between the lunar calendar and the seasons, one does not need to add the extra month every other year, but one does need to add it more frequently than one year in three. This will be the average. It would be a great mistake, however, to infer that in ancient times leap years occurred in an orderly fashion and were always separated by one or two years. Two years in succession could be declared leap years, and though there was a rule against three years in succession being declared such, there was a tradition that Rabbi Akiba (d. A.D. 135), who was reckoned a great authority on the calendar, had done precisely this when in prison, and had intercalated three years in succession (*t. Sanh.* 2:8; Bar. in *b. Sanh.* 12a). When Akiba's pupil, Rabbi Simeon ben Yohai, reports this, it is met with protest. Yet there does not seem to be any adequate reason to deny this tradition. And if this could happen after the temple had been destroyed, how much more could it happen before that, when the many reasons for intercalation that related to the temple would have had much more importance?

The old sources mention, in all, eleven reasons for adding a thirteenth month. Six of these are regarded as primary reasons: (1) the immaturity of the corn crops, (2) the immaturity of the fruit trees, (3) the remoteness of the equinox, (4) the Passover ovens being not yet dry, (5) Jews from the Dispersion on their way to Jerusalem having not yet arrived, and (6) the roads and bridges leading to Jerusalem still needing to be repaired after the winter (*t. Sanh.* 2:2, 12; Baraitas in *b. Sanh.* 11a–b). We have seen that two of the first three reasons had to apply, before intercalation was considered appropriate, and the same may be the case with the other three. Four subsidiary reasons are also mentioned: (7) the kids or lambs being too thin, (8) the turtledoves being too young, (9) the weather being cold or snowy, and (10) the Jews of the Dispersion having not even been able to set out (*t. Sanh.* 2:4–6, 12; Baraitas and letters in *b. Sanh.* 11a–b). These ought only to serve as auxiliary reasons for intercalation. But if intercalation is based on these alone, as the saying of Rabban Simeon ben Gamaliel II quoted above indicates that it sometimes was, the decree is considered valid. Finally, a disputed reason for intercalation is mentioned: (11) danger of a large part of the nation being unable to eat the Passover because of uncleanness (*t. Sanh.* 2:10; Bar. in *b. Sanh.* 12a–b). Rabbi Judah ben Ilai, who usually represents the older view, supports this reason. If it is more than merely theoretical, it probably goes back to temple times, as all the reasons that relate to sacrifices and the pilgrimage to Jerusalem (at least six of the other ten) certainly do.

With so many reasons why a thirteenth month could be added, and such irregularity in the adding of these months, it is virtually impossible to say in which years one was added and in which years one was not. Negatively, we know that one would not be added in a sabbatical year or a year of famine (see nn. 17 and 18), and though there seems to have been no famine in the relevant period, the year A.D. 33–34 was probably a sabbatical year, so there would not have been a thirteenth month before the Passover of A.D. 34. Positively, many of the reasons for intercalation imply that the rainy season had begun or ended late, with late cold or snow, or delayed crops, or thin lambs and kids, so if we knew in which of the relevant years (if any) such conditions were present, we could regard it as probable that a thirteenth month was then added. However, neither the New Testament nor Josephus supplies this information.

Such being the case, it is possible that the Passover in any of the years A.D. 30–36, except A.D. 34, may have been delayed by the addition of the thirteenth month. And since it was a well-known practice to have two leap years in succession, and not unheard of to have three leap years in succession, it is necessary to reckon with this possibility as well. It has to be realized, however, that in such cases the Passover would probably have fallen only a month after the equinox, not two or three months after it.[19]

Before seeing what effect all this would have, we need to consider the question of the length of the thirteenth month. In later times it was an ordinary month, and its length (whether thirty days or twenty-nine) was determined by the moon. This is the reckoning advocated by Rab Papa (fourth century A.D.) in *b. Sanh.* 11a. Later still, after the calendar had been regulated astronomically, the thirteenth month was fixed at twenty-nine days, and the twelfth month (normally twenty-nine days long) was in leap years given an extra day, making it thirty days long. This seems to be the reckoning that underlies the discussion in *b. Roš Haš.* 19b, where the argument turns on the length of the twelfth month, not the thirteenth. However, the two letters written by Rabban

19. Two leap years in succession would be due to such causes as the normal incidence of leap year followed the next year by a late spring, or the normal incidence of leap year preceded by a leap year delayed by the sabbatical year or a year of famine. If the latter sequence were followed the next year by a late spring, one would have leap years three years in succession. In each case, however, the final or penultimate factor is the normal incidence of leap year, so even after the last of the leap years Passover would only be a month later than the equinox, not two or three months later.

Gamaliel II and Rabban Simeon ben Gamaliel II announcing the addition of a leap year, long before the calendar was regulated astronomically, both say that it has been decided "to add thirty days to this year," that is, to add a thirteenth month of that length. Moreover, lest this should just be taken as a coincidence, there is also the habitual saying by the second of these patriarchs, "it is advisable in my opinion to add thirty days to this year" (see above, p. 191). It looks, therefore, as if this is another of the old calendrical traditions characteristic of to the family of Rabban Gamaliel (like that mentioned in n. 17). As the family of Rabban Gamaliel held the patriarchate for most of the first two centuries A.D., this probably means that it was normal first-century practice to use a thirteenth month of fixed length, namely, of thirty days.

There was at the time a rival view, reflected by a baraita quoted in *b. Šabb.* 87b, that the thirteenth month should have a fixed length of twenty-nine days. A similar view is attributed by Rabbi Joshua ben Levi (third century) to "the holy community of Jerusalem" (*b. Roš Haš.* 19b). Indeed, it is possible that the view that the thirteenth month should have a *variable* length also goes back to early times, since Rab Nahman bar Hisda (fourth century) transmits a saying of Rabbi Simai (first to second century) to this effect (*b. Roš Haš.* 19b). A reference to one or other of these rival views is made in a baraita quoted in the same context, where Rabban Simeon ben Gamaliel is strangely represented as holding the rival view: "How long is the period of the prolongation of the year? Thirty days. Simeon ben Gamaliel, however, says a month."

Since, however, we have the letters to show what the family of Rabban Gamaliel (and Rabban Simeon in particular) really held, it is likely that the name of some opponent of Rabban Simeon should stand here in place of his. At least the baraita represents thirty days as the standard reckoning, and the reckoning of the family of Rabban Gamaliel would certainly have been standard for as long as the patriarchate was in their hands. While that period lasted, the thirteenth month would have had a fixed length of thirty days.

Why this should be, is not so easy to answer. However, a possible reason is the amount of time necessary for the messengers announcing the thirteenth month, or the new year itself, to get to the Jews of the Dispersion. The observance of holy days at the right time caused great problems to the Jews of the Dispersion, because often the news that the preceding new moon had been sighted in Palestine failed to reach them soon enough. The Passover, the most important festival of all, was only thirteen days after the new moon of Nisan, and there was no way that the messengers could get to a distant part of the Dispersion such as Rome in thirteen days. The best way to Rome was by sea, but even during the most favorable season for sailing the journey would take them twice this length of time. The beginning of Nisan was so far from being the most favorable season for sailing that it was only days after the season when the seas were completely closed.[20] The messengers might well have to travel by the overland route, and if they covered about fifty Roman miles a day, like the Roman imperial post, the journey to Rome would take them about 42 days.[21] By giving the thirteenth month a fixed length, it would be possible to ensure that at least when there was a leap year the news would arrive in time for Passover, since it would give the messengers forty-three days before the festival for their journey, instead of thirteen. So this may perhaps have been the motive for giving the thirteenth month an unchanging length.[22]

Applying these considerations to the problem in hand, and working once more from the figures for the appearance of the new moon provided by Humphreys and Waddington, we see that there are three years in the period A.D. 30–36 when the announcement of a thirteenth month before the Passover could have been significant. In A.D. 34, though the fourteenth day of the lunar month immediately after the equinox would have been a Wednesday (March 24), the insertion of a thirty-day intercalary month would have moved the fourteenth day of the first month to a Friday (April 23). However, it was noted above that the Passover of A.D. 34 probably fell in a sabbatical year, and if so it would not have been preceded by a thirteenth month. More significant, therefore, is the case of A.D. 31. This is the year favored by Jeremias, who argues that Nisan 14 in that year could have been a Thursday if it was preceded by a thirteenth month and if the announcement of the new moon of Nisan that year was delayed for a day by poor visibility. The latter of these requirements can be forgotten, however, if the thirteenth month had a fixed length of thirty days, for a delay of thirty

20. See Beckwith, "The Origin of the Festivals," 15–16.

21. See A. M. Ramsay, "The Speed of the Roman Imperial Post," *JRS* 15 (1925) 60–74. Among the journeys she instances is an overland journey in winter from Rome to Alexandria (perhaps 3,177 miles), which took 63 days. From Jerusalem to Rome is about two-thirds of this distance, and follows a similar route.

22. Of the other major holy days, Pentecost would have created no problem, since it was fixed by counting fifty days from the Passover. But Trumpets, the Day of Atonement, and Tabernacles, on Tishri 1, 10, and 15 respectively, would have caused difficulty. The Mishna says that, in order to fix Trumpets, messengers went out to announce the sighting of the new moon of Elul, the previous month (*m. Roš Haš.* 1:3), and this makes one wonder whether the family of Rabban Gamaliel also gave a fixed length to Elul. Certainly, there was a tradition that in practice Elul always had twenty-nine days (*b. Roš Haš.* 19b), and the tradition perhaps arose out of a rule.

days would, in itself, move Nisan 14 from Tuesday, March 27, to Thursday, April 26. Nor should the case of A.D. 35 be wholly ignored. For though, in that year, a delay of thirty days would have moved Nisan 14 from Tuesday, April 12, to the very late date of Thursday, May 12, we are not in a position to say that toward the end of March that year, after an exceptionally late spring, it might not have seemed necessary to add a thirteenth month.

Reconciling the Passion-Week Chronology

The chronology of Passion Week is a difficult and complicated problem, and this is no place to explore the whole question. The purpose of the present essay is simply to counsel caution before too hastily rejecting certain solutions or accepting others. As I have tried to demonstrate, the idea that astronomical and calendrical considerations cut the Gordian Knot by confining the Nisan 14 of the Passion to a Friday in A.D. 30 or A.D. 33, thus excluding the synoptic chronology, is a mistake. On the contrary, if the Passover fell before the equinox in A.D. 33, Nisan 14 was a Thursday; and if the Passover was delayed by a thirteenth month in A.D. 31 or A.D. 35, Nisan 14 was a Thursday. Moreover, if the Passover fell before the equinox in A.D. 30, and the announcement of the new moon was delayed for a day by poor visibility, Nisan 14 was a Thursday in that year also. Of course, it could be conjectured that poor visibility made the other three Thursdays Fridays, in accordance with the "Johannine" chronology. But then, the two favored Fridays were subject to the same danger, and could have become Saturdays!

If one is not content to posit a contradiction between John and the Synoptists (a position that has its own difficulties, not the least of them being the indications, listed on pp. 202-3 below, that John himself knows, and sometimes follows, the synoptic chronology), various possible ways of reconciling them are worthy of consideration. One way, which is much in vogue at the present time, is that of rival calendars. This takes various forms. Occasionally it has been maintained, on the grounds of a misunderstanding of the rabbinical evidence, that some Jews sacrificed the Passover lamb on Nisan 13, not Nisan 14. This would be contrary to the express command of Exod 12:6, Lev 23:5, Num 9:3, 28:16. Occasionally again, it has been conjectured that the Sadducees or Boethusians (related groups, if not indeed the same) had a controversy with the Pharisees over the date of the Passover, just as they did over the date of Pentecost. However, this is pure conjecture. Since the voluminous rabbinical literature so often specifies matters on which these rival groups contended, including of course the date of

Pentecost, it would be strange for it to say nothing about a controversy over the date of the still more important festival of the Passover. What the rabbinical literature does say (and Josephus, quite independently, supports; see *Antiquities* 13:288, 296, 298, 401–2; 18:15, 17), is that in practice the Sadducees gave way to the views of the Pharisees. If so, such a controversy could hardly have any bearing on the date of the Last Supper, for one can scarcely think of Jesus as the one *Sadducee* who had the courage of his convictions.[23]

Then again, an explanation of the discrepancy between the gospels has occasionally been sought in the fact that some Jews reckoned the twenty-four-hour day from nightfall and others from daybreak; or, to speak more accurately, that some *preferred* one reckoning to the other, for they were not treated as mutually exclusive.[24] The fallacy here is that it would only have led to a difference in the dating of the night and not of the day. Since (except on rare occasions like the Passover meal) all activity took place in the daytime, it is the day that would be dated, and the night—whether the night preceding or the night following— would take its date from the day. Especially must this have been so if both reckonings were used, as they were, by the same people. Since the Pentateuch required that the lamb should be slain on the fourteenth and eaten the following night (Exod 12:6–10), and since the slaying had, by the first century, been moved forward from the evening of the fourteenth into the afternoon of that day (Philo, *On the Special Laws* 2:145, 149; *Questions and Answers on Exodus* 1:11; Josephus, *Jewish War* 6:423; *m. Pesaḥ.* 5:1), it would make no difference in practice whether the following night was reckoned part of the fourteenth or part of the fifteenth, for it would still be the night after the day which, on both reckonings, was called the fourteenth, and on which the Passover lamb was slain.

These conjectural differences of calendar have now been pushed into the background by the demonstration of a real difference of calendar between the predominant Jewish schools of thought and the

---

23. The reason for the controversy over the date of Pentecost was that the Pentateuch does not give Pentecost an explicit date, and that the word "sabbath" that it uses in this connection (Lev 23:11, 15–16) is open to more than one interpretation. Nothing of the kind applies to the Passover. There is late evidence (tenth century) that the Sadducees favored a rough solar calendar of 360 days, which would need to be intercalated in a different way from the lunar calendar (see L. Nemoy, "Al-Qirqisani's Account of the Jewish Sects and Christianity," *HUCA* 7 [1930] 363); but as the dates in this calendar would usually have diverged by much more than one day from those in the lunar calendar, it would not help solve the chronology of Passion Week.

24. In proof of this see my article, "The Day, Its Divisions and Its Limits, in Biblical Thought," *EvQ* 43 (1971) 221–27.

Essenes. The credit for demonstrating this belongs mainly to Annie Jaubert. In her book *La date de la cène* and various related articles she has proved, to the satisfaction of most scholars, that the solar calendar expounded in 1 Enoch and the Book of Jubilees, and actually practiced at Qumran, assigned exactly fifty-two weeks (or 364 days) to the year, and that its new year's day was a Wednesday. A consequence is that the fourteenth day of its first month, when the Passover lambs were due to be slain, was a Tuesday, and Jaubert tries to use this fact to explain the difference between the Synoptics and John, by suggesting that Jesus followed the Essene calendar and his opponents the standard lunar one.[25]

Unfortunately, this ingenious proposal proves to be open to very weighty objections. First, though many events follow hard upon one another between the Last Supper and the death of Jesus, all the gospels place his death on a Friday (Matt 27:62, 28:1; Mark 15:42; Luke 23:54; John 19:31, 42), and they all imply that the Last Supper took place the night before, not three nights before. Second, the links between primitive Christianity and Essenism, though interesting, are relatively few, and Jesus' own links with Essenism do not appear to be any stronger. In particular, on the many occasions when he goes up to Jerusalem for the feasts (as J. T. Milik points out), he always goes up with the festival crowds and not at some unusual time.[26] Third, it is very questionable whether the Essenes did go up to Jerusalem for the feasts, or whether Jesus, had he shared their views, would have done so. The Essenes followed the beliefs expressed in the older sections of the Book of Enoch, where the sacrifices offered in the Second Temple are described as "polluted and not pure," and the seer is unable to tell whether God's people enter Jerusalem any more (1 Enoch 89:67, 73).[27] The temple authorities, for their part, excommunicated the Essenes (Josephus, *Antiquities* 18:19), and this may well have happened before the time of Jesus' ministry. Fourth, the assumption of Jaubert that, though the Essenes held the Passover on a different day from other Jews, they would have held it in the same week, is quite gratuitous and in all probability wrong. It is based on the supposition that the Jews of our Lord's day had the same proficiency as some of their neighbors abroad in astronomical science, and so would have been well aware that the true length of the solar year was not 364 days. As shown above, such a

25. See *La date de la cène* (Paris: Gabalda, 1957).

26. J. T. Milik, *Ten Years of Discovery in the Wilderness of Judaea* (London: SCM, 1959) 112–13.

27. The Book of Enoch consists of five distinct sections, all of which have been found at Qumran and agree with Essene thinking, except for the Book of Parables (1 Enoch 37–71).

supposition is not in accordance with the unsophisticated and pragmatic approach to the calendar that Jewish evidence from the first few centuries A.D. actually reflects.

Even in a country like Egypt, where astronomy was much studied, it seemed quite acceptable until the final decades of the first century B.C. to use a solar (or stellar) calendar of 365 days, and to allow its ¼ day deficiency to accumulate. In the Rome of Republican times, which was like Israel in that astronomy was not studied there, a quasi-solar year with an average annual excess of 1¼ days was employed. The excess of the Roman year was thus exactly the same as the deficiency of the Essene year. By the time of the Julian reform of 46 B.C., the Roman calendar was two months out of line with the seasons, so there is reason to think that the same discrepancy may have had a similar effect in the case of the Essene calendar. The natural inference to be drawn is that the Essene calendar would likewise have grown out of line with the seasons. There is evidence in 1 Enoch 18:15, 80:2-8 that it soon did get out of line with the seasons, although, because the Essenes thought their calendar perfect, they attributed the discrepancy to the seasons going astray rather than their calendar! The perfection of their 364-day calendar, so that it would not ever go astray even by a day, and would never need to be adjusted, is very strongly stated in 1 Enoch 72:32, 74:12, Jub. 6:30-32; and in illustration of this, the number of days in periods of three, five, and eight years are totaled up, the total in each case being a multiple of 364 (1 Enoch 74:13-16). To minds that thought like this, the idea of intercalation would be an offence. The various forms of intercalation that have recently been proposed for the Essene calendar are not only entirely conjectural, but are in several cases directly at variance with the Essene evidence.[28] Without intercalation, however, the Essene calendar would rapidly have diverged from the seasons. Since the calendar is first found in the oldest section of 1 Enoch, and so dates back to the third century B.C., the idea that it would still have been sufficiently in line with the seasons by the time of the Last Supper for it to have placed the Essene Passover in the same week as that of other Jews, is in the highest degree improbable.

But if the hypothesis that rival calendars are the clue to reconciling the chronology of Passion Week finally breaks down, one is thrown back upon the old solution that the Synoptists really agree with John,

---

28. See my "The Modern Attempt to Reconcile the Qumran Calendar with the True Solar Year," *RevQ* 7 (1970) 379-96; "The Qumran Calendar and the Sacrifices of the Essenes," *RevQ* 7 (1971) 587-91; and "The Earliest Enoch Literature and its Calendar," *RevQ* 10 (1981) 365-403. The first and second of these deal also with the question how the Essenes handled the practical difficulties of using a calendar that was out of line with the seasons. The third of the articles owes much to the writings of J. M. Baumgarten.

or that John really agrees with the Synoptists. Since the great Christian students of Judaism (Edersheim, Strack-Billerbeck, Dalman, Jeremias, to name only recent examples) are virtually unanimous in holding that the Synoptists represent the Last Supper as a Passover meal,[29] the only way of maintaining that the Synoptists really agree with John that the Passover meal came a day later, is to say that Jesus, on his own authority, held his own Passover meal a day early. This would have involved holding it on a different day from that which the Old Testament prescribes, and killing a lamb outside the sole sanctuary that the Old Testament recognizes (for the priests of the temple would never have offered a lamb a day early, and Jesus would never have had it deceitfully presented as some other kind of sacrifice). Nevertheless, such was the sovereign authority with which Jesus acted that no one can call this solution impossible.[30] What makes me hesitate about it, apart from the apparent implications of Mark 14:12 and Luke 22:7-8 to the contrary, is the fact that the Fourth Gospel itself appears to contain indications of a chronology other than that which lies upon its surface—a chronology that would make the Last Supper not an anticipated Passover meal but the official one, and would make John agree with the Synoptists, not the Synoptists with John.

The chief of these indications, pointed out by Jeremias,[31] are the following: (a) The Last Supper, as John describes it (and not just as the

29. The evidence that Jeremias, *The Eucharistic Words of Jesus*, 41-62, presents to prove that the Last Supper was a Passover meal (and on pp. 62-84 to answer the customary objections) has really destroyed the older alternative hypothesis that the Last Supper was just a "kiddush-meal" or a "haburah-meal." It cannot have been anything but a Passover meal, even if an anticipated one.

30. R. T. France has recently argued the case for this solution in his essay "Chronological Aspects of 'Gospel Harmony,'" *Vox Evangelica* 16 (1986) 43-59, with the difference that he uses the argument from silence that there was no Passover lamb at Jesus' Passover meal, pointing out that this would have made it easier for him to hold it before the Passover sacrifice was offered; and he interprets Mark 14:12 and Luke 22:7-8 accordingly. However, the argument from silence is far from strong, since the Evangelists naturally concentrate on those parts of the meal ceremony that Jesus significantly modified, not on those he left unchanged, such as the eating of the lamb. France also speaks rather unguardedly about a lamb-less Passover meal being normal after the destruction of the temple, and probably normal even in temple times among the Jews of the Dispersion. It is true that after the lamb could no longer be sacrificed at the temple it became a much less important part of the meal, and efforts were made to distinguish it from a sacrificed lamb by the way it was cooked (*m. Pesah.* 4:4, 7:1; *m. Beṣa* 2:7; *t. Beṣa* 2:15); and it is possible that such practices were anticipated among the Jews of the Dispersion and in separated groups like the Essenes. This is hardly the same, however, as having no lamb at all, and especially in a Passover meal like Jesus', held in the proximity of the temple while it was still standing. See also n. 32.

31. *The Eucharistic Words of Jesus*, 53-54, 80-82.

Synoptists do), has many of the peculiarities of the Passover meal. It is held in Jerusalem, despite the crowds, and not in Bethany (John 18:1; contrast John 12:1-2); it is apparently held later than the usual evening meal, going on into the night (John 13:30); and the participants recline instead of sitting (John 13:12, 23, 25). (b) The assumption of the disciples that what Jesus had sent Judas out from the Last Supper to "do quickly" might have been to buy the necessities for the feast (John 13:27-30) is hardly intelligible if this was only the night following Nisan 13 and not that following Nisan 14, for it was the custom in Judea to work on Nisan 14 until midday (m. Pesaḥ. 4:1, 5). Nisan 15, on the other hand, was a solemn rest day, in accordance with Lev 23:5-8, so if this was the night following Nisan 14, Judas would already have been late in buying the necessities for the festival day and the sabbath following it, and needed to make haste. (c) The statement of John 19:31, "the day of that sabbath was a high day," is curiously vague if it refers to Nisan 15 and not Nisan 16. John has already stated seven times that they have come up to Jerusalem for the Passover (John 11:55 [twice]; 12:1, 13:1, 18:28, 39; 19:14). It would surely have been more natural, therefore, to say "the day of that sabbath was the Passover" or "the day when they ate the Passover," had he thought of it as such. If, however, it was Nisan 16, the day of the offering of the Sheaf (Lev 23:9-14), his expression is a very natural one.[32]

What, then, should be made of the two passages in John that seem to state the direct opposite: John 19:14, which calls the day of the Crucifixion "the Preparation of the Passover," and John 18:28, which says that on the same day the chief priests and Pharisees have yet to "eat the Passover"?

"The Preparation of the Passover" (John 19:14) is a phrase that naturally recalls the rabbinical expression "the Eve of the Passover," meaning Nisan 14, the Passover itself being Nisan 15. However, the rabbinical form of language is curiously at variance with the Old Testament, where it is Nisan 14 that is the Passover, and Nisan 15 is the

---

32. Point (a) does not directly conflict with the hypothesis of an anticipated Passover meal, but points (b) and (c) do. Indirectly, however, point (a) also conflicts with it, for it is hard to think that John would have referred to the Passover meal taking place on two distinct days without giving any hint of the explanation, though the explanation lay in a quite unique decision by Jesus (which could hardly be guessed) to hold it a day early. The Evangelists are accustomed to emphasize unconventional actions by Jesus, and to explain the reason for them, not to refer to them in this deceptively allusive way. Similarly, in Mark 14:12 and Luke 22:7-8 the absence of any such hint of an unconventional decision by Jesus makes it natural to understand the verses as meaning that Jesus' Passover meal took place after the sacrificing of the Passover lambs, in accordance with custom, and not before it.

first day of Unleavened Bread (Lev 23:5–8, Num 28:16–25); and there is no clear example of the rabbinical phraseology in the New Testament. So, as the Preparation (Gk. *paraskeuē*) commonly means Friday (the preparation for the *sabbath*), and as the word is used twice in this sense in the very same chapter of John (John 19:31, 42), it seems better to understand "the Preparation of the Passover" as meaning "the Friday of Passover week."[33]

"Eat the Passover" (John 18:28) is more difficult, for there is no doubt that it would usually mean "eat the Passover lamb." But since it turns out, in the light of the foregoing evidence, that this interpretation would make John contradict himself about the chronology, a less usual interpretation becomes a distinct possible. The sacrifice of the Passover lamb, and the meal that followed, were only the first (though the most important) of the many sacrifices and sacred meals that, since Old Testament times, took place throughout the week of Passover and Unleavened Bread. In the first century, it was held that the command not "to appear empty" before the Lord at the pilgrim feasts (Exod 23:15, 34:20, Deut 16:16) had a precise meaning: it meant that each male Israelite was to bring a burnt offering and a peace offering, in addition to the Passover lamb. This obligation is the subject of the tractate Hagigah in the Mishna. Those referred to in John 18:28 as wanting to remain ceremonially clean so as to "eat the Passover" are the chief priests and the Pharisees (cf. v. 3). The Pharisees would have been very scrupulous about the *hagigah* duty, and as it involved a peace offering, which necessarily included a sacred meal, they would certainly have wanted to remain ceremonially clean so as to be able to eat it. This would have concerned the chief priests even more, since a share of every peace offering went to the priest who offered it. Moreover, the

---

33. The baraita in the Babylonian Talmud stating that "On the Eve of the Passover Yeshu was hanged" (*b. Sanh.* 43a) would tell against this explanation if one could be sure that it referred to Jesus of Nazareth (as some of the rabbis supposed) and that the date had not been altered for apologetic reasons. However, the rest of the baraita, which states that he was first stoned, and that his execution was delayed for forty days while a herald went out inviting anyone to say a word in his favor, suggests that it may refer to a different Yeshu altogether. In Jeremias's view (*The Eucharistic Words of Jesus*, 19), it refers to the Yeshu who was a disciple of Rabbi Joshua ben Perahiah (ca. 100 B.C.) and who fled with his master to Alexandria from the persecution of Alexander Jannaeus, but afterward fell into idolatry, as is related in *b. Sanh.* 107b and *b. Sota* 47a. A more reliable parallel to John 19:14 is found in the Gospel of Peter (mid-second century A.D.), which unambiguously says that Herod (rather than Pilate) delivered Jesus to the Jews "on the day before the Unleavened Bread, their feast." However, the Gospel of Peter is dependent upon the canonical gospels, including John, and this would not be the only example of it misunderstanding its sources.

peace offering might be an ox from the herd, rather than a lamb or goat from the flock (for all these details of the law of the peace offering, see Lev 3:1–17, 7:11–36).

The question, therefore, that one faces is, Was it possible to use phrases like "to sacrifice the Passover" and "to eat the Passover" to cover these other sacrifices and sacred meals as well? In Old Testament times, Deut 16:2–8 shows that it was; and since the Old Testament was the Bible of Judaism and the Pentateuch was reckoned its most important part, it was always possible for pentateuchal phraseology to be echoed or copied. Deut 16:2–3 reads,

> You shall *sacrifice the Passover* unto the Lord your God, of the flock *and the herd*, in the place which the Lord shall choose to cause his name to dwell there. You shall *eat* no leavened bread *with it* [i.e., with the Passover]; *seven days* shall you *eat* unleavened bread *with it*, even the bread of affliction.

Here the phrase "sacrifice the Passover" is actually used, and the phrase "eat unleavened bread with the Passover" (and therefore "eat the Passover" itself) is clearly implied. In both cases the reference is to what goes on for seven days, and includes the sacrificing and eating of oxen from the herd as well as lambs and kids from the flock. The usage is found again in the Hebrew of 2 Chr 30:22, in the account of Hezekiah's Passover, where the literal meaning is, "So they *ate the festal sacrifice* [i.e., the Passover] for the *seven days*, offering sacrifices of *peace offerings*, and giving thanks to the Lord, the God of their fathers." Moreover, the earlier example occurs in biblical Greek as well, since Deut 16:2–3 is literally translated in the Septuagint (whereas 2 Chr 30:22 is paraphrased).

It does not seem impossible, therefore, that "eat the Passover" in John 18:28 means "eat all the sacred meals of the festival," as those concerned would go on doing for seven days. Whether this interpretation is *likely* or not, may partly depend on whether John assumes in his readers a knowledge of the Synoptic Gospels, or at least of the synoptic tradition. If so, he could have used the phrase in this less common sense without expecting to be misunderstood. Of course, some today deny that John assumes a knowledge of the synoptic tradition, but the traditional dating of his gospel and the remarkable selection of material it contains strongly suggest that he does. If so, this most problematical verse of his is probably in only apparent conflict with the synoptic chronology.

Paul

The First Missionary Voyage of Paul: Historical Reality or Literary Creation of Luke?

S. Dockx†

The Ascent to Jerusalem in 48

The first missionary voyage of Paul is narrated by Luke (Acts 13:4–14:28) *after* Paul's ascent to Jerusalem to bring the results of the collection organized at Antioch, in view of the great famine predicted by the prophet Agabus (Acts 11:27–30). On the other hand, this first missionary voyage is inserted by Luke *before* the ascent of Paul to Jerusalem for the general council that dealt with the problem of the circumcision of the Gentiles who had become Christians (Acts 15:1–33).

There would be no problem in this arrangement, if the ascent of Paul to Jerusalem to remit the collection to the apostles and the elders were distinct from his ascent to discuss there the problem of the circumcision of the Gentile converts. This facile solution, based especially on the account of Acts, is undermined, however, by Paul's categorical affirmation (Gal 2:1) that he had only been back to Jerusalem fourteen years after his conversion (or fourteen years after his first visit).

Exegetes have been more and more united in identifying the ascent of Jerusalem of Acts 11:27–30 with that described in Acts 15:1–4.[1] But this identification is based on literary traits, which are not always able to lead to an assured conclusion. It is fortunate that we do have the possibility of establishing the chronology of Acts 11:27–30, as well as Acts 15:1–33, in rapport with the facts of secular history.

Ascent to Jerusalem in View of the Great Famine (Acts 11:27–30)

If we can determine the date of "the great famine" that affected the entire empire under the reign of the Emperor Claudius (Acts 11:28),

Father Dockx passed away on 7 November 1985. The translation from French to English was made by Edwin Yamauchi, and checked by Professor Anne Pratt of the French Department, Miami University.

1. Cf. J. Dupont, *Etudes sur les Actes des Apôtres* (Paris: Cerf, 1967) 67–72.

we would be able to know in which year Barnabas and Saul went up to Jerusalem to bring the collection made at Antioch to provide for this calamity.

The reign of Claudius was often affected by local famines, but never by a universal famine affecting the entire empire in the same year.[2] But the great famine under Claudius can only be viewed as that famine that raged in the empire following the drought that took place in 49 in the East and in 50 in the West.[3]

To compound the problem, the drought of 49 in the East had been preceded in Palestine by the suspension of sowing in the spring of 48, as this fell in the course of a sabbatical year. It follows then that for Jerusalem there had not been any sowing in the year 48, and because of this fact a resulting lack of provisions. Then in 49 a disastrous drought followed, which only aggravated the situation created by the preceding sabbatical year.

The difficulties of provisioning at Jerusalem in 48 were foreseen. It was the same catastrophic situation every seven years for the poor who did not have the financial resources to lay up provisions, and who had to buy expensive produce imported from neighboring countries at their hour of need. It was for this reason that Queen Helena of Adiabene bought grain in Egypt and figs from Cyprus to distribute to the hungry population at Jerusalem (Josephus, *Antiquities* 20:51 and 101).[4] The catastrophic drought of 49 in the East, on the other hand, could not have been humanly foreseen. Thus it was the prophet Agabus, who came from Jerusalem to Antioch in 47, who predicted it (Acts 11:27–28). It was likewise following a revelation that Paul is said to have ascended to Jerusalem (Gal 2:2). This revelation may well have been the prophecy of the prophet Agabus. Paul says that the Apostles—James, Cephas, and John—asked him to care for the poor of Jerusalem (Gal 2:10), probably in view of the "famine" of the coming sabbatical year. The Letter to the Romans, written at Corinth during the winter of 54–55, alludes to the collection organized by Paul in Macedonia and in Achaea (Rom 15:26) in view of the "famine" of the sabbatical year in 55.

The ascent to Jerusalem then ought to have taken place in the spring of 48, before the prices of the victuals had become prohibitively expensive for the poor among the saints of Jerusalem.

2. E. Haenchen, *The Acts of the Apostles: A Commentary* (Philadelphia: Westminster, 1971) 62 n. 5: "One may not speak of a famine covering the entire Roman Empire."

3. See my study, *Chronologies néotestamentaires et vie de l'Eglise primitive* (Gembloux: Duculot, 1976) 62–63. See also Dupont, *Etudes*, 163.

4. This action then probably did not take place in 49, the year during which the drought affected the East, but rather in 48, the sabbatical year, which did not affect either Egypt or Cyprus.

The insertion of Acts 12:1-24, narrating the imprisonment of Peter by King Herod Agrippa I and the ignominious death of the latter (in 44) can in no way constitute an assured chronological base, as if that which had been *narrated* before Acts 12:1 were chronologically anterior to the year 44, an error that many scholars writing on St. Paul have committed.

Ascent to Jerusalem for the Apostolic Assembly (Acts 15:1-29)

Acts 18:12 records Paul's appearance before Gallio, who was pro-consul of Achaea from May 51 to May 52.[5] Inasmuch as Paul was brought before Gallio early in the beginning of his administration, perhaps in May 51, and as Paul had already been at Corinth for one and a half years at least (Acts 18:11), Paul must have arrived in Achaea about November 49.

For Paul to be in Corinth about the fall of 49, he must have left Antioch (Acts 15:40) at the latest in the spring of this same year. Five months would have sufficed to traverse the high Anatolian plateau, Macedonia, and Achaea.

From Antioch (Acts 15:40) to Troas (Acts 16:8), Paul advanced by forced marches (Acts 16:1, 6, 7), held back only for a time in the country of the Galatians by illness (Gal 4:13-15). Three months, at the most, were necessary to make the journey from Antioch to Troas. Paul then ought to have arrived about mid-August. There remain then two and a half months for the visits at Philippi, Thessalonica, Beroea, and Athens, which corresponds to the historical probabilities.

As the apostolic assembly at Jerusalem must have taken place, at the latest, in the year that preceded the departure of Paul from Antioch for Corinth, this assembly ought to have taken place in 48, and more probably in the spring of this year. For, after the general assembly, the delegates from Jerusalem, Judas and Silas, had had the time to report to Antioch, to visit the churches of Syria and of Cilicia, and to return to Jerusalem.

Thus it is historically certain that the year 48 is the date of the ascent of Paul to Jerusalem and his bearing the collection for the great famine there. Acts 11:30 and Act 15:1-29 represent then the one and same visit of Paul to Jerusalem. This correlates with the categorical affirmation of Paul that he only went up twice to Jerusalem, the first time, three years after his conversion (Gal 1:18).

5. This has been the opinion most widely held by scholars such as Deissmann, Jeremias, Groag, Haenchen, and Finegan. Since the discovery of four supplementary fragments of the same letter to Gallio, doubt is no longer possible. It is then a case of the proconsulate of Gallio extending from May 51 to May 52. See B. Schwank, "Der sogenannte Brief an Gallio und die Datierung des I Thess," *BZ* 45 (1971) 265-66.

J. Jeremias, faithful to his theory of sources, thinks that Acts 11:30, 12:25, and 15:1–33 constitute doublets recounting the one and the same journey.[6] Instead it seems to me that the actual journey of Barnabas and Paul is recounted only once, namely in Acts 12:25. The passage in Acts 11:27–30 recounts that which took place at Antioch before this journey, and Acts 15:4–33 that which took place at Jerusalem after this journey. Acts 12:25 is the link that is bound to Acts 11:27–30, as one sees by the very Pauline use of the term *diakonia* for the 'collection' in 12:25 and 11:29, and which is linked at the same time to 15:4 as one sees by the mention of the return to (*eis*) Jerusalem at 12:25 and the arrival in this city at 15:4.

For greater clarity, it will help to reproduce the passages of the source used by Luke (as I have reconstructed them) in regard to the narrative of the ascent to Jerusalem.

> [Acts 11:27] During this time some prophets came down from Jerusalem to Antioch. [28] One of them, named Agabus, stood up and through the Spirit predicted that a severe famine would spread over the entire Roman world. (This happened during the reign of Claudius.) [29] The disciples, each according to his ability, decided to send a *collection* for the brothers living in Judea. [30] This they did, sending their gift to the *elders* by *Barnabas and Saul*. . . . [12:25] When they had completed delivering the *collection*, they returned to *Jerusalem*, taking with them John, also called Mark.
>
> [15:4a] When they came to *Jerusalem*, they were welcomed by [. . .][7] the apostles and the *elders*. . . . [15:12b] They listened to *Barnabas and Saul* [the Greek text reads Paul] recount all that God had done [. . .][8] among the Gentiles, by them.

Who are the Gentiles among whom God manifested himself? If we consider the letter of the apostles and the elders, sent with the delegates of the apostolic council, they are the Gentiles of the regions of Antioch, Syria, and Cilicia whom Barnabas and Saul had evangelized before ascending to Jerusalem (Acts 15:23, Gal 1:21). If, on the other hand, we consider Acts 13:4–14:27, they are the Gentiles of Cyprus (Acts 13:4–

---

6. J. Jeremias, *Abba* (Göttingen: Vandenhoeck und Ruprecht, 1966) 251.

7. The term *church* seems to be an interpolation of Luke. Later on (Acts 15:6, 23; 16:4) it is solely the question of apostles and elders. At Acts 15:22 it is again a question of the church mentioned with the apostles and the elders, but in spite of this, the church is not mentioned in the apostolic letter.

8. Σημεῖα καὶ τέρατα 'signs and wonders' is a favorite formula of Luke in the Acts of the Apostles (2:22, 43; 4:30; 5:12; 7:36; 14:3). I suppose that it was he who introduced it in 15:12.

12), Pamphylia (Acts 13:13), Pisidia (Acts 13:14), Lycaonia (Acts 14:6), among whom God had done great things according to Luke (Acts 14:27).

Luke is inspired by Acts 15:12b, ὅσα ἐποίησεν ὁ θεὸς [. . .] ἐν τοῖς ἔθνεσιν δι᾽ αὐτῶν, which alludes to the work of God in favor of the Gentiles of Syria and of Cilicia, to compose his finale of chaps. 13–14: ὅσα ἐποίησεν ὁ θεὸς μετ᾽ αὐτῶν, which alludes to the Gentiles of Asia Minor. The Lucan formula (Acts 14:27) is also repeated by him (Acts 15:4) to describe the Gentiles of chaps. 13–14.

The text, which is perfectly intelligible as far as Luke's source is concerned, becomes ambiguous indeed by his insertion of the narrative of the missionary voyage of chaps. 13–14. It is necessary to understand the sequence of events at the level of Luke's source, a source of great historical value, rather than at the level of the present text of Acts.

That Luke's source is concerned with a single journey—recounting the following motifs: the famine predicted by Agabus, which took place under Claudius (Acts 11:28), and the welcome given the envoys from Antioch at Jerusalem (Acts 15:4)—is seen from the fact that it was Barnabas who was the head of the mission (Acts 11:30, 15:12b). It is Luke, wishing to stress Paul's prominence, who cites the two apostles in reverse order (13:13, 43, 46, 50; 14:3).[9]

The First Missionary Voyage

If there was only one ascent to Jerusalem, the account of which begins at Acts 11:27 and ends at 15:30, one is confronted with the following problem: Where to place chronologically the missionary voyage of Acts 13:4–14:27—before the Council of Jerusalem (Acts 15:1–30) or after it (11:27–30)?

The missionary voyage of Acts 13:4–14:27 cannot have taken place *before* the Council of Jerusalem. Indeed, before the ascent of Barnabas and Saul to Jerusalem in the spring of 48, they had taught as teachers together (Acts 13:1) an entire year at Antioch (Acts 11:26). There could then be no question in the year 47–48 of a missionary voyage to Cyprus, Pamphylia, Pisidia, and Lycaonia. The preceding year, 46–47, Barnabas, delegated by Jerusalem to Antioch (Acts 11:22), worked there alone for a while (Acts 11:23), then went to look for Paul at Tarsus (Acts 11:25) to aid him in his work of teaching at Antioch. Paul had

---

9. The order: Barnabas/Paul in Acts 14:12, 14 is due to the fact that Barnabas was compared to Zeus and Paul to Hermes. As the order of the gods was Zeus/Hermes, Luke has placed Barnabas before Paul here. Acts 13:7 serves as a transition between the order Barnabas/Saul, and Paul/and his companions (Acts 13:13).

been sent by the brothers to Tarsus (Acts 9:30) a dozen years before. During all this time, Paul seems to have established his headquarters in his native city to journey from there to evangelize the regions of Syria and of Cilicia, as he himself says (Gal 1:21). No mention is made of any activity whatsoever in Cyprus, Pamphylia, Pisidia, or Lycaonia. However, the letter of credentials sent with Judas Barsabbas and Silas by the apostles and the elders is addressed only to the believers of Syria and of Cilicia (Acts 15:23). This would have been entirely abnormal if the first missionary journey had taken place before the Council.

J. Jeremias has very ably defended the hypothesis that the first missionary voyage took place *after* the Council.[10] E. Haenchen has also followed this approach.[11] But if one takes into account that the Council of Jerusalem had taken place at the time of the Passover feast in 48 (= April 17), Barnabas and Saul would have been able to return to Antioch only toward the end of May at the earliest. They had begun by working together at Antioch with the support of Judas and Silas (Acts 15:33). It is more than probable that Judas, Silas, Barnabas, and Saul had visited the churches of Syria and Cilicia, where Saul had converted numerous Gentiles. Indeed, Judas and Silas, delegated by the apostles James, Peter, and John, were bearers of the apostolic letter destined for the Gentiles of these countries.

If one assigns the months of June/July to the apostolic tour in the regions of Syria and Cilicia, Barnabas and Saul would have been able to leave for Cyprus not earlier than the month of August, assuming the historicity of this voyage. Even if the missionaries had not been delayed on this island, they could not have arrived at Perga in Pamphylia before the end of this month. They could have been on the return trip from Perga to Attalia (Acts 14:25) at the latest toward the end of October, if they wished to return to Antioch by sea, as travel by sea was generally ended by November 11. In Asia Minor they would then have had at their disposal for their apostolic labors only the two months of September/October. It is not necessary, with Julius Wellhausen and W. M. Ramsay, to require many years for the first missionary voyage, but to posit just two months, for their activity in Asia Minor, as Luke has described it, is completely improbable.

It remains then to accept the conclusion that the first missionary voyage never took place, *neither before nor after* the Council of Jerusalem,

---

10. J. Jeremias, "Untersuchungen zum Quellenproblem der Apostelgeschichte," *ZNW* 36 (1937) 205–21; reprinted in his *Abba*, 238–55.

11. Haenchen, *Die Apostelgeschichte* (Göttingen: Vandenhoeck und Ruprecht, 1959) 380–81.

but is a literary creation of Luke in his desire to give an image of the ideal Apostle: first, preaching to the Jews in the synagogue (Acts 13:14–41); then their hostility toward the apostles (Acts 13:45–47); then, the proclamation of the gospel to the Gentiles, who are converted (Acts 13:48–49); finally, the persecution of the apostles and their expulsion from the city (Acts 13:50–51). This ministry of preaching and conversion is crowned by the establishment of elders in every city visited (Acts 14:23).

Luke's Literary Creation

Luke and His Sources

But if it is Luke who on his own initiative has designed the portrait of an apostle in chaps. 13–14, why has he taken Cyprus, Pamphylia, Pisidia, and Lycaonia as his backdrop?

The answer to this question seems to lie in the fact that Luke, in order to exalt his heroes, always makes them the pioneers in evangelizing a pagan region. As he had read in his source (Acts 15:40b) that Barnabas left for Cyprus accompanied by Mark, he made Paul leave with Barnabas and Mark for this country before the Council of Jerusalem (Acts 13:4–5). As this setting is only the background of the portrait of the Apostle Paul and Barnabas depicted by Luke, this does not give any detail of their missionary activity. Luke contents himself with saying that from Salamis, where "they proclaimed the Word of God in the synagogue of the Jews" (Acts 13:5), the apostles "traversed the entire island as far as Paphos" (Acts 13:6).

Luke, who had read in his source that there were already believers at Lystra and Iconium before the arrival of Paul (Acts 16:2), designed a portrait of the latter as active in the cities of Lycaonia before the Council of Jerusalem (Acts 14:1–7, 21, 23). He made Paul and Barnabas travel from Paphos to Perga (Acts 13:13) and thence to Antioch in Pisidia (Acts 13:14–51) in order to move from Cyprus to Iconium and Lystra.

We can see that the missionary activity of Paul and Barnabas on Cyprus and in the cities of Pisidia and Lycaonia is a literary creation of Luke by the fact that it is Paul who is represented as the head of the mission, as he appears in the order Paul/Barnabas (Acts 13:13, 46, 50; 14:3, 20)—the same order of precedence in the pairing certainly re-edited by Luke (Acts 15:2).

Historically speaking, it was Barnabas who was the head of the mission: It was he who was commissioned by the religious leaders of

Jerusalem (Acts 11:22), it was he who went to seek Saul at Tarsus (Acts 11:25-26), and it was he who was named first (Acts 11:30; 12:25; 15:12, 23).

The first source, called Antiochian by Adolf Harnack, and which I prefer to call the "Acts of Barnabas," gives Paul the Aramaean name "Saul" (Acts 11:25, 30; 12:25; 13:1-2), while the second source, which serves as the reference for the second part of Acts (chaps. 16-28), gives Paul the Roman name "Paul."[12]

If it was Mark who edited the account concerning Barnabas, he understood the use of the name "Saul," which he and Barnabas (both of Jewish origin) employed to designate their apostolic companion. And perhaps Timothy, of Greek origin, was the author of the source of the second part of Acts, where the name "Paul" is used. Luke, in joining these two sources, improved his redaction of the voyage of Paul to Cyprus by substituting the name Paul for Saul (13:9). This is also an indication that it was Luke who edited the account of the voyage to Cyprus before the Jerusalem Council (13:4-12), while it took place, in reality, after the council (15:39) for Barnabas and Mark, but not for Paul.

The Chronology of Paul's Travels

For clarity's sake, table 1 shows the chronology of events that immediately preceded and followed the Council of Jerusalem. In this chronological summary one will note that the events of the departure of Paul from Antioch toward the middle of May 49 to his settling at Corinth, where he arrives toward the middle of November, take up only six months.

I disagree with the chronology proposed by R. Jewett, which requires the journey from Jerusalem to Corinth to take 201 weeks, or at the very least, 91 weeks.[13] This results from the fact that Jewett makes the journey by a series of forced marches,[14] with a sequence of evangelistic campaigns comparable in length to the sojourns at Corinth and at Ephesus.

12. I believe that Acts was reedited by Mark, the cousin of Barnabas, at the request of Luke during Paul's stay at Rome in the course of the two years, 56-58 (see Phlm 24). I attribute the second source to Timothy. See my "Luc a-t-il été la compagnon d'apostolat de Paul?" *NRT* 103 (1981) 390.

13. R. Jewett, *Dating Paul's Life* (London: SCM, 1979) 61; idem, *A Chronology of Paul's Life* (Philadelphia: Fortress, 1979).

14. "He went through Syria and Cilicia" (Acts 15:41); "as they traveled from town to town" (Acts 16:4); "they traveled throughout the region of Phrygia and Galatia" (Acts 16:6); "so they passed by Mysia" (Acts 16:8).

TABLE 1.   *Chronology of Events Surrounding the Council of Jerusalem*

Event	Acts	Date
Barnabas is sent to Antioch	11:22	46
Barnabas goes in search of Saul at Tarsus	11:25	spring 47
Barnabas and Saul preach at Antioch for a year	11:26	spring 47 to spring 48
Agabus predicts the great famine in Judea that will take place under Claudius in 49	11:28	spring 47
The collection at Antioch for Jerusalem	11:29–30	spring 47 to spring 48
Barnabas and Saul ascend to Jerusalem	12:25	spring 48
Barnabas and Saul arrive at Jerusalem	15:4	Passover 48 (= April 12)
Barnabas and Saul, with Judas and Silas, return to Antioch	15:30	spring 48
Barnabas and Saul, with Judas and Silas, visit the churches of Syria and Cilicia	15:23	summer 48
Judas and Silas return to Jerusalem	15:32	fall 48
Peter leaves for Antioch; the incident at Antioch (Gal 2:11–14)		March 49
Barnabas leaves to evangelize Cyprus, his native country	15:39b	May 49
Paul leaves for Macedonia and Achaea	16:9	mid-May 49
Paul arrives at Corinth	18:1	mid-November 49
Paul encounters Gallio at Corinth	18:12–17	May 51

The unusual length of this voyage forces Jewett to identify the ascent to Jerusalem for the apostolic Council with the ascent indicated by Acts 18:22, "when he landed at Caesarea, he went up to greet the church," an ascent that would have taken place after the stay of a year and a half at Corinth. But this view is contradicted by Paul as well as by Acts. Paul writes, "Then, I went to Syria and Cilicia" (Gal 1:21), "then I went up to Jerusalem with Barnabas" (Gal 2:1). It was immediately after having worked in Cilicia with a stay at Tarsus (Acts 11:25), and in Syria with Barnabas with a stay at Antioch (Acts 11:26), that Paul went up to Jerusalem for the apostolic Council. According to the Epistle to the Galatians there is no way of placing, as Jewett wishes to do, a voyage of evangelizing from Antioch to Corinth and a stay of eighteen months there between the evangelization of Syria and Cilicia and the ascent to Jerusalem. The silence of Paul over this supposed evangelistic activity before the Council at Jerusalem would be entirely inexplicable.

Acts also maintains the same significant silence over this matter. The letter of authorization sent with the delegates from Jerusalem is addressed to the only Christians won from the Gentiles, who were resident at Antioch in Syria and in Cilicia (Acts 15:23). Finally, why would not the Christians won from the Gentiles in Asia Minor, Macedonia, and Achaea have been mentioned, if it had been in these areas that Paul had already worked? And why does Paul speak of Barnabas as his companion in the apostolate (Gal 2:1), when the latter had not been working with him, particularly during the year and six months at Corinth (Acts 18:11)?

That it is perfectly possible to place the voyage of Paul from Antioch to Corinth between the spring and the winter of the year 49 can be seen in table 2. At first glance it would seem clear that one could prolong the length of the journey from the Cilician Gates to Athens by some months and shorten, on the other hand, the length of the stay at Ephesus. But a detailed examination of this hypothesis shows that this is not possible.

There are, in truth, two possibilities: either Paul passed through the Cilician Gates immediately *before* winter (September 51), or he traversed them immediately *after* winter (June 52). In any case, it is necessary to hold to the one or the other chronology, for the departure of Paul from Ephesus for Troas took place a short time after the feast of Pentecost (1 Corinthians 16) of the year 54 (May 30), the year that preceded the ascent to Jerusalem in 55, a sabbatical year. According to the first chronology, which I prefer, we have the following data:

Arrival at Corinth	mid-November 49
Sojourn of eighteen months at Corinth	mid-November 49 to mid-May 51
Encounter with Gallio	May 51
Departure from Corinth for Antioch	June 51
Departure from Antioch for Ephesus	August 51
Passage through the Cilician Gates	September 51 (*before* the winter of 51–52)
Arrival at Ephesus	mid-November 51
Paul preaches in the synagogue for three months (Acts 19:8), a winter rest	mid-November 51 to mid-February 52
Paul preaches in the school of Tyrannos for two years (Acts 19:9, 10)	mid-February 52 to mid-February 54
Paul rests again for "some time" at Ephesus (Acts 19:22) until Pentecost" (1 Cor 16:8) for four months	30 May 54

TABLE 2. *Chronology of the Voyage of Paul in Spring–Winter 49*

Points of Travel and Sojourn	Distance (km/mi)	Duration	Date
Passage through the Cilician Gates[a]			early June
Cilician Gates to Lystra	240/149	1 week	
Sojourn in Lystra		2 weeks	
Lystra to Antioch	242/150	1 week	late June
Antioch to Galatia	220/137	1 week	early July
Sojourn in Galatia		3 weeks	late July
Galatia to Troas	634/394	3 weeks	mid-August
Troas to Philippi by sea		2 days	
Sojourn at Philippi (Acts 16:12)[b]		2 weeks	mid/late August
Philippi to Thessalonica	140/87	3 days	
Sojourn at Thessalonica (Acts 17:1; Phil 4:16)[c]		3 weeks	
Thessalonica to Berea	70/43	2 days	late September
Sojourn in Berea (Acts 17:14)[d]		1 week	early October
Berea to Athens	500/311	3 weeks	late October
Totals	2,046/1,271	10 weeks of travel + 11 weeks of sojourn = 21 weeks = 5 months = 205 km/127 mi per week	

[a] In order to draw up this table it is necessary to take into account the fact that one cannot pass through the Cilician gates before the month of June. At the same time it is necessary to assume that Paul must have arrived at Athens at least a fortnight before the cessation of navigation. Recall that Paul sent Timothy from Athens to Thessalonica (1 Thess 3:2), in all probability by sea, for the round-trip journey from Athens to Thessalonica is 1,100 km (684 mi), or five weeks of land travel, whereas it would have taken only a dozen days by sea if the winds were favorable.

[b] Acts 16:12: "we passed a few days in this city." The continuation of the narrative (Acts 16:13-40) is a composition by Luke, in which the first person plural continues to be used (Acts 16:13-16), although the voyage is no longer by sea. At Acts 16:17 one sees the transition from "we" to "Paul and Silas" for the remainder of the narrative, omitting Timothy. That Acts 16:13-40, recounting the imprisonment of Paul at Philippi, is from the hand of Luke is seen by observing 1 Thess 2:2, where Paul speaks of "sufferings and insults endured at Philippi," but not of imprisonment.

[c] The sojourn of Paul at Thessalonica was quite brief. For he had only preached in the synagogue to the Jews during three sabbaths, without having had the opportunity to address the Gentiles also. Moreover, the believers of Philippi, a city situated three days journey from Thessalonica, had only two occasions to send Paul his part of the weekly collection from the church at Philippi. For the existence of such a collection during the Eucharistic celebrations, one may refer to 1 Cor 16:1-2.

[d] Since Berea is no further from Thessalonica than about a two-day walk, Paul's revolutionary preaching on the Sabbath could have been reported to the Jews of Thessalonica on the following Tuesday, who then could have been in Berea on Thursday of the same week. That Thursday, not the following day, Paul fled from Berea, which does not allow a missionary activity lasting two months at Berea (contra R. Jewett).

Thus, Paul remained at Ephesus according to Acts a total of two years and seven months.

According to a hypothetical chronology of five months and more for the distance from the Cilician Gates to Athens (see Table 2), one obtains the following chart:

Arrival at Corinth	mid-April 50
Stay of eighteen months at Corinth	mid-April to mid-October 51
Encounter with Gallio	October 51
Departure from Corinth for Antioch	end of October 51
Stay at Antioch	November 51 to May 52
Departure from Antioch for Ephesus	May 52
Passage through the Cilician Gates	June 52 (*after* the winter of 51–52)
Arrival at Ephesus	July 52
Stay at Ephesus	July 52 to June 54 (after Pentecost, 30 May 54)

According to this second hypothesis, Paul remained at Ephesus a total of one year and two months.

This second chronology, ascribing a duration longer than five months to the journey from the Cilician Gates to Athens, presents the anomaly of the departure of Paul by sea from Corinth to Antioch at the end of October, that is, at the time when snow is already about to fall on the Cilician Gates. Paul, a realist, would never have begun his journey under such circumstances. Moreover, the total duration of one year and two months for the stay at Ephesus ill accords with the times mentioned in Acts: "three months" (Acts 19:8), "two years" (Acts 19:9–10), "some time" (= four months; 19:22)—or two years and seven months total.

As the only variant possible for the duration, the hypothesis of five months for the journey from the Cilician Gates to Athens does not agree with the chronological facts of Acts and of 1 Corinthians, it is necessary to retain the assured date of the arrival of Paul at Corinth toward mid-November 49.

As Paul had evangelized the Gentiles at Antioch, Syria, and Cilicia immediately before ascending to Jerusalem about Passover 48, this leaves no possibility of an evangelization of Cyprus and of the provinces of Asia Minor before the Council of Jerusalem, and, on the other hand, since he visited the churches of Syria and Cilicia immediately after the

Council during the second half of 48, with his departure in May 49 to return to Corinth, there was neither before nor after the Council of Jerusalem a place for a missionary journey to Cyprus and the provinces of Asia Minor. This journey (Acts 13:4–14:28) is not a page of history, but a painting by Luke.

A New Chronology
for the Life and Letters of Paul

Dale Moody

Several significant reviews of Pauline chronology have been published in recent years. Many commentaries and articles have touched upon particular points, but a summary of the situation may be gained from three books. In 1964 Bo Reicke of Basel published his *Neutestamentliche Zeitgeschichte*, and Paul is included in this survey from 500 B.C. to A.D. 100.[1] *The Chronology of the Life of Paul*, published by George Ogg in 1968, gathers most previously published materials and proposes a chronology that differs little from traditional views.[2] The most recent revision is by John J. Gunther, whose *Paul: Messenger and Exile* makes some radical departures from those adopted by Reicke and Ogg, but there are still some problems left unsolved.[3]

Though it may seem presumptuous to say so, in such a brief essay, I conclude that all three of the above studies rely too much on secondary sources and fail to go directly to the original documents for a fresh start. The discussion that follows assumes the original sources are true unless there is overwhelming evidence to the contrary. It is amazing how things fall together like pieces in a jigsaw puzzle when this is done. At the risk of being called a compulsive harmonizer, I am making the effort to solve the problem of Paul's chronology.

It is well to begin with four crucial dates as common ground for investigation. These dates may be supported by evidence that is both canonical and extracanonical. This will be followed by a new thesis on

Dale Moody is Emeritus Professor of Christian Theology at Southern Baptist Theological Seminary.

1. B. Reicke, *The New Testament Era* (Philadelphia: Fortress, 1968).
2. Published in America under the title *The Odyssey of Paul* (Old Tappan, NJ: Revell, 1968).
3. Valley Forge, PA: Judson, 1972.

the chronology and structure of the Acts of the Apostles. The final step is a reconstruction of the origin, date, and setting of each Pauline writing.

Crucial Dates for Pauline Chronology

The first crucial date to be considered is the three-year period during which Paul was in Damascus and Arabia. This includes the date of his escape from Damascus.

Paul's conversion was vitally related to the martyrdom of Stephen. Reicke has rightly dated the stoning of Stephen at the time Pontius Pilate was deposed in A.D. 36.[4] His removal created a power vacuum that enabled the Jews to launch an attack on the new sect that followed Jesus. This was perhaps followed by Paul's conversion late in 36 (Acts 8:1-3, 9:1-22, 22:4-16, 26:9-18; Gal 1:13-17; cf. Eusebius, *Historia Ecclesiastica* 2:23).

Reicke also dates Paul's return to Jerusalem in A.D. 38, but 39 makes room for the full three years of Gal 1:18. The escape of Paul from Damascus would need to be dated before A.D. 40, for Damascus was then under the jurisdiction of Aretas IV, who died in 40 (Acts 9:23-25; 2 Cor 11:32).[5]

The same New Testament sources speak of Paul's trance in the temple on his return to Jerusalem (Acts 22:17; 2 Cor 12:1-4), and it will be later shown that the fourteen years of 2 Cor 12:2 are included in the years late A.D. 39 to 53.

The second date to be established by both the New Testament and extracanonical sources is the death of Herod Agrippa I in A.D. 44. He was the grandson of Herod the Great and the Maccabean Mariamne. His reign was four years under Gaius Caligula (37-41) and four under Claudius (41-44). Josephus mentions his death in *Jewish War* 2:218-19, but the details are given later in *Antiquities* 19:343-52. Some details differ in Acts 12:20-23, but there is little doubt that Josephus and Acts speak of the same event in 44.

The third date for common ground centers on the coming of Gallio as proconsul of Achaia in Corinth, about A.D. 51. Ogg's careful study of

---

4. Reicke, *New Testament Era*, 192. Cf. Josephus, *Antiquities* 18:88-89. Hugh J. Schonfield, *The Pentecost Revolution* (London: Macdonald, 1974) 308, is correct on the date of Stephen's death despite his errors on the dates of John the Baptist and Jesus.

5. Josephus, *Antiquities* 18:109-25. Cf. G. Lancaster Harding, *The Antiquities of Jordan* (rev. ed.; London: Lutterworth, 1967) 124. Ogg follows Emil Schürer and others in the belief that between 37 and 40 Caligula gave Damascus to Aretas IV (see *Odyssey of Paul*, 22-23).

Paul's eighteen months in Corinth concludes that Gallio was proconsul there between May 51 and May 52.[6]

If this date be correct, then Paul must have arrived in Corinth in late A.D. 49. This links up with Claudius's edict in 49 in which the Jews were expelled from Rome for rioting over *Chrestus* (that is, Christ), and agrees with the statement that Aquila had "lately come from Italy with his wife Priscilla, because Claudius had commanded all Jews to leave Rome" (Acts 18:2; cf. Suetonius, *Claudius* 25:4).

The date of Paul's imprisonment in Caesarea is the most debated of the four crucial questions. Ogg again sees clearly when he argues that the *dietia*, the 'two-year period' of Acts 24:27, has reference to Paul's imprisonment in Caesarea, not to the length of Felix's term as procurator.[7] The *dietia* is the last of a series of time references to Paul's imprisonment, and there is no evident concern about the length of Felix's term. Note the phrases: "put them off" (24:22), "when I have opportunity" (24:25), "sent for him often" (24:26), and "when two years had elapsed" (24:27). It would be strange indeed if the last reference suddenly became interested in how long Felix was procurator.

These references are preceded by Paul's speech, which begins by saying Felix has "for many years" been a judge over the Jewish nation (24:10). Does this mean that Paul's imprisonment was as late as A.D. 58–60, as many say, or does it substantiate the statement by the Roman historian Tacitus (*Annals* 12:54), who says Felix had ruled in Samaria and possibly Judea from about A.D. 48? Most writers declare Tacitus in error. Ernst Haenchen says dogmatically that "Tacitus' version of these events is well nigh worthless."[8]

L. H. Feldman, in the Loeb Classical Library edition of Josephus, has a note that is more restrained than that of Haenchen. He notes that Josephus said in *Jewish War* 2:247 that Felix was sent in A.D. 52 "to be procurator of Judea, Samaria, Galilee, and Perea" and that "this would not necessarily be inconsistent with his having served as procurator of one of these districts previously" (*Antiquities* 20:137 n. e).

It is amazing how many writers resort to special pleading to lengthen the time of Felix from A.D. 52 onward. Endless references can be found that say he was procurator from 52 to 60, but no documentation is given. About the only argument to support this long term for Felix goes back to the brief statements by Josephus about the term of Festus. Festus gets little space, so it is argued that he served a short term, A.D. 60–62.

6. Ogg, *Odyssey of Paul*, 111.
7. Ibid., 149.
8. E. Haenchen, *The Acts of the Apostles* (Philadelphia: Westminster, 1971) 70.

If this be the case with Festus, why does Florus get more space than Felix, although he also had only a two-year term, A.D. 64–66? It is more likely that the atrocities under Felix and Florus got the space while the stability under Festus was passed over lightly (*Jewish War* 2:247–335). Haenchen makes the same observation, but he reduces Felix to a two-year term, 53–55.[9]

A careful comparison of Josephus's *Jewish War*, written about A.D. 77–78, with his *Antiquities*, written about A.D. 94, will indicate that the former is far more reliable, but neither work by Josephus has material to refute the above conclusions (cf. *Antiquities* 20:137–258). It is altogether possible that Felix was procurator of Judea and Samaria from A.D. 48 and of all of Palestine from A.D. 52 to 57. Festus would then be procurator from 57 until his death in 62. This conclusion would agree with Acts 24:10.

Support for this point of view may also be found in extracanonical sources. The Latin version of Eusebius' *Chronicle* rendered by Jerome says that Festus succeeded in the second year of Nero's reign, that is, A.D. 56. This does not contradict the paragraph above. It would have been May 57 before Festus arrived in Caesarea, which agrees with the pictures given in Acts 24:27 and also does not contradict the evidence found in Josephus (*Jewish War* 2:271, *Antiquities* 20:185–203).[10] Ogg rejects this so-called antedated chronology, advocated so vigorously by Adolph von Harnack, but Ogg's collection of evidence does not require his own conclusion.[11]

The date on which Festus succeeded Felix may on Ogg's evidence be A.D. 54, 56, or 59.[12] Ogg allows for a date as late as the summer of 61 for the actual arrival of Festus, but this contradicts the careful argument of Reicke for the date of Colossians. Ogg thinks of Colossians as of Roman origin, but Reicke says there was no Colossae after A.D. 60. It was destroyed by the same earthquake that destroyed Laodicea (Tacitus, *Annals* 14:26).[13] Festus must have arrived in Caesarea by 57.

9. Ibid., 71.

10. If J. Vardaman (personal communication) is correct that the Festus coin of A.D. 58 reads "in the fifth year of Nero" and "the third year of Marcus Porcius Festus," the issue is settled in favor of A.D. 56 and Eusebius is vindicated. The references in Eusebius are in Rudolph Helm (ed.), *Die Chronik des Hieronymus, Eusebius Werke* (Berlin: Akademie-Verlag, 1956), 7:182, 185. Cf. Jack Finegan, *Handbook of Biblical Chronology* (Princeton: Princeton University, 1964) 315–25; idem, *The Archeology of the New Testament: The Mediterranean World of the Early Christian Apostles* (Boulder, CO: Westview, 1981) 14.

11. Ogg, *Odyssey of Paul*, 146–70.

12. Ibid., 153.

13. Cf. Reicke, "The Historical Setting of Colossians," *RevExp* 70 (1973) 429–38.

Pauline Chronology and Acts

If it is possible to relate these four crucial dates with the data of Acts, it would seem that such a correlation is more reliable than views that harp about the "errors" of Acts. It is with gratitude that I pay tribute for clues given by two British scholars.

In 1898 C. H. Turner of Oxford noted that the structure of Acts includes six panels or books. Each book closes with a summary of progress (6:7, 9:31, 12:24, 16:5, 19:20, 28:30-31).[14] Turner's outline has long been the structure for my understanding of Acts, but I do not accept the chronology he proposed.

The views of a second British scholar came to my attention from a passing reference in Haenchen. In 1918 C. J. Cadoux, also of Oxford, advanced the view that these panels were five years each, with summaries at the Pentecosts of A.D. 34, 39, 44, 49, 54, and 59. In 1937 he revised his analysis by one year forward, as he advanced the date of the Crucifixion from A.D. 29 to 30.[15]

The date of 30 for the Crucifixion does not upset this pattern if 30 is included in the first five years, A.D. 30-34. Haenchen dismissed Cadoux's views as "recondite,"[16] but he missed a good clue. Even Cadoux did not work out the full consequences of his clue.[17] The division into five-year cycles, however, has more evidence than the date of Pentecost.

A third step was reached in seeing the quinquennial chronology of Acts by the reading of Josephus's *Jewish War*. Josephus described the games of Caesarea by parallels between Zeus and Caesar and by dating the beginning of such games in the hundred and ninety-second Olympiad, that is, 10-9 B.C., the third year of the Olympiad (*Jewish War* 1:415).[18] These games, which began in 9 B.C., continued in five-year cycles until New Testament times. The Greeks had their Olympiad every four years, but the Romans had their quinquennium every five.

---

14. C. H. Turner, "Chronology of the New Testament," *Dictionary of the Bible* (ed. James Hastings; New York: Scribner, 1898), 1:421.

15. C. J. Cadoux, "The Chronological Division of Acts," *JTS* 19 (1918) 333-41; and, "A Tentative Synthetic Chronology of the Apostolic Age," *JBL* 56 (1937) 177-91.

16. Haenchen, *Acts of the Apostles*, 60 n. 1.

17. Cadoux, "Chronology of the Apostolic Age," 182-83.

18. The translation of *pentaeterikous* as 'four-yearly' in the new popular translation of Josephus by G. A. Williamson (*Josephus: The Jewish War* [Baltimore: Penguin, 1970] 77) is an error. The four-yearly celebration of the Romans was known as the Actiad (see *Jewish War* 1:398).

These three clues opened up the chronology of Acts in agreement with dates arrived at along different lines. It is a key that unlocks many other riddles. The quinquennial chronology of Acts follows.

Book I (1:1–6:7) has been used to refute the importance of the six summaries pointed out by Turner. The short summaries at 2:43, 46–47; 4:4; and 5:5b, 12, 13b, 14 belong to what Harnack called a doublet on the beginnings of the church. Harnack thought he saw two Jerusalem sources in the early chapters of Acts. The first at 1:6–2:47 + 5:17–42 he called B, because it was later, and the second at 3:1–5:16 he called A.[19]

G. H. C. Macgregor points out the parallels in the summaries: 2:43a with 5:5b, 2:43b with 5:12a, 2:46a with 5:12b, 2:47a with 5:13b, 2:47b with 5:14.[20] All of this may be accepted if doublets, so frequent in Luke–Acts, are not called duplicates. Indeed, it may be that the summaries in Book I suggested the summaries at the end of the six books. No effort is made to determine what happened each year, but the events of Book I seem clearly to fit the years A.D. 30–34.

Book II (6:8–9:31) begins with the preaching of Stephen, and it would take about two years of that type of preaching to bring about his martyrdom in A.D. 36. The date of A.D. 39 has already been reached as the date of Paul's return from Damascus, which comes at the end of Book II (9:23–30). Meanwhile the gospel was spread to Samaria and the seacoast (8:1b–40).

The convergence of Acts with a quinquennial celebration comes at the end of Book III (9:32–12:24). Book III begins with the preaching mission of Peter (9:32), and this would be after the famous fifteen days where Paul visited Peter in Jerusalem in late A.D. 39 (Gal 1:18). Book III has a peculiar chronological problem that may be illustrated by listing some established dates:

40–42   Peter's preaching mission (9:32–11:18)
   45   Paul's "whole year" in Antioch (11:19–26)
   46   Relief mission during the famine "in the days of Claudius" (11:27–30; Josephus, *Antiquities* 20:49–55)
42–43   Death of "James the brother of John" in the days of unleavened bread (12:1–19)

19. A. Harnack, *The Acts of the Apostles* (London: Williams and Norgate, 1909); the German edition (*Die Apostlegeschichte*) was released in 1908.
20. G. H. C. Macgregor, "The Acts of the Apostles: Introduction and Exegesis," *The Interpreter's Bible* (ed. George A. Buttrick; New York: Abingdon, 1954), 9:69.

44 Death of Herod Agrippa I, August 6 (12:20–23; Josephus, *Antiquities* 19:343–52)

Book III, as noted, closes with the death of Herod Agrippa I in A.D. 44 (12:24). It is obvious that the events of 11:19–30 are not in chronological order. Why? The answer is simple. A page of papyrus got misplaced in the transmission of the text! When 11:19–30 is placed after 12:24, Book III becomes a book on the preaching of Peter, A.D. 39–44. Acts 11:19–30 becomes the introduction to Book IV, beginning with "the persecution that arose over Stephen," as in case of Book II (6:8).

Book III marks the end of the Acts of Peter, and Book IV marks the beginnings of the Acts of Paul. This idea was suggested by R. B. Rackham as long ago as 1901, in a commentary that anticipated Harnack by seven years.[21] Without Turner and Cadoux, Rackham and Harnack, our understanding of Acts would be greatly reduced. Later works catalogued in Haenchen are often less acute.

The end of Book III touches on the second question of common ground between Josephus and the New Testament. Here Haenchen sees the problem of dating the death of James at Passover of A.D. 44, as many say. Nisan 15 came on April 1, and Herod Agrippa died on March 10, three weeks before.[22]

The problem, however, is not as Haenchen suggests, for the account in Acts 12 makes clear that some time elapsed between the death of James and the death of Herod Agrippa I. James died in Jerusalem, but Herod Agrippa I died in Caesarea, and it was not until Herod "went down from Judea to Caesarea, and remained there" (12:19) that he made his oration "on an appointed day" (12:21). Indeed, there would be no conflict with the evidence if the death of James were pushed back to A.D. 42, and that is precisely what Bo Reicke does.[23]

21. R. B. Rackham, *The Acts of the Apostles* (Westminster Commentaries; London: Methuen, 1901).
22. Haenchen, *Acts of the Apostles*, 62. However, a private communication from J. Vardaman on Ostraca Petrie 271 demonstrates that Marcus Julius Alexander, the son-in-law of Agrippa I who married Bernice, was still alive in mid A.D. 44. This ostraca, published in G. A. Tait, *Greek Ostraca in the Bodleian*, vol. 1 (Oxford: Clarendon, 1930), is dated Pauni 22, the fourth year of Claudius (16 June A.D. 44). Josephus said that Marcus died before Agrippa I, hence ca. early August 44 for Agrippa's death seems necessary (but after August 1, on which Josephus reports that Agrippa I celebrated the emperor's birthday).
23. Reicke, *New Testament Era*, 194, 196–97.

Book IV really begins with the coming of Paul to Antioch in A.D. 45 and the famine relief in A.D. 46. If Joachim Jeremias is correct in pointing out that A.D. 47-48 is a sabbatical year in which there would be no harvest until early A.D. 49, the famine of A.D. 46 was the beginning of an acute period.[24]

It is not impossible that this condition continued and became the basis for the great collection requested of Paul in A.D. 49 (Acts 24:17, Gal 2:9). It is not necessary to confine the collection of A.D. 46 to Barnabas alone, as Haenchen suggests, for the only text extant says "by the hand of Barnabas and Saul" (11:30).[25]

The preaching of Barnabas and Paul in Cyprus would be dated in A.D. 47, but there is no help from inscriptions and other literary sources. The connection between Sergius Paulus and the changing of Paul's name from Saul remains still an area of speculation.

Most scholars today identify the Jerusalem conference of Acts 15 with the one in Gal 2:1-10, which occurred most likely in A.D. 49. Paul and Barnabas "remained no little time" in Antioch after their return from the first missionary journey of A.D. 47, so that would almost eliminate A.D. 48 for the date of the Jerusalem Conference. A date between A.D. 46 and early A.D. 48 would be possible for the first missionary journey.

Paul said it was fourteen years after his conversion in A.D. 36 that he went up to Jerusalem to see Cephas and James again (Gal 1:18-19; 2:1, 9). This does not exclude him from a visit to the brethren and elders in A.D. 46 (Acts 11:24-30). If the year A.D. 36 is included, fourteen years from A.D. 36 would be A.D. 49. Pierre Benoit argues that Acts 11:27-30 belongs between Acts 15:2 and 3, but this is not obvious.[26]

The problem of how to relate the three years of Gal 1:18 to the fourteen years of Gal 2:1 is solved when it is recognized that Paul used a concurrent chronology in which his conversion in A.D. 36 became the starting point for each. Gal 1:11-17 indicates how this event was a dating event for him. The fourteen years included the three.

24. J. Jeremias, "Sabbathjahr und nestestamentliche Chronologie," *ZNW* 27 (1928) 98-103; idem, "Untersuchungen zum Quellenproblem der Apostlegeschichte," *ZNW* 36 (1937) 205-21; Haenchen, *Acts of the Apostles*, 63.

25. More details about the many famines that made up the great famine may be found in L. H. Feldman, *Josephus* (Loeb Classical Library; Cambridge: Harvard University, 1965), note *a* on *Antiquities* 20:51.

26. P. Benoit, "La deuxième visite de Saint Paul à Jérusalem," *Bib* 40 (1959) 778-92; repr. in *Studia biblica et orientalia*, vol. 2 (AnBib 11; Rome: Pontifical Biblical Institute, 1959) 210-24; also repr. in *Exégèse et Theologie* (Paris: Cerf, 1968) 285-99.

The summary of Acts 16:5, at the end of Book IV, would then represent what happened between late A.D. 49 and 54. It is not necessary to push the Jerusalem Conference back to A.D. 48 for this chronology. If the Jerusalem Conference were early in A.D. 49, then there was time for Paul to reach Corinth by late A.D. 49. This would include the "some time" of 15:33 and the "some days" of 15:36.

This time frame makes for a tight schedule, but the purpose in Paul's travel at this point was to deliver "to them for observance the decisions which had been reached by the apostles and elders who were in Jerusalem" (Acts 16:4). Days, not months or years, fit the mission best.

It is still a tight schedule to get Paul to Corinth by late A.D. 49, but nothing in the text of Acts makes it impossible. They "went through the region of Phrygia and Galatia" and went on to Macedonia "immediately" after Paul's vision at Troas (16:10). The "following day" they came to Neapolis and went to Philippi for "some days" (16:11–12). The slave girl pestered Paul for "many days" (16:18) before he was put in jail.

In Thessalonica Paul spent "three weeks" before the brethren sent him "immediately" to Berea (17:2, 10). The Bereans examined the scriptures "daily" (17:11), but trouble soon took him "immediately" to Athens (17:14). There Paul was "waiting for them" as he argued in the synagogues "every day" (17:16–17) before the occasion of the Areopagus address.

The second missionary journey would have been A.D. 49–51. Reicke says 50–53, so he must date the third journey 54–58 to fit his long chronology.[27] His proposal would require Paul's appearance before Gallio toward the end of his two years as proconsul, a conclusion reached by adding the "many days longer" (Acts 18:18) to the "year and six months" (18:11). This seems unlikely, as Reicke is forced to place the edict of Claudius in A.D. 50, but most scholars prefer A.D. 49.[28] On this point Ogg is to be preferred.[29] Acts 18:11 is a summary of Paul's time in Corinth and his appearance before Gallio came during that time, about May 51, soon after Gallio arrived.

Another tight schedule is the "great detour" to Syria in Acts 18:18–23. After getting Paul out of Corinth by the autumn of 51, Ogg leaves Paul in Syria for three years, A.D. 51–53, to fit his long chronology.[30] Will the text in Acts support such a long stay in Antioch? Paul

27. Reicke, *New Testament Era*, 219.
28. Ibid., 205.
29. Ogg, *Odyssey of Paul*, 99–126.
30. Ibid., 132.

was obviously in a hurry to get back to Ephesus when he left in May 51. He was unable to stay "a longer period" at that time (Acts 18:20), but he rushed on to Caesarea and "went up" to Jerusalem (?) before he "went down" to Antioch (18:22).

It is not possible to know how much time is "some time" (18:23), but after that Paul left Antioch and went "from place to place through the region of Phrygia and Galatia" (16:6). If the time was much the same on the second journey, he could have been in Ephesus by late 51. Haenchen requires no more time than that required for the trip from Antioch to Ephesus.[31] Ogg agonizes in a sea of fantasy to show why it took so long this second time, but he is not convincing.[32] He is really forced to retain his long chronology.

In Ephesus Paul argued in the synagogue "three months" (19:8), at the end of 51 or beginning of 52. This was followed by "two years" in the hall of Tyrannus (19:10). If the quinquennial chronology is correct, the summary at 19:20 would be about Pentecost, A.D. 54. This could be the Pentecost of 1 Cor 16:8, but A.D. 53 is more likely for 1 Corinthians. Paul stayed on for nine months more. On 13 October 54 Claudius died. Seneca, Nero's tutor, became immediately the most influential man in the Roman Empire. Was this why Paul resolved to see Rome? Seneca was the brother of his friend Gallio.

Here it is necessary to reject one of the most widely used arguments in Pauline chronology. This is the most crucial date in my new chronology. Josephus says Pallas, the brother of Felix, continued in highest honor under Nero, and that explained for him how Felix was spared in Rome on his recall (*Antiquities* 20:182–83). If Pallas did save Felix, it was much earlier than A.D. 59. Tacitus, however, gives a very different picture (*Annals* 13:2, 14, 15). According to Tacitus, Pallas was rejected from the very beginning of Nero's reign, and Seneca became the man of power, even writing Nero's inaugural oration! Ogg is no doubt correct when he calls Josephus's statements "a misrepresentation."[33]

Paul's resolution in Ephesus at the end of 54 must be compared to the vision of Macedonia in 49 (Acts 16:9) and the one in Achaia when Gallio became proconsul in May 51 (Acts 18:9, 12). At the end of exactly three years in Ephesus (Acts 20:31), A.D. 51–54, Paul left for Macedonia to finish his collection and after that for Rome! So Paul left

31. Haenchen, *Acts of the Apostles*, 71.
32. Ogg, *Odyssey of Paul*, 121–34.
33. Ibid., 159.

Ephesus for Macedonia; it is even possible that he went to Illyricum (Rom 15:19). If so, he went via Salonae in Illyricum or Dyrrhachium or Apollonia in Macedonia on his way from Corinth from the west.

After Passover in 55 Paul was on his way to Jerusalem with the great collection (Acts 20:3-6). The time phrases in Acts give a good picture of the time required: "five days" (20:6), "seven days" (20:6), "the following day" (20:15), "and the day after that" (20:15). He was rushing to be in Jerusalem by Pentecost (20:16). After Miletus the time notes continue: "the next day (21:1), "seven days" (21:4), "one day" (21:8), "on the morrow" (21:8). "After these days" he made the journey from Philippi to Jerusalem between the feast of Unleavened Bread and Pentecost (21:15).

Between Pentecost 55 and Pentecost 57 he was a prisoner in Caesarea in Herod's praetorium. The *dietia*, 'the two years' of Acts 14:7, had reference to Paul's time in prison and not to the time Felix was procurator (see above).

In the fall of A.D. 57, September or October, the sea voyage to Rome with the shipwreck took place. By 58 Paul was already in Rome: "and he remained two whole years at his own expense" (Acts 28:30). By late 59, it is possible that he was released by the good offices of Seneca who may be the Theophilus to whom Luke–Acts is dedicated (Luke 1:3, Acts 1:1). Only government officials are called "excellent" (cf. Luke 1:3, Acts 23:26, 26:25).[34]

Pauline Chronology and the Pauline Epistles

Paul's letters present no problem for the above revision of Pauline chronology. Indeed, they support it. Paul's letters may be grouped into four periods. The first group is the primary letters of 1 and 2 Thessalonians. The most debated historical question is the reference to God's wrath upon the Jews at the time Paul wrote that "God's wrath has come upon them at last" (1 Thess 2:16).

What does Paul have in mind? The Jewish persecution of Christians is interpreted much as in the early chapters of Acts (2:23, 3:15, 4:10, 5:30-31, 6:8-8:1). The Jews "killed" Jesus, and now they persecute his disciples. Ernest Best suggests the edict of Claudius in A.D. 49 as the

34. Nothing is said about the two years in a *praitōrion*, as in Caesarea, for a *praitōrion* in the New Testament means a governor's palace, and there was no governor's palace in Rome. Phil 1:13 uses *praitōrion* as it is used in all other places in the New Testament: Mark 15:16; Matt 27:27; John 18:28, 33; 19:9; Acts 23:35.

likely event that Paul has in mind.[35] This would fit the year 50 for 1 Thess 2:16.

The second Thessalonian letter discloses a matter of great literary importance. Arguments about date and authorship often involve computer data on style, as if Paul wrote his letters with his own hand. In reality, if evidence from Paul's letters is followed, Paul wrote very little with his own hand.

At the end of 2 Thessalonians a clue is given in these words: "I, Paul, write this greeting with my own hand. This is the mark in every letter of mine; it is the way I write" (3:17). Who then wrote the rest of the letter? Things take on a new look if one notes the name of the possible amanuensis at the beginning of each letter. This would be Silvanus or Silas with the possible help of Timothy in 1 and 2 Thessalonians. Silvanus also wrote 1 and 2 Peter (1 Pet 5:12, 2 Pet 3:1).

The second group of Paul's letters are the pillar letters of 1 and 2 Corinthians, Galatians, and Romans. If the role of the amanuensis is noted in these letters, then Sosthenes was the composer of 1 Corinthians and Timothy of 2 Corinthians. 1 Cor 16:21 has Paul's signature as in 2 Thess 3:17. A previous letter was written to Corinth (1 Cor 5:9), and 2 Cor 6:14-7:1 may be a page of that letter. 1 Corinthians fits perfectly between Passover (cf. 5:7) and Pentecost (cf. 16:8 in A.D. 53). 2 Corinthians 10-13 meets the conditions of the painful letter mentioned in 2 Cor 2:4, 9; 7:8. It should be dated in late A.D. 53 or in 54. 2 Corinthians 1-9 with the exception of 6:14-7:1 would then come from Macedonia after Paul left Ephesus in A.D. 54 (cf. 2 Cor 2:13, 8:1).[36]

It was a prolific time in A.D. 53-54 as Paul dispatched four or five letters to Corinth, and it seems that a letter went to Galatia about the same time, in the summer of 54 after 2 Corinthians 10-13 went to Corinth.[37] The conflict with Judaism is certainly very much the same. It is not possible to determine the amanuensis for 2 Cor 6:14-7:1 and 7:10-13 and Galatians, but it is certain Paul did not write Galatians with his own hand (6:11). It is a good guess to give Timothy (or Luke) the credit here.

35. E. Best, *A Commentary on the First and Second Epistles to the Thessalonians* (New York: Harper and Row, 1972) 120.

36. J. A. Fitzmyer, "Qumran and the Interpolated Paragraph in II Corinthians 6:14-7:1," *CBQ* 23 (1961) 271ff., thinks the passage is non-Pauline. See W. G. Kümmel, *Introduction to the New Testament* (London: SCM, 1965) 211.

37. C. K. Barrett, *A Commentary on the First Epistle to the Corinthians* (2d ed.; New York: Harper and Row, 1971) 5, dates the Corinthian correspondence in A.D. 54. Barrett has a careful consideration of the possibility of two letters in 1 Corinthians.

The most impressive example of the amanuensis role is found in the letter to the Romans, the most important letter of "the big four" or pillar letters. It may be that Romans 16 is a covering letter, but there is no reason to doubt the common amanuensis for the last chapter and the rest of the letter. His identification is clear: "I, Tertius, the writer of this letter, greet you in the Lord" (16:22).

Any reader of 1 Corinthians and Romans will see the very different style of Romans, especially as it relates to in the Stoic diatribe. C. K. Barrett has called attention to this at many places, and I have developed it in my own commentary on Romans.[38] The role of the amanuensis makes this difference understandable, but the computer approach that resorts to word counting runs into problems. Different styles are possible within one year if the amanuensis is different.

The third group of Paul's letters have long been called the prison letters. They are Philippians, Colossians (with the covering letter of Philemon), and Ephesians. Paul's imprisonment is mentioned in each letter (Phil 1:7, Col 4:18, Phlm 9, Eph 4:1), but there is no agreement about the location of the prison. Rome is the traditional location, but a large number follow G. S. Duncan in his Ephesian theory.[39]

Another minority theory, which locates the prison letters in Caesarea, is gaining ground. The theory has generally been associated with the name of Ernst Lohmeyer, but it was advocated by H. E. G. Paulus in 1800 and D. Schulz in 1829 before Lohmeyer gave it strong support around 1928–30. John J. Gunther has recently revived it, but his dates are two years too late.[40]

If the amanuensis theory is combined with the quinquennial theory, Timothy wrote Philippians from Caesarea in late A.D. 55. The *praitōrion* of Phil 1:13 was Herod's *praitōrion* mentioned in Acts 23:15, the only *praitōrion* in which the sources say Paul was a prisoner. The traditional view that this letter came from Rome has led many great scholars astray.

---

38. Barrett, *A Commentary on the Epistle to the Romans* (New York: Harper and Row, 1957) 5, dates Romans in A.D. 55. I suggested A.D. 57 in my commentary in *Broadman Bible Commentary* (Nashville: Broadman, 1970) x, but I now agree with Barrett. The sequence of letters outlined above (but not the dates) are much the same in Udo Borse, *Der Standort des Galaterbriefes* (Koln-Bonn: Peter Hanstein, 1972).

39. G. S. Duncan, *St. Paul's Ephesian Ministry* (London: Hodder and Stoughton, 1929) 59–60.

40. Gunther, *Paul: Messenger and Exile*, 98–107, dates the work by Paulus in 1700, but this is no doubt a misprint. J. L. Houlden, *Paul's Letters from Prison* (Harmondsworth: Penguin, 1970) 1–44, summarizes the previous studies.

Even J. B. Lightfoot argued that *en holō tō praitōriō* should be translated 'throughout the whole praetorium guard', and most later translations have followed him.[41] The Authorized (King James) Version
without the influence of Lightfoot says correctly 'the palace'! The
correct translation does not go beyond a footnote in the Revised Standard Version.

Reicke argues strongly for Caesarea in the case of Colossians and
Ephesians, but he retains the Roman captivity for Philippians. He is
driven to the conclusion that Philippians was written later than Colossians and Ephesians! The reference to "those of Caesar's household" in
Phil 4:21 is the last stronghold for the Roman theory, but this could
have reference to Cornelius and his household described in such detail
in Acts 10 and 11 or any other saints in the service of Nero, a point
made by G. S. Duncan.[42]

A special problem is confronted in Phil 3:1b–4:9, but it is not
insurmountable. It seems that an earlier letter to Philippi got incorporated into the second letter from Caesarea of late A.D. 55. The best
location for that so-called "dog letter" in the midst of the "joy letter"
is the late summer of 54, about the time Paul sent 2 Corinthians 10–13
to Corinth and Galatians to Galatia. The conflict with Judaism is much
the same with all three. Phil 4:10–23 got put under this earlier letter,
a very plausible thing when one looks at a papyrus copy. It sounds
like 2 Cor 6:14–7:1 all over: compare 2 Cor 6:13 and 7:2 with Phil 3:1a
and 4:10.

The eschatology of this Philippian correspondence makes an interesting comparison with that of the Corinthian letters. Phil 3:1b–4:9 is
strong on the resurrection of the body (3:17–21) as in 1 Corinthians 6
and 15, but the later letter to Philippi, over a year later, agrees with the
teachings on immortality in 2 Cor 5:1–10 (cf. Phil 1:23). Doctrinal
development alone is not a safe guide to chronology, but here it agrees
with the evidence. Timothy seems to be the amanuensis of all the
Corinthian and Philippian correspondence except 1 Corinthians (cf. Phil
1:1, 2 Cor 1:1).

Reicke has argued strongly for Colossians and Ephesians coming
from Caesarea, but his date of A.D. 58–60 is too late. His appeal to
Tacitus, *Annals* 14:28, and other references to the earthquake of 60 do
fit the latest possible date for Colossians. Colossae was not able to
rebuild as was wealthy Laodicea. Timothy again appears as the amanu-

41. J. B. Lightfoot, *Saint Paul's Epistle to the Philippians* (London: Macmillan, 1868)
99–104.
42. Duncan, *St. Paul's Ephesian Ministry*, 110–11.

ensis (Col 1:1), and Paul gives his signature and greeting as usual (Col 4:18).

The relation between Colossians and Ephesians is most complex. For many years the theory associated with the names of E. J. Goodspeed and his student John Knox was appealing. They assigned Ephesians to Onesimus in the tenth decade. C. L. Mitton later worked out more details.[43] Charles Moule, still holding for the traditional date for Colossians, well nigh demolished the Goodspeed-Knox-Mitton theory on Philemon and Colossians.[44] It now seems passé.

A new beginning has been made by locating the origin of Colossians and Ephesians in Caesarea. If Colossians was composed by Timothy around Passover 57, it is possible that it contains materials of a Passover liturgy. This would explain the emphasis upon the cross and the resurrection.

It would also explain why there is only one passing reference to the Spirit in Colossians (1:8) and thirteen in Ephesians (1:13, 14, 17; 2:18, 22; 3:5, 16; 4:3, 23; 5:18, 6:17, 18). If the old notion that Colossians and Ephesians were written not far apart is accepted, then a good suggestion would be that Ephesians contains much material from the Pentecost liturgy of 57.[45] Peter Rhea Jones has compared the Greek style of Ephesians with that of Luke–Acts and concluded that Luke is the writer of both![46] Was it his style to withhold his name? Did he compose the Pastoral Letters also? 2 Tim 4:11 would suggest that possibility.

The chronology of Günther Bornkamm is correct and near correct at some places, but his claim that the death of Paul was in 60 has no evidence to support it.[47] With his chronology and methodology Paul is deprived of six of his thirteen letters.[48] In the year 60 the great and just Seneca was the major influence in Rome, and it is all but impossible to date the death of Paul before the burning of Rome on 19 July 64.

However, after cordial correspondence with S. Dockx of Brussels, Belgium, I have been persuaded that Eusebius was correct not only on

43. C. F. Mitton, *The Epistle to the Ephesians* (Oxford: Oxford University, 1951).

44. C. F. D. Moule, *The Epistle of Paul the Apostle to the Colossians and to Philemon* (London: Cambridge University, 1957) 13–37. Evidence for many ideas in Ephesians having a close relation to Qumran may be found in Jerome Murphy-O'Connor (ed.), *Paul and Qumran* (London: Geoffrey Chapman, 1968) 115–31, 159–78. Therefore, the argument of Eduard Lohse, *Colossians and Philemon* (Philadelphia: Fortress, 1971), for a late date does not stand.

45. Both of these suggestions have been explored in unpublished papers by Gilbert Sanders.

46. In a seminar paper and in further oral communications.

47. G. Bornkamm, *Paul* (New York: Harper and Row, 1971) xl–xli.

48. Ibid., 241–24.

the appointment of Festus in 56 but on the death of Peter and Paul in the fourteenth year of Nero's reign, between 13 October 67 and 9 June 68.[49] The old Gallican tradition of 18 January 68 is not impossible. My differences with Dockx focus on the imprisonment of Paul in Caesarea and the origin of the prison letters. His requirement of a return of Paul to the Lycus Valley after his release from Rome and before his work in Spain seems most unlikely. Paul's appeal to Nero made it impossible for him to follow the plans so plainly stated in Colossians and Philemon.

After Paul's release from house arrest in early 60, he perhaps went directly to Spain for three to five years, but he then returned to the East, stopping first in Crete, where he left Titus (Titus 1:5), and in Ephesus, where he left Timothy before going to Macedonia (1 Tim 1:3). While in Macedonia, perhaps in Philippi, he wrote a letter to Titus. He spent the winter in Nicopolis (Titus 3:12) and wrote a letter to Timothy—1 Timothy. Later he came back to Ephesus before going to Troas where he was arrested while Nero was touring Greece, 67-68. He was then taken to Rome, where he was executed.

Table 1 shows the Pauline chronology when all references in Paul's letters are taken at face value. There are no sources available against this chronology. The idea of a second imprisonment is often dismissed on the grounds that Eusebius first mentioned it (*Historia Ecclesiastica* 2:22), and Jerome followed his view (*De Viris Illustribus* 5), but there is much evidence before Eusebius.

Clement of Rome said that both Peter and Paul died in Rome after Paul had gone to the limits of the West (1 Clement 5). Ignatius of Antioch indicates the importance of both Peter and Paul for Rome (*Romans* 4:2). Dionysius of Corinth describes how both Peter and Paul died at the same time (*Historia Ecclesiastica* 2:25:5–8). Irenaeus traced the apostolic succession of Rome from Peter and Paul (*Against Heresies* 3:1:2, 3:3:1). Some details of Paul's death at Tre Fontane and his burial outside the wall are perhaps preserved in the apocryphal "Acts of Paul" before the end of the second century. Tertullian says Paul suffered death in Rome, but he is not clear on a second imprisonment (*Apology* 5, *Prescription Against Heresies* 35). After Eusebius, Cyril of Jerusalem, Epiphanius, John Chrysostom, and others support this tradition, against which there is no evidence.

Against this background, the formation of the Pauline corpus and the composition of Luke–Acts may be seen in a different light. A first collection of Paul's letters was possible in 55 when Romans was written from Corinth. Robert L. Lindsey has argued that Mark, the author of the Roman gospel, knew about 1 and 2 Thessalonians, 1 and 2 Corin-

---

49. Helm, *Die Chronik des Hieronymus, Eusebius Werke*, 7:182, 185.

TABLE 1.   *Pauline Chronology, Spring 60–January 68*

Spring 60–Spring 64	Paul in Spain with headquarters in Cadiz
Spring 64–Spring 65	Paul in Crete where he leaves Titus (1:5)
Spring 65–Summer 65	Paul in Ephesus where he leaves Timothy (1 Tim 1:3)
Summer 65	Paul goes through Macedonia on the way to Nicopolis (1 Tim 1:3; Titus 3:12)
Winter 65–66	Nicopolis (1 Timothy)
Spring–Autumn 66	Ephesus (2 Tim 1:4, 18; 4:9–10)
Winter 66–67	Troas (2 Tim 4:14; cf. 1:19–20)
Spring 67	Paul arrested (2 Tim 4:20)
Spring–Autumn 67	Taken to Rome via Corinth; Paul a prisoner in Rome; 2 Timothy composed (1:4–5)
Summer 67	Paul before the tribunal; adds to 2 Timothy (4:6–22)
Autumn 67	Timothy and Mark arrive in Rome (2 Tim 4:9, 13, 21)
18 January 68	Paul executed (2 Tim 4:17–18)

If Peter was executed at the same time as Paul, then the following dates can be given for him:

42	Peter goes to Rome (Acts 12:17; Eusebius, *Historia Ecclesiastica* 2:14, 15, 17)
49	Peter expelled from Rome with all the other Jews (Acts 18:2; Suetonius, *Claudius* 25:4)
54	Peter returns to Rome after the death of Claudius, 13 October 54
67–68	Peter executed with Paul

thians, and Romans.[50] It just could be that Phoebe took all these writings, written either from or to Corinth, when she left for Rome (Rom 16:1–2).

If the prison letters came from Caesarea, as outlined above, a second collection of three letters could have been made by Tychicus when he and Onesimus left Caesarea for the Lycus Valley with Colossians (4:7), Philemon, and Ephesians (6:21). With the addition of Galatians, written from Ephesus(?), and Philippians, the collection of ten letters was complete.

E. J. Goodspeed made a good case for a collection of ten Pauline letters by Onesimus in Ephesus, but he dated the collection too late, in the tenth decade, his date for Luke–Acts.[51] All of this is possible in the early sixties before the composition of the pastoral letters.

50. R. L. Lindsey, *A Hebrew Translation of Mark* (2d ed.; Jerusalem: Dugith, 1973) 52.
51. E. J. Goodspeed, *The Meaning of Ephesians* (Chicago: University of Chicago, 1953); idem, *The Key to Ephesians* (Chicago: University of Chicago, 1956).

Goodspeed was also correct in seeing a short Pauline corpus in the polemic of Tertullian against Marcion. Book 5 of Tertullian's five books *Against Marcion* discussed the ten letters to seven churches from the longest to the shortest, with the exception of Galatians at the beginning, where it displaced Ephesians and Ephesians replaced Galatians. It is doubtful that Marcion dropped the pastorals. He used the letters of Paul first collected by Onesimus.

One other possibility is suggested before bringing this survey to a close. It is possible that Marcion did not mutilate the Gospel of Luke as much as the vehement Tertullian accused him. If he used the first edition of the Gospel, which Luke composed in Caesarea, and Tertullian used the second edition composed at Rome, many of the omissions in Marcion are without blame. This is a question to be discussed by specialists in Luke and Tertullian, but Marcion's Luke begins at 3:1, where many have seen an earlier beginning. An appendix to Tertullian's attack against Marcion by a modern master of the great Carthaginian is a helpful place to begin an examination of this question.[52]

This picture of the life and letters of Paul with the implications for other problems has usually taken the New Testament writers, the Greek and Latin Fathers, and the classical authors at face value, allowing things to fall in place without major amputations. It is true that respect for Eusebius is obvious all the way, but indeed, it was developed as the evidence was examined.

The excessive subjectivity of an author like Bornkamm makes it possible to prove any point of view by dismissal of all evidence that does not agree with the author's presuppositions. Eusebius deserves to be read afresh, not because he is always correct but because critical orthodoxy ignores his conclusions too frequently without sufficient reason.

52. See Ernest Evans, *Tertullian Adversus Marcionem* (Oxford: Clarendon, 1972) 643–44.